BENEATH
THE SURFACE

BENEATH THE SURFACE

The Hidden Realities of Teaching Culturally
and Linguistically Diverse Young Learners
K–6

KEN PRANSKY

HEINEMANN
Portsmouth, NH

Heinemann
361 Hanover Street
Portsmouth, NH 03801–3912
www.heinemann.com

Offices and agents throughout the world

The author and publisher wish to thank those who have generously given permission to reprint borrowed material:

Table 1–1: "Contrasting Cultural Assumptions Chart" originally appeared in *Theory into Practice*, 44 (1). Copyright © 2005. Published by Taylor and Francis. Reprinted by permission of the publisher. www.informaworld.com.

Figure 2–1: "Apple Comparison Problem," Figure 5–7: "Organization of Dots," and Figure 6–4: "Samoeuth's Work with Fruit Problem" originally appeared in a Unit of Feuerstein Instrumental Enrichment Program. Reprinted with permission of Professors Reuven Feuerstein and Louis Falik.

Figures 5–1 through 5–4: Cover image and excerpts from *Fire! In Yellowstone: A True Adventure*. Published by Houghton Mifflin Harcourt. Reprinted with permission of Gareth Stevens Publishing.

Excerpts from *MCAS Prep: Grade 5 Mathematics, Second Edition*. Reprinted with permission of Queue, Inc., One Controls Drive, Shelton, CT 06484. 800-232-2224. www.qworkbooks.com.

Library of Congress Cataloging-in-Publication Data
Pransky, Ken.
  Beneath the surface : the hidden realities of teaching culturally and
linguistically diverse young learners, K–6 / Ken Pransky.
    p. cm.
  Includes bibliographical references and index.
  ISBN 13: 978-0-325-01202-5
  ISBN 10: 0-325-01202-4
  1. Multicultural education—United States. 2. Early childhood
education—United States. 3. Critical pedagogy—United States. I. Title.
LC1099.3.P73 2008
372'.0117—dc22   2008013274

Editor: Leigh Peake
Developmental editor: Cheryl Kimball
Production: Elizabeth Valway
Cover design: Bernadette Skok
Cover photo: David Stirling
Composition: Cape Cod Compositors, Inc.
Manufacturing: Steve Bernier

Printed in the United States of America on acid-free paper
12 11 10 09 08   RRD   1 2 3 4 5

This book is dedicated to the all students whom I have taught, and their families. I'm sure I have learned far more from them than they have from me.

Contents

Acknowledgments

THERE ARE many people to thank, and I'm sure I will miss some, for which I apologize in advance!

First, I would like to thank my Fort River Elementary School colleagues for their dedication and skill, and for how much they have inspired and taught me over the years—I am truly fortunate to have worked at this wonderful school and with these wonderful educators! In particular, I want to thank Torie Weed and Seiha Krouch for their friendship, support, and insights. It has been a gift to work so closely with such lovely, skilled educators for so many years. I also want to thank Laurie Hickson for putting up with my bizarre sense of humor as the ESL half of our ESL-inclusion first-grade classroom partnership since 1991, and for all she taught me about working with young children. Others to whom I am grateful for having willingly taken on the challenge of ESL inclusion with me and for the students are José Cantillo, Amy Jackendoff, Judah Hughes, Rick Last, Pam Szczesny, Peter Lamdin, Linda Yeh, and Bill Read.

Another very important gift I have received from some Fort River staff is better learning the difference between what in this book I call an *empathetic* as opposed to a *sympathetic* understanding of issues of race, class, and other issues of diversity and difference. These thanks in particular go to Roger Wallace, José, Sue Markman, Tom Chang, Lianne Suarez-Werlein, Tara Luce, and Sokhen Mao, whom I would also like to thank for so freely sharing his infectious laughter and smile, and his expertise about Cambodian history and culture.

Many thanks are due to my friend and sometime coauthor Dr. Francis Bailey, for his very important guidance and thought-provoking perspectives over the last fifteen or so years. His commitment to inquiry and reflection enabled me to really grow as a teacher at a critical time in my career and expand the boundaries of my thinking. Every teacher should have someone like Francis as a sounding board and resource to grow and evolve with. Thanks are also due to Dr. Dave Martin, who initiated me into the wonderful world of mediated learning and the Feuerstein Instrumental Enrichment (FIE) program.

I need to thank those giants in their fields whose ideas and insights have profoundly influenced who I am as a thinker and educator: Lisa Delpit, Barbara Rogoff, Lev Vygotsky, Reuven Feuerstein, Alexi Kozulin, Teresa Perry, Shirley Bryce Heath, Jerome Bruner, Katherine Nelson, James Gee, Michael Cole, Sonia Nieto, and Mary Gauvain, to name just some of them. And overarching all of my professional thinking are the teachings of S. N. Goenka, my teacher, to whom I am eternally grateful.

Many people helped in the evolution of this manuscript. In particular, I appreciate Mike Morris for his willingness to be my guinea-pig first reader and also Lisa Hannahan, Pam, Laurie, and Torie for the time they took to read and comment on various parts of the book.

I am very grateful to the expert guidance and friendly whip cracking of my editor, Cheryl Kimball. Without her, I'm not sure where I'd still be in this process—though I am absolutely sure I would not be in nearly as good a place! I consider myself fortunate, indeed, to have had the opportunity to work with such a perceptive and supportive editor.

I would like to also express my appreciation to the friends I made in Iran, Spain, Mexico, and Japan, who taught me what true friendships are that transcend cultures, ethnicities, and religions, and in some cases that have outlasted thousands of miles and decades of separation. With more people like them, the world would surely be a kinder, more peaceful place.

Finally, I would like to thank my parents for raising me with love and helping me develop a social conscience, and my family for their support putting up with my long stretches of absence ensconced in front of the computer screen!

Introduction

AT LEAST one thing about our profession is for sure: it is not easy being a teacher in the twenty-first century. Never mind the growing, intrusive influence of government regulation, the movement toward more and more testing, the increase in the quantity of what must be taught, and the reduced respect for our profession within society. Our student population has been changing for many years. More and more of our students are "other people's children," in the words of Lisa Delpit (1995), an African American educator who writes eloquently about identity, language, and culture. For example, according to U.S. Census Bureau projections, the percentage of the non-Hispanic white population will have shrunk from 69.4% in 2006 to 50.1% by 2050 (www.census.gov/ipc/www/usinterimproj/natprojtab01a.xls).

Many of our students are from linguistically and culturally diverse communities. Many are academically underachieving. The majority of us teachers, however, are white. We must learn the challenging dance of working with students whose experiences, cultures, and language backgrounds are not what we know or understand well, if at all. It is not an easy task, and our options are limited: we can resent it as a burden, ignore it (to the detriment of some of our neediest students), or adapt ourselves to this new reality with open heart and mind.

To an ever-increasing degree, the simple fact is that our schools and classrooms no longer reflect who our students are.

But even if we willingly choose the latter course, what road map do we have? Although the things we think are most right about teaching may indeed be right for the students most like ourselves, they may not be so right for those students unlike us. This is true no matter who we are. No Child Left Behind (NCLB) and high-stakes testing want to force us down prescribed or ill-conceived paths, which are not in the best interests of our students.

This book lays out a road map that is in the best interests of students and our profession.

My Challenges

This book is not intended as a how-to guide, nor is it a foolproof recipe for instant classroom success—as if there were any such thing! It is meant to provoke thought and stimulate reflection while staying grounded in practice. It starts from the premise that we know our craft well. As dedicated professionals, most of us willingly grapple with new ways of understanding the teaching-learning process if we feel it will help us be more effective. When we come to new understandings, we naturally make instructional decisions that reflect them. The question becomes: How do we reach new, respectful, and meaningful understandings about our students and the teaching/learning process? To address this question, the book proposes a general framework within which we can broaden and integrate our understanding of our students, ourselves, our classrooms, the curriculum, our teaching, and language within the context of what we *already* do. But the first step *must* be to reexamine what we "know" to be true, identifying our assumptions about ourselves, our classrooms, our students, and the learning process.

That said, it is very difficult to reorient our fundamental assumptions about our students, ourselves, language, teaching, and learning, especially if we have not lived in a subordinate position, experienced racism, or at least lived in another culture and tried learning another language. How many of us take classes in multicultural education and, even if we are positively affected in the short term and our heart is in the right place, we do not fundamentally change how we approach our teaching practice, or how we try to understand our students, even if we make some "window dressing" changes? Yet that level of empathy and knowledge is what it takes to be a successful teacher of "other people's children." We must be willing to deconstruct, rethink, and reconstruct many things that we take for granted as being natural and right. This or that new program or methodology is not the answer. So how do we do it?

We need to approach teaching from the inside out, thinking differently first, not just doing differently.

To more successfully teach diverse learners, we must at least be sympathetic; that is, we know that all our students do not have equal opportunity, we believe in equity, and we want all our students to learn in a classroom that welcomes and values them. But that is just the starting point, and it misses much. From that springboard of sympathy, we must try to become more empathetic: we need to try to form genuine, understanding, and interested relationships with students based on who *they* are, and recognize and understand the impact of difference, disempowerment, and racism (maybe unintentionally even in my own classroom), not only a sympathetic acknowledgment that they exist (but not in *my* classroom); we realize we need to *create* an equitable classroom. We need to recognize and be honest (with our students and ourselves) about the intricate web of social and political inequities many families from diverse communities face on a daily basis, because that forms the backdrop of all we do regardless of our own good intentions. And beyond that, we must become more knowledgeable about our students *and ourselves*, their language *and our own*, their cultures *and our own*, and the teaching-learning process. In other words, we need to cultivate an open-minded, reflective practice. This book is designed to help you move along the *sympathy-empathy-knowledge* continuum from wherever you may presently be. And if you need convincing, one of my challenges is to convince you that it is worth the effort to start peeling away the layers of this particular onion.

Another challenge is being a white educator trying not to enact my white, dominant-culture, and middle-class privileges through what I say or how I say it. Related to this, we all have strong preconceptions and opinions about these issues and can easily misinterpret what others say. The words themselves can generate strong feelings and provoke hair-trigger reactions. I certainly understand how I could be misinterpreted or misunderstood and why that could happen. So, knowing there may be expectations of what I will or won't say or how I should or shouldn't say it, and that some of what I do say may be misinterpreted or misunderstood, all I can do is lay out my guiding philosophical beliefs (in no particular order), letting the chips fall where they may:

- *All* children can learn.

- If a child fails to learn, it's on the *teacher's* shoulders.

- I have the deepest respect for all the children and families with whom I work.

- As a member of the empowered, dominant culture, I'm sure I'll make mistakes when talking about issues that affect disempowered, nondominant groups, but I go where my heart, mind, and experience take me.

- *Any* teacher can learn to be successful working with *any* student not like him if he keeps his heart and mind open.

- *Deficit thinking* is poison.

- Teachers can and should learn from their students and their students' families.

- There is no end to what I can learn about the teaching-learning process, especially with regard to students not like me.

- Being social constructs, most schools inevitably have some racist structures and practices that, whether unintentionally or not, erode the confidence and achievement of many children of color.

- The school success paradigm is governed by dominant-culture assumptions and expectations, is based on dominant-culture knowledge and experiences, and is reinforced by NCLB and high-stakes testing regimens; by definition, that disempowers many children of color, yet in the end they must learn the appropriate skills they need to become *independently* successful within that paradigm and, more important, to have optimum choices in our society.

- For a student to become school successful does not mean that she has to abandon her primary identity; in fact, she should not.

- I want all children to succeed academically within the present structures of schools, the society at large, and government regulation, even if I do not agree with these structures or regulations, or like the context of education today.

Another challenge I faced is that given the scope and size of this book, I could not say everything I wanted to say or connect all the theoretical dots as explicitly as I'd have liked. I have tried to include what is necessary to help us think about teaching, learning, and language in a different way, and if there seem to be gaps in my logic or in the conclusions I've drawn, I ask for a leap of faith that the background dots are all connected and that everything has roots in some theory and practice.

I also want to reiterate that this book is intended to provoke thought, personal and professional reflection, and discussion. So even if something I write does not resonate with your experience, with your students, with your reflection, or breaks down in collaborative discussion with others, my purpose has been served. Although I believe very deeply in what I have written, I neither expect nor want this book to be swallowed hook, line, and sinker. Without a reader's willingness to develop a reflective practice around these issues, this book—indeed, *any* book about working with other people's children—is rendered useless!

Who Are English Language Learners?

Another of my goals in writing this book is to broaden the understanding of who constitutes the second language learner population in our schools. Of course, there are ELLs (English language learners),[1] but that is just part of it. As our student population changes, the education field as a whole must reorient itself to this new reality by reconsidering what it means to teach and learn in culturally and linguistically diverse classrooms.

Too often, we just end up superimposing old ways of thinking on the new realities of our classrooms.

In the classic view, ELLs are students who are dominant to a greater or lesser degree in their native language and have less than native-speaker proficiency in English. The goal is to help students acquire English, and when they have enough English skill, they can meaningfully profit from classroom instruction. The field of ESL has a well-developed theory, and there are many great resources that help classroom teachers adapt their classrooms to ESL students.

However, the paint on this broad brush is too thin. Although there are many classic English-as-a-new-language learners for whom ESL theory and practice are very appropriate, language *acquisition* per se can no longer be the defining concept of the entire field for two reasons. First, we often see two "tracks" of ELL student progress: students from professional and affluent families with academically influenced first languages tend to achieve grade-level proficiency more quickly, while students with less academically influenced first languages, often from poor or working-class families, struggle more academically. The roots of this achievement disparity are not totally described by classic ESL theory, nor, at least in my and my colleagues' experience, mediated solely by good ESL instruction. Beyond that, there is a large and growing population of students who are English dominant, or even monolingual English speakers, who come from homes where English is not the shared or preferred language of the adult community. They are students whose dominant or first language is English as a second language or some combination of English and their parents' first language(s). Aside from default thinking—some special program or other, remedial attention, or even special education—there is not a widely held, coherent way of viewing or working with this population of students that places *them* at the center of our

The English of students who speak ESL as a first or dominant language and the English of school are not really the same "English."

thinking as users of language; first and foremost, we must *understand* them as thinkers and users of language.

While English-dominant students are often not viewed as qualifying for ELL programs because of their English status or their lack of (their parents') first language (which is also referred to in this text as L_1) skills, they are really second language learners too, and, in fact, may be much needier than many ELLs over the long term. "English" stands in the way of their realizing their full academic potential, too, and in a deeper way. Not because they speak an objectively inferior English, but because "school English" is defined by a certain type of linguistic expertise, and while students from certain backgrounds are trained to have it, they are not. I have always found it thought provoking that, for example, a recently arrived, monolingual Japanese-speaking first grader at our school tends to be positioned *much* closer to a path of academic success in a public school classroom in this country than some English-dominant first-grade students of diverse cultural and linguistic backgrounds who were born here. It seems counterintuitive, yet ironically, the Japanese student's Japanese is actually more matched to school English, and at a deeper level, his culture closer to the culture of an American public school classroom, than are the English and culture of many English-dominant students.

This interplay of diverse cultures, languages, and socioeconomic status[2] creates a significantly large percentage of our nation's students that demands a coherent, theoretical perspective to guide our practice. I call this enlarged, more inclusive language-learning population *culturally and linguistically diverse*, or CLD, students. The term *CLD* has been used in the literature, such as in a very important book about bilingual education and ESL by Ovando, Collier, and Combs (2003), but it is not so widely known. Any student from a home community with linguistic or cultural differences from the dominant culture or language is a CLD student, to a greater or lesser degree. It is quite likely that many CLD students will be mismatched or mispositioned in some way within the classroom language or culture in a classroom predicated on dominant-culture norms. The greater the number of mismatches across a broad range of cultural, linguistic, cognitive, and social factors, the more challenging classroom learning will be.

Successful teaching of many CLD students by definition has to be centered in issues of culture, class, and race, and language form, dialect, and register, as much if not more than obvious second language learning, and in a cohesive, proactive way.

While it is very true that culture and language clarify a major fault line between achieving and underachieving student populations in many of our schools, it is not by virtue of this or that language or culture, but rather whether it is *literacy oriented* or not, that matters more (all things being equal in terms of programs and staffing and the rudimentary understanding that a lack of academic English proficiency is not a deficit or special need). The term *literacy oriented* as well the companion term *school matched* are deeply analyzed and defined in succeeding chapters.

I do not mean to imply that ESL programs and teachers have no value: I, myself, am one! ESL teachers perform an *essential* service for students who are acquiring English, and the insights of the ESL field are important for all teachers to know insofar as they help classroom teachers moderate the classroom learning environment and positively affect the performance of second language learners. But we also need to have a CLD-inclusive perspective on culture, language, and learning that stretches past ELLs, one that holistically thinks about the entire range of CLD students from their inside out, as best and as humbly as we can. That view is grounded in these three key questions: (1) What constitutes school-matched English? (2) What constitutes dominant-culture classroom culture? and (3) How should the process of teaching and learning be conceptualized in a diverse classroom?

Unless we rub out and redraw the lines demarcating how we view teaching, our students, and the language of our classrooms, we will continue to misunderstand the needs of non-literacy-oriented students—ironically, the very students we need to *most clearly* think about. When the lines are redrawn, we get CLD² (which still includes ESL and the need to support language acquisition), instead of just ESL (which often misses CLD): it is a more informative way of looking at ourselves, students, language, and learning.

> *There is no getting around it: to work more effectively with "other people's children," we must either have changed or be willing to change.*

For those of us who are approaching change from a purely intellectual perspective (as opposed to it being an outgrowth of personal experience), the framework presented in this book gives enough detail to hang new thinking on. We can learn to feel ourselves deepening our *empathy* and *knowledge* as we develop a reflective practice. Further, this framework enables us to see that the onus of responsibility must be shifted *off* the shoulders of our students and their families (who can neither change their culture nor become school-matched speakers of English with the wave of a wand—nor should they).

> *Many dominant-culture students walk into kindergarten as academic successes waiting to happen. There isn't anything special that defines them as a group of successful learners other than the fact that they are lucky!*

Literacy-oriented, dominant-culture students are lucky to have been acculturated in homes where the language and cognitive skills of literacy-oriented communities were part and parcel of their development, because successful, independent, formal school learning requires those same skills. And certainly, they were lucky to be born into the dominant culture, with all its attendant privileges and various forms of social, economic, political, and cultural capital. There is certainly nothing objectively better about them, or worse about home acculturations that do not develop those skills, or have those advantages. It's just the way it is.

This awareness alone should profoundly affect how we view our role as teachers. The onus of responsibility we take off non-literacy-oriented CLD students and their families gets shifted onto the intersection of students, teacher, language, and learning dynamics in the classroom, where it belongs. And *we* must shoulder the initial burden of change—not as a burden of guilt, but as a proactive responsibility for trying to equalize the luck advantage for the sake of the children in our charge. This shift of responsibility helps us turn away from viewing students and their families as having deficits we need to fix or blaming parents for the way they raise their children. Instead, we are moved to ask, "What are our students' home language and culture strengths, and how can we bridge the gaps between those and the requirements of the classroom language and culture so we can turn CLD students' home experiences and language acculturation into another form of classroom luck?" How can you blame anyone, or think to fix anything about him, because he is not holding a winning lottery ticket, or even worse, because his family has been mugged by the system?

I blame only myself *if I choose not to become more empathetic and knowledgeable.*

This is extremely important, because deficit thinking is poison. It may move us to think that parents don't care about their children's education because their caring looks different than what we think is right, or we just make blind, stereotypical misjudgments about them. We mis-see our students and their potential—after all, if they are missing so much, we need to think first about "filling their holes" instead of first understanding better *who they are.* If we start with such a negative perspective, how can we proactively change ourselves and our classroom environment to enable CLD students to "get lucky," too—and if we think our way is best and right, why would we change? By avoiding deficit thinking, we avoid the mistake of teaching from our students' outside in, instead of from their inside out.

But we also need the flexibility to understand at a deeper level what language and culturally influenced thinking skills non-literacy-oriented CLD students must have to be able to achieve *independently* at higher levels in dominant-culture learning spaces. My experience at my school has been that not all young CLD learners are ready to profit equally from good, multiculturally sensitive instruction, strong, positive relationships, and high expectations. We must acknowledge the full continuum along which our students fall, albeit it in an empathetic, knowledgeable, and nonjudgmental way.

My Journey

To help you better understand where I am coming from, how I think, and why I think it, I offer up this quick bio. Between 1974 and 1987, I lived and taught EFL (English as a foreign language) internationally, in Iran, Spain, Mexico, and Japan, as well as teaching ESL for a time at a language institute in Colorado. When my wife became pregnant, we decided to return to the United States to put down roots in western Massachusetts.

Before going overseas to teach, I had received my master's in teaching English as a second language from the School for International Training in Brattleboro, Vermont (1981), perhaps the best-known ESL-related master's program in the states at that time. Now back stateside, I felt confident in my teaching ability, my experience, and my knowledge of the field. Most of the ESL jobs, to my surprise, seemed to be in public schools, which had higher salaries than private language schools. Some of my experiences overseas had been challenging, like being in the Peace Corps in a remote desert site in Iran, and I remember thinking, "Teaching children in an affluent town in the United States after teaching overseas, once with a class of more than forty in a desert oasis town with nothing more than a few pieces of chalk, a blackboard, and an outdated book? And for a better salary than I'd expected, too?! Lucky me!"

I got hired to start the ESL program at one of the four elementary schools in town. In the mid-1980s, the first Cambodian immigrants had begun to settle in the area, sponsored by local churches. They had escaped the horrors of the Khmer Rouge and then spent a long time in squalid refugee camps. By the time I came to the school, there were about twenty ELL students at the school, mostly traumatized Cambodian immigrants. But as I said, with my background in languages, English teaching, and multicultural education, I thought it would be pretty easy. . . .

It did not take me long to realize how wrong I was! Some of my students came to school in the frigid winter wearing sandals and skimpy T-shirts. I recall a couple of kids hiding under tables, they were so overwhelmed. Within three years, the number of ELL students on my caseload had jumped to sixty-four. (Since then, our school has added more ELL staff, while the ELL population has fluctuated between forty-five and sixty-five students.) I remember having a pullout group of seventeen mixed kindergarten and first graders that first year! But the biggest issue was how difficult learning at our school seemed for many of them.

I felt quite frustrated with myself in my first years there because of the uneven results I got. Our international students from professional and education-oriented families (there are five colleges in the area) did very well academically, while students from Cambodian immigrant and other socioeconomically struggling families did much more poorly, even those that had more speaking skills in English. I could not help that gap close, in spite of using "cutting-edge" teaching practices for working with children, being quite knowledgeable about the ESL side of my field, learning as much as I could about literacy development and early childhood education, and the students being in an otherwise excellent school, that, while not perfect, was at the forefront of putting progressive pedagogy (whole language, constructivism, etc.) into practice. The Cambodian students even had a Khmer TBE[4] program. While helpful, all this was not enough to overcome whatever other issues were at play that kept that population so underperforming.

Even after several years, the Cambodian families were still recuperating from the horrors of the Cambodian holocaust and refugee camp experiences, which explained a lot. However, as that horror has receded in time and children born here have started coming to our school, disparities in achievement have typically *remained* (if not to the same degree), even within that community: children from families who have been more culturally grounded (regardless of class), and/or who had more educated parents, have been significantly more academically successful than students who were less well grounded culturally, and/or whose parents were not as well educated. Our school has experienced this pattern not only with Cambodian students, but also among children from the Latino community and more recently our Cape Verdean immigrant students. (I should note that there is some achievement disparity between different [social] classes of white students as well.) All of my professional energy has gone into trying to understand what is going on in classrooms with language and learning, and with students, that creates this phenomenon at my otherwise high-achieving school.[5] In this book I have tried to put all that I have since learned from a variety of different fields into a framework that I wish I had when I first started teaching at my school. It is certainly one I continue to work with and add to.

The Layout of the Text

The book is essentially organized in two parts. The first three chapters combine to create the sociocultural framework that I propose as a lens for developing a reflective practice.

Chapter 1 sets out a framework for understanding ourselves, our students, and the learning process as deeply influenced by cultural norms, assumptions, and expectations. It analyzes classrooms as primarily cultural sites of learning, and learning tasks as cultural tasks. Further, it connects culture to the development of cognition (problem solving) and language by grounding them in the learning-focused language interactions young children have with their parents or other significant adults.

Chapter 2 looks at a framework for more fully appreciating the meaning of language. First it describes the process of second language learning and factors that either enhance the process or make it more problematic. Then it identifies various domains of language beyond basic language acquisition, such as academic versus communicative language, dialect and register, and vocabulary that may be mismatched to the English of schooling and therefore have a negative impact on learning either due to the mismatch itself or the resultant value judgments of uninformed teachers. The focus is on understanding literacy language better.

Chapter 3 looks at the learning process. Understanding a fuller range of legitimate instructional directions that a teacher might skillfully move in within a given learning interaction—toward the students, instructional task, language, or academic content—extends the conceptual framework set out in Chapters 1 and 2. It explores the difference between *quantity* and *quality* in learning and presents three learning models that are particularly conducive to conceptualizing the teaching of underachieving CLD students.

Chapters 1–3 start with one or more framing anecdotes. Out of these anecdotes, various questions are raised. To answer the questions, a set of principles is proposed that develops the sociocultural and language framework. Interactive exercises are interspersed to foster deeper engagement with the ideas. The book is designed to help further your own reflective practice—a process more about asking good questions than about getting answers!

Your answers can be right only when you have thought about yourself *and your own particular CLD students more deeply.*

This is where we make the important move from sympathy to empathy and knowledge. The deeper we understand our students, ourselves, language, and culture, the more successful we can be teaching CLD students. The framework presented in these first three chapters is one way to enact what African American author and educator Gloria Ladsen-Billings (1994) refers to as *culturally relevant* teaching. Terms such as *culturally responsive* and *culturally congruent* convey a similar meaning. (Another great source for thinking through this idea is Sonia Nieto.)

In her wonderful book *The Dreamkeepers: Successful Teachers of African-American Children*, Ladsen-Billings profiles several extraordinary teachers. What characterizes them is *not* that they all teach in the most progressive or modern way; indeed, they teach in many different styles. What characterizes them as great teachers of African American students is

- the obvious *caring* they have for their students,

- the *understanding* they have of them,

- the *strong relationships* they form with them,

- the strong sense of *social justice* they foster, and

- building on the previous qualities, the *high academic expectations* they hold, with *appropriate support* as needed.

I have tried to flesh out this five-pronged structure to apply to any culturally and linguistically diverse young learner in the form of the sociocultural framework developed in Chapters 1–3.

The second part of the book, Chapters 4, 5, and 6, applies the framework developed in Chapters 1–3 to literacy (mainly reading) and math. Illustrative classroom anecdotes are used as a realistic backdrop for the process of reconceptualizing reading and math instruction. The idea is not to *replace* sound reading and math programs with the ideas presented in these chapters, but rather to deepen their effectiveness with CLD students, to have more targeted and appropriate instruction within them.

If we don't smell the burning wood, it is likely that real reflection and inquiry have stopped.

As we develop a reflective practice around these ideas, I like to keep in mind something I once heard Ted Williams, whom many consider the greatest hitter in baseball history, say. He was aware of a momentary burning smell when he hit a pitch well. The friction of the ball caused a sudden, fleeting burn on the wood of the bat. We have to smell the burning wood as teachers. It is the friction between old assumptions and new understandings, effortfulness versus comfort.

Our field often encourages us to take a best practices menu approach to our teaching—we want something from this list and something from that. Teachers often ask me, "So, what can I *do*?" That is part of the problem when working with CLD students. Before *doing* anything, we need to rethink who our students are, who we are, what it is we *already* do, and why it is or isn't working. The following anecdote illustrates this dilemma.

A friend once went to hear Lisa Delpit speak. In her seminal book *Other People's Children* (1995), one of the issues she raises is that white, middle-class teachers may need to speak in a more directive way with some of their students than they are typically comfortable with (this issue is described in more detail in Chapter 2). He reported that she opened her talk by saying something like, "I get lots of emails and letters from white teachers saying, 'I speak more strongly to my students, but nothing changes!'" In other words, they had overlooked her *foundational* message: we must make strong, continual efforts to understand our students as empathetically and knowledgeably as possible. If the effort to develop empathy and knowledge is missing, just talking more strongly changes *nothing*. It may even be counterproductive if it is seen just a technique from column B of working better with African American students tacked on to what we otherwise do, without reflection or inquiry.

We have to resist looking for the easy way out—it's a waste of time, because there is none! That is why, in this book, although I do give some suggestions and illustrate issues that arise with examples from classrooms at my school, my main emphasis is on a framework for inquiry and reflection more than a how-to guide. The emphasis is not on the *what* of teaching, but the *why*.

Context

Another reason that the emphasis on this book is on rethinking language and learning, not on describing technique or methodology, is context. I should say that there are two relevant issues about context. The first is the all education is set within an inequitable society. If we teach CLD students, the social justice component of our work can never be forgotten. This aspect of context is front and center of many books on multicultural education and social justice, and is a separate study that I encourage all of us to undertake.

The second aspect of context is simply where we teach. Not enough emphasis is given to this aspect of context in books on pedagogy. There are so many different contexts in which we all teach, and so many different combinations of students in our classrooms. Some teachers work with large numbers of CLD students in inner-city schools that are underfunded and have overtly racist structures, and their hands are tied; others work in inner-city schools where there is a possibility of positive transformation, such as 90-90-90 schools. Some work in affluent districts with smaller numbers of CLD students. Some work in schools with bilingual programs, while others, like those in Massachusetts and California, now have laws severely restricting the possibility of first language use in instruction and materials. Some work in well-funded districts with low student-teacher ratios, while others work in less well-funded districts that have large class sizes. Some work in states or districts with highly controlled curricula, while others have a freer hand.

How could any one program or approach possibly fit every teacher's students and context? How can someone—me or anyone else—who does not know your students tell you the best way to work with them, especially at the detail level of instruction? There is no one, correct thing to do that unites teaching across all these different contexts. We need to

- know ourselves, our students, and their families;

- understand the characteristics of learning enacted in our classrooms;

- understand the sociocultural context of schooling;

- help students develop a capacity to critically reflect on the world around them;

- understand the curricula of school, both the overt as well as the hidden curriculum;

- know that issues of disempowerment are *always* present in diverse classrooms and institutions;

- know the characteristics of the classroom language that CLD students must learn; and

- know how to think in a different way about the learning process.

Then whatever we do will be positive.

Inevitably, my particular context (as described earlier) has strongly influenced this book. The teaching and learning moments used to illustrate the principles in the text are drawn from my own and some of my colleagues' experiences with the particular CLD students who attend my particular school. If my context were a school in which CLD students were the majority population, I'm sure I would enact my teaching differently. However, the frame and process of my thinking would not be different.

In some respects, getting equitable achievement across race, class, and ethnicity in a dominant-culture school in a relatively affluent town with smaller numbers of CLD students can seem more problematic than at a high-poverty school where the will to change exists. Achievement is generally higher for children of color in my town's schools than the state and certainly the national average, but the levels of achievement are still inequitable. However, power holding dominant-culture parents are mainly satisfied with schools whose classrooms that reflect who *their* children are, and the likelihood is that fundamentally altering the learning dynamics and language use of these classrooms to the benefit of small numbers of (often poorer) students of color is not going to happen, regardless of the intent and efforts of some educators. Therefore, my work has grappled with the contextual questions of how to overcome the remaining impediments to independent, higher levels of achievement by my students within dominant-culture learning spaces, and my examples are drawn from these experiences. In fact, this looks to be one of the major trends in education—learning to work with growing percentages of CLD students in historically white districts.

That said, a sociocultural framework for developing a reflective practice should describe *all* teaching contexts. In the service of this goal, the text addresses these overarching questions, which apply to *any* context: How can we more genuinely and respectfully learn more about our CLD students? What are the characteristics of learning in our own classrooms, and how can we learn more about those characteristics? Who are we as cultural beings, and how can we learn more about ourselves in that way? What are the salient characteristics of the English we use in our classrooms, and how can we identify them? How do we positively enact that new knowledge and awareness through our teaching? It is our responsibility to close the gap between what we presently know and all we can know about each of these questions in whatever context we teach in.

Why Only Diverse *Young* Learners?

I have chosen to confine this book to working with diverse young learners, K–6. As children grow and mature, they become more linguistically, socially, culturally, and politically self aware. In addition, the language and concept systems of older students have largely formed, while they are in the process of forming—and are profoundly interrelated—during a student's early years at school. So identifying, highlighting, and working with the differences in language use and cultural patterns that strongly color classroom learning experiences becomes the elementary teacher's job because what is being learned, how it is being learned, and the language through which it is being learned are all so closely intertwined. Most young children do not have the capacity or maturity to sort those things out, let alone recognize them. While I am sure some things in this book may apply to older CLD learners as well, I make no claims for anything being automatically applicable to older learners, with whom I do not have much experience in an American public school setting.

Of course, I do not mean that young children do not feel it or know it when they are excluded by others, the recipients of racist comments or actions, or made to feel invisible within the classroom community. They most certainly do! I am referring to the ability to be analytical about one's cultural environment—especially the interconnection of language and learning, and subtle differences in learning norms and expectations—which implies a level of maturational development that does not usually arrive until a child gets older.

So . . . Let's Begin

I have the utmost respect for classroom teachers—what a job! The amount you have to juggle, keep on top of, and understand is extraordinary. It seems to get harder all the time.

I am also very aware that educational fads are always coming down the pike. You get some training, then your district abandons you to it with no support or drops it and rushes on to something else. It seems like many of these programs are meant to close the gap for underachieving CLD populations, but do they really work, at least as well as you'd like? And the quantity of what you are expected to teach increases all the time. Who wants more of that?

This book does not go with that flow, but rather goes against it, and in a positive way. The secret is really having the space to increase the *quality* of our teaching, a way of thinking about teaching that forms the backbone of the discussion in the first three chapters. It is my hope that this book will help you begin to carve out that space and, by doing so, enhance the learning experience of *all* the students in your classroom. This book is not meant as the end of the process—rather, it's a beginning.

Notes

1. The name changes with the times. It is also called English as a second language (ESL), and some programs are called English learner education (ELE).

2. This is *not* to imply that all culturally and linguistically diverse students are academically underachieving or need special attention.

3. As an example, the rate of overall reading readiness of preschool-age children doubles between the lowest 20 percent and the highest 20 percent of household incomes (Jacobson Chernoff et al. 2007).

4. A transitional bilingual education program, where students split their day between working in their first language (Khmer) and working in English. TBE programs—or any instruction or teaching materials in a child's first language—have essentially been outlawed in Massachusetts since the Question 2 referendum passed in 2002 by adding onerous regulations that make first language instruction very hard to get approved.

5. These general achievement patterns hold across our state, and the country as well.

Children as Thinkers, Learners, and Users of Language

A SOCIOCULTURAL MODEL

What Is Culture?

CONSIDER THESE two scenarios from a first-grade classroom, both experiences of mine related in Bailey and Pransky (2002–3):

> As a way to get the class to focus on appropriate behavior in cooperative groups, the teacher is hamming up a demonstration of inappropriate behavior, such as yanking a book away from someone or saying, "You didn't do that very well!" Almost all the children are laughing, and when the teacher asks the students to comment on what she was doing wrong, almost everyone's hand shoots up. The few Cambodian children in the group look very uncomfortable. At one point, the teacher asks them if they can say what she was doing wrong, but they all look down in apparent embarrassment. They know English well enough. So what don't they get? What is their problem?

> A Latina girl often sits quietly in class with a shy smile on her face. She seems to need an adult to help her through most academic tasks, though she's certainly

active enough in social situations and proactively offers to help the teacher during cleanup and other procedures. As the year goes on, there is little appreciable change in her academic behavior. Does she have special needs?

There are many lenses through which we can view child development and how children learn. For those of us who teach culturally and linguistically diverse students, a sociocultural model is the most revealing. It shows us that most learning is characterized by and enmeshed with linguistic and cultural norms. The culture and language of a classroom may well be mismatched in one or more or ways to any CLD student in it. Indeed, it is often these clashes between the child's cultural and linguistic development and identity on the one hand, and the teacher's and classroom's on the other, that cause the learning of CLD students to become problematic. This chapter focuses on the theme that cultural norms, beliefs, and values deeply influence a child's development, cognition, use of language, and identity, and form the parameters within which children learn best.

A sociocultural perspective centers the discussion in the child for who she is as a thinker and user of language, instead of just in relation to any deficit she seems to have juxtaposed against the dominant classroom language or culture.

Reading the introductory anecdotes, one might have wondered why the Cambodian children were having difficulty even understanding such an obvious lesson and whether the Latina student had special needs. Actually, the Cambodian children were uncomfortable because in their culture, it is shameful for young children to comment on, or especially question, adult behavior. In the girl's case, I learned that positive, caring attention from adults in her home community is often attracted by different behaviors from what we value in the typical classroom at our school, such as independence in learning. As a young girl, she was merely enacting her appropriate role in adult-child relationships as she had been trained to do.

These anecdotes give rise to several questions that must be considered when viewing learning as a sociocultural process:

- Just what is culture, and what is its effect on or relationship to learning, cognition, and language?

- What are the ways that CLD students are positioned differently within the classroom learning environment?

- How are classrooms and culture related?

- Aren't there best practices that are applicable to all children in all learning contexts? Don't all children naturally prefer to learn in a similar way, suggesting that if the learning environment is constructed in a certain way, it will foster the best learning of all students?

• Isn't learning primarily a personal and intellectual process?

These questions are addressed through the following principles:

1. Culture has deep, often hidden elements.

2. Culture, learning preferences, language, and cognition are inextricably intertwined and develop through learning interactions between children and parents or other significant adults.

3. Cultures strongly influence patterns of learning (though we must dance lightly with this idea to avoid stereotyping).

4. Real student-centered learning is learning centered in who students are, not in a particular way of organizing classroom learning dynamics.

5. Disempowerment is a natural characteristic of diverse classrooms unless and until the teacher takes active steps to combat it.

6. We are most comfortable thinking the norm is what we believe and value, and we base our assumptions about best learning on this norm.

7. Successful teachers of CLD students form genuine, interested relationships with them on the students' own terms, both personally and as learners.

8. Equity does not necessarily mean equal.

Before reading what I have to say about each one of these principles in more detail, it might be helpful to think about how each of them resonates with you, or does not, as the case may be.

Principle 1: Culture has deep, often hidden elements.

The first step in understanding a sociocultural framework must be to explore a deeper meaning of culture. The image of an iceberg helps illustrate this concept (see Figure 1–1). Just as we see only a tiny portion of the whole iceberg, our senses recognize only a small part of culture.

At the tip of the iceberg are the sensory elements people most often associate with culture. For instance, if we think of Chinese culture, we might think about certain types of cuisine, brushwork painting, music in a different scale,

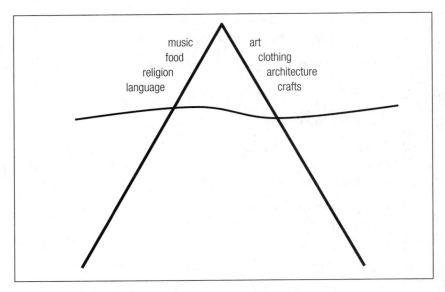

music   art
food   clothing
religion   architecture
language   crafts

FIGURE 1–1. *Cultural Iceberg*

and so on. It has been my experience that when teachers refer to multiculturally sensitive classrooms, they often mean giving prominence to these iceberg-tip elements of their CLD students' cultures. Diverse students feel more comfortable and respected when they see their culture being valued and celebrated along with that of the dominant culture. Indeed, this is a necessary step we must take to create a truly multicultural classroom community where all students are clearly welcomed. It is one basic manifestation of the sympathy I referred to in the book's introduction.

Each teacher brings to the classroom a great deal of "cultural baggage." This baggage may cause the teacher to take certain things for granted and to behave in ways and manners which he/she may not be aware of. The teacher must explore his/her values, opinion, attitudes, and beliefs in terms of their cultural origin. (Locke, in Hollins 1996, 153)

Yet while these visible elements of culture are very important, of more significance to us as teachers are the more subtle, hidden elements of culture—the ones below the surface, where belief systems take shape. Many scholars have realized how culture strongly molds how people should ideally think, feel, behave, act, value, and use language (Rogoff 2003; Gauvain 2001; Au 1980; Feuerstein et al. 1980; Lave and Wegner 1991; Pease-Alvarez and Vasquez 1994). Figure 1–2 shows a more complete cultural iceberg with these deeper, hidden elements.

Though it is easy to overlook when we are part of the dominant culture, it's not just our CLD students who are products of cultural conditioning. We no more represent the norm or the way things should be than anyone else.

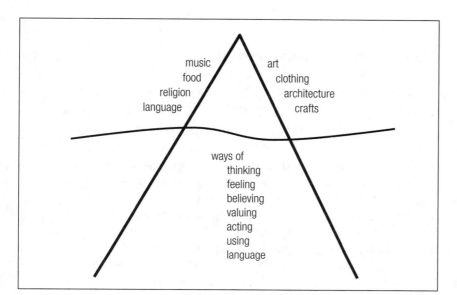

FIGURE 1–2. *Cultural Iceberg with Hidden Elements*

DISCOURSE COMMUNITY

The sociolinguist James Gee developed the concept of discourse community (1990), which is one helpful characterization of culture. (The terms *discourse community* and *culture* will often be used synonymously in this book.) According to Gee, a discourse community is a "socially accepted association among ways of thinking, feeling, believing, valuing and acting that can be used to identify oneself as a member of a socially meaningful group" (46). These ways are expressed both explicitly and implicitly through the shared language of the community.

We sometimes need to negotiate conflicting discourse community identities. As CLD students integrate more into the school discourse community, they often need to reconcile their traditional family and new school identities, especially as they get older. So, two issues arise for CLD students: (1) school discourse community norms may not be clear, and (2) even if clear, they may be in conflict with the students' own norms. Classroom discourse communities most often reflect norms shared by the teacher and majority student population. Without the teacher consciously making the implicit explicit for them, CLD students often remain unaware of the shared understandings of the majority members and the teacher in the dominant-culture classsroom, both with regard to language and the norms upon which learning is predicated. And even if they did understand on their own, they still could not become a member of that new discourse community without the "permission" of the members.

(Continues)

DISCOURSE COMMUNITY *(Continued)*

How Discourse Community Relates to Your Teaching

As a means of initiating a personal process of inquiry and reflection about this important concept, it might be helpful for you to stop for a moment and think of your predominant discourse community memberships, which are likely reflected in your classroom discourse community. Start with gender, race, class, culture, and religion, then think of friends, professional affiliations, hobbies, and so forth. Then take a step back and reflect on the animating beliefs, values, ways of acting, and ways of thinking that underlie your most important discourse community memberships and see how you may be enacting them in your classroom; in other words, your basic expectations of learning, interacting, behaving, etc.

A primary need is to understand our CLD students and their discourse community identities better. But we need to develop a sense of positive, caring interest in who they are at a deeper level than just the broad brush of Japanese culture or Cambodian culture or French culture, which can lead to stereotyping (for more about this, see Principle 3). It's like peeling an onion—as we learn more about ourselves and our students, we ask more questions. There's no place to stop. We should never assume "Now I've figured it all out!"

Thinking Through the Hidden Elements

In one sense, the first three chapters of this book are all about ways to conceptualize the elements hidden below the tip of the cultural iceberg and how they relate to our classrooms. However, following are some brief examples to jumpstart your thinking.

The appropriateness of language and its meaning are held externally as a shared understanding by discourse community members, who use language that conforms to the collective norms of the community. Discourse communities are defined as much by what understandings are shared implicitly by its members as by what is communicated explicitly.

Thinking

Much of this chapter addresses the issue of patterns of thinking developed through cultural activity. As adults who teach, we enact our discourse community expectations of how children should think in the process of learning by the ways we structure learning activities; much more rarely do we *teach* what we expect in terms of how students should think about and process information. After all, why do that if we assume all children are naturally enacting the same patterns of thinking in the process of their learning (barring a special need) or that a particular type of learning task will signal a certain type of thinking and all students will know what that is?

For example, many of us in the dominant culture develop a strength in learning more independently at young ages. Not only is that not a universal, but it is undesirable in some cultures for children not to closely follow the lead of adults. Some of these students might be sitting in our classrooms! We might think of them as passive learners or even question their desire or effort, when the fact is they are just looking for something different. The real problem is that while we and the rest of the class are dancing the polka, some of our CLD students are waltzing. They are disempowered if we do not highlight our classroom discourse community's preferred ways of thinking and give them time to practice them.

The ways we think about experience may differ dramatically according to discourse community. Our CLD students may be thinking about and interpreting classroom interactions and what they have heard in very different ways than we or our dominant-culture students are. They might be feeling excluded even as we think we have included everyone or given everyone equal choice. Just think of the seemingly simple question many of us ask our students after a vacation, "So, what did you all do over the break?" Intentionally or unintentionally, we may end up emphasizing the experiences of students who did special things or went on long trips because, to members of our discourse community, that is what vacations are for when possible. However, some of our students might not stray beyond the walls of their house or the parking lot of their apartment complex, and such conversations bum them out.

Feeling

Along with the ways we think, we do not all feel in similar ways about similar experiences. Political affiliation is a discourse community identity that frequently gives rise to strong feelings and thus illustrates the point. Think of the word *abortion*. How we react to that word emotionally is part and parcel of our political discourse community identity. In conversation with other members of our political discourse community, we group think and feel that word, and thus speak and act accordingly, but we do not need to rehash our shared thoughts, feelings, and beliefs about it. Rather, they are a jumping-off point for conversation, a part of the unspoken ether of the community's interactions. Throughout the day, we frequently access our feelings or generate new feelings about our experiences and toward others, often grounded in our discourse community orientation.

Based on collective experience and for very good reason, people of color often react to the same situations with very different perceptions and feelings than those of us from the dominant culture, even for something as simple as walking into a store and having the shopkeeper look in your direction. In a classroom, it can play out as our feeling that we are being fair and equitable with all our students at the same time that our students of color are feeling ignored, underappreciated, underchallenged, or misunderstood. We may not be aware of how our CLD students are feeling because our own discourse community expectations blind us to the possibility of difference, and so we don't look for signs to the contrary. We think we've tapped into positive feelings, while we've inadvertently stimulated negative ones, like those evoked in the student who did nothing over a break when the experiences of his already more privileged classmates are honored. We need to be humble yet vigilant!

Believing

Strongly connected to ways of feeling and thinking are shared ways of believing. We think, feel, and act based on our beliefs. The students in the anecdotes that kicked off this chapter were acting out very different belief systems than those of the discourse community norms in their classrooms.

Beliefs about time are important underpinnings of our worldview. For example, our dominant culture measures time precisely, almost conferring ownership of time to the individual, which gives rise to concepts of *maximizing time* and *wasting time*. We say "time flies"; Cambodians say "time walks." When I lived in Iran, I couldn't "waste time" or "kill time." Our beliefs about how we can use time pervade our thinking, propel us forward, and deeply affect how we think, plan, and act. It is a touchstone of how school curricula are enacted, and success in school is measured. But not all communities carry that same fundamental belief system about time, which in turn affects the way they think, plan, and act. Our desire to control and "maximize" time plays a key role in the way our culture approaches teaching, curriculum design, and assessment.

There are other examples that may affect how we view students and/or how they act and learn in our classrooms. A Japanese person's sense of identity is defined in large part by the group(s) he belongs to, as foreign as that may seem from our cultural vantage point, where individuality is the prime descriptor. Cambodians "know" that karma rules their lives just as we "know" that free will, talent, and effort make our future, and some people of color "know" that the latter can really be just white privilege talking. We do not easily perceive our culture's deep influence on our (usually) unquestioned core beliefs about the world or how the language we use is grounded in them.

Valuing

Just as feelings color thinking, values color beliefs. I have always been aware of this with many of my older Cambodian parents. For example, at parent conferences, they first want to know if their child has been respectful and behaved well. All else is secondary, including the details of what their child is doing in math or reading. Another way that values may impact our classroom is how we deal with religion or values-related issues. We can easily and quite unintentionally step on the toes of other communities' values.

Acting

How we act expresses how we think, feel, believe, and value. The Cambodian students in the opening anecdote looked down in shame because of their thoughts, beliefs, and feelings regarding that experience, while the other students laughed and actively sought to be called on. And think of the way the Latina student acted, which directly reflected her community beliefs and values. Because of our own cultural lens, however, it was quite easy to misinterpret her behavior and negatively value judge her as a student.

When you were asked to start thinking of your own discourse community identities earlier, you were also simultaneously being asked to think of your profile of a good learner in your classroom: how good learners should think and act in the learning process. Through our instruction, we enact what we think, feel, believe, and value about good learning based on our discourse community assumptions (be they cultural, professional, etc.). When students are not matched to the behaviors and ways of thinking we expect—indeed, even count on—in the way we organize the learning environment, they are disempowered and flounder.

Using Language

Language use is the signal fire of the shared discourse community norms of thinking, feeling, believing, and valuing. Shared ways of using language are what most identifies members of a discourse community.

When I'm with my mother and I'm frustrated, I say, "Oy!" When I'm with friends and frustrated, I'm more likely to say things I would not dream of saying in front of my mother. When I'm with other meditators in my tradition, I use words like *sweep* and *sensation* without needing to explain I do not mean them in the usual sense. And in that context, our usually unverbalized, shared beliefs form the backdrop for our conversations, which would be hard to understand for folks who do not *sit*. Teacher jargon inevitably infuses our professional discourse community identity. Sometimes when I sit in on special education meetings, I realize that the teachers are communicating as a discourse community in ways that the parent does not really get, especially if English is not her first language.

It can be surprising what some CLD students *don't* know about the language of the classroom discourse community and what we take for granted. Take the word *listen*. It seems pretty obvious. However, in their homes, some of my CLD students experience *listen* as a command that is associated solely with *behavior*: for example, "Listen to me! I told you never to do that again!" At school, its dual function is not automatically understood. At school, the command to listen regathers class (or an individual student's) focus (behavior), but for the more important end of *thinking*; in other words, it's really synonymous with *learn*. Many of my underachieving CLD students just hear when they really should listen. Further, when we use a common teacher expression like "Listen—eyes on me," it confuses some students, who then think that you use your eyes to listen at school. In fact, I've had some CLD students name "eyes" and "body" even before "ears" when I ask them what part of their body they use to listen. But I want them to realize that the most important part of the body in listening is the *brain*! We need to try to pay careful attention to classroom uses of language and not always assume we have communicated clearly to and with our CLD students.

> *To become a member of a new discourse community, one needs to become initiated into the appropriate ways of using language and interacting. That means that as teachers, we need to take the lead as best we can in making explicit the implicit values, beliefs, and ways of thinking, acting, and using language of our classroom discourse community and openly act as our CLD students' strongest advocates for full inclusion in the community.*

Chapter 2 is devoted to deconstructing some of the dominant-culture classroom's preferred ways of using language. It cannot be emphasized enough that our language use in the classroom reflects the shared, often implicit, norms of our classroom discourse community, that is, our shared ways of thinking, feeling, believing, valuing, and acting.

It's not that we should be expected to know all the details of our students' discourse community identities or even our own. But when we discover that discourse communities exist and strongly influence how we and our CLD students think, feel, learn, and use language in our classrooms, we should *want* to start. The development of this type of empathy and knowledge is what a reflective practice of inquiry is for.

A Hidden Dimension

As a great educational thinker, Jerome Bruner (1996), once wrote, "The chief subject matter of school, culturally speaking, is school itself." Besides language use and interaction norms, the curriculum itself has this hidden dimension. A very interesting study by Anyon (in Hollins 1996) in the early 1980s revealed the symbiotic relationship between schools and the discourse communities in which they are set. Although the schools in Anyon's study nominally all had the same explicit academic curriculum, he found that students were being socialized to learn in very different ways.

In "working class" schools, the students primarily engaged in mechanical activity, with little questioning. Conforming to procedure and following rules were emphasized. Anyon concluded that these students were being prepared for mechanical and routine adult jobs. In "middle class" schools, the emphasis switched to getting the right answer. Work that required students to follow a lot of directions was common. These students, Anyon surmised, were being prepared for adult jobs in bureaucracies, handling paperwork, and technical tasks.

In "affluent professional" schools, the focus switched again, with an emphasis on creativity and originality. Based on the emphasis on developing artistic, intellectual, and scientific creativity, he surmised that those students were being prepared for professional careers. Finally, in "executive elite" schools, students engaged in problem solving and a wide range of critical thinking skills, and in mastering high-status knowledge. They were being trained to manage systems and people.

The roots of those different hidden curricula stretch back directly into the majority students' families. The way children are apprenticed to learn in the home most often extends into the schools that are based in their communities and represents the dominant discourse community norms. It is a seamless and often implicit connection for some students, but invisible and disconnected for others.

As teachers, it should be part of our reflective practice to uncover the explicit and implicit norms of our schools and classrooms and communicate them clearly to students.

The most successful students practice selective acculturation into the dominant culture while maintaining their own (cultural) identity (Lee 2006). We need to help foster this proactive, positive biculturalism. We certainly should not be out to remake CLD students in our own image, or think that we are giving them something of any objective or transcendent value if we initiate them into our classroom discourse community. Of course, given what it takes to be successful at school, we must try to make the implicit norms of our classrooms comprehensible and accessible—just with all the humility and perspective we can muster. My goal is to help students become as independently successful as they can be within the system while supporting the growth of a healthy, positive, bicultural identity, so they can become stake-holding members of society in the future and help transform society in positive ways.

Principle 2: Culture, learning preferences, language, and cognition are inextricably intertwined and developed through learning interactions between children and parents or other significant adults.

A couple of years ago, I was at the post office during the Christmas rush. The line was long and slow moving. A man behind me had brought his young child along, who looked to be about three or four years old. After running around a few minutes, the child asked, "Why are we here?"

"To send presents for Christmas."

"Why are we doing that?"

"Families like to send each other presents at Christmas."

"Why?"

"We like to get presents, don't we? So it's important to be kind and give presents, too."

"Why?"

The conversation continued in this vein for a while. Every answer of the father prompted a new "Why?" from his son. Anyone who has his own child or has been around a child of this age is familiar with this stage of child development.

Clearly, more was going on than a simple conversation. The child was developing his social awareness, practicing language and new vocabulary, and learning social norms, all of which in turn were intimately connected to the construction of the child's concepts and worldview. The child was also learning the value placed on asking questions in his culture. (This is not a universal; my Cambodian cultural informant tells me that in the local Cambodian community, adults do not often answer young children's why questions and instead cut them off, which socializes those children to a completely different understanding of the use and value of children's questions to adults!) There is no point at which the development of cognition, language, sociocultural beliefs, values and ways of acting, and learning preferences can be uncoupled.

Formal school academic achievement in our culture demands high degrees of metacognitive awareness, which is closely tied to independence in learning, which is fostered by our culture as well.

Language and culture connect directly to cognition. Children develop a cluster of independent critical thinking skills based on the type of culturally familiar problem-solving activities and language interactions they engage in with

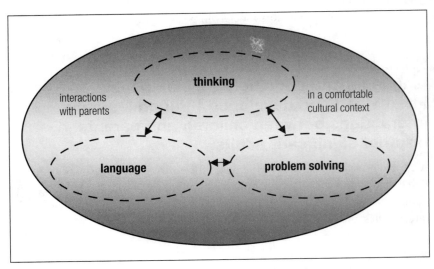

FIGURE 1–3. *Language—Thinking Skills—Problem-Solving Style Tripod*

their parents. The imprint of these patterns helps form the deep impact culture has on each of us, on our ways of thinking, believing, and acting. We could say that while we enact culture, culture enacts us. (That is not to say that people do not also have their own individuality. They are not mutually exclusive concepts, and dwelling on any apparent dichotomy is ultimately just a red herring.) As children interact with significant adults, they develop the preferred ways of using the language, thinking, and problem solving of their community through the ways the adults organize, direct, and participate in those interactions. Figure 1–3 on page 12 shows the connection between cultural experience, ways of thinking, and ways of using language.

CULTURE SHAPES HOW CHILDREN LEARN

In his book on fostering cognitive competence, Prem Fry (1992) cites John Ogbu, who has written extensively and powerfully about immigrant communities in the United States, saying that "children's sociocultural ecologies pose problems and tasks that function to organize and channel the child's intellectual processes in given ways" (63). Cultures are organized to support children's integration into the preferred activities and ways of their community (Rogoff 2003). Rogoff notes that in more traditional societies, children learn to become meaningful contributors to their societies over time by watching and copying adult models and participating directly in adult society. For instance, a child will begin to work on the farm from an early age, long before any actual labor of hers has a corresponding payoff for the adult community.

Westernized, industrial, literacy-oriented society no longer has such an immediate contributory role for children. In the same way that the observe-and-copy model prepares children for future meaningful integration into many traditional cultures, schooling prepares children for meaningful integration into literacy-oriented society. Stake-holding parents in literacy-oriented societies naturally prepare their children for success within that cultural paradigm through the ways that they construct learning tasks and use language. That only

makes sense, but the home community acculturation and apprenticeship of all the students in our classrooms is not necessarily literacy oriented.

Take metacognition. Metacognition is a person's awareness of her own learning, both process and content. While all people develop metacognitive awareness, not all cultures expect, set out to develop, or even desire high degrees of metacognitive awareness *in children*. Some studies indicate that an earlier development of metacognitive skills may be correlated with higher socioeconomic status (Werdenschlag 1993; Wang 1993; Portes et al. 1994; Sinha, in Valsiner 1988).

Higher socioeconomic status is often an indicator of the parents' education level. Specifically, western middle-class and affluent adult-child problem-solving interactions often include parental distancing strategies, which encourage young children's metacognitive development. In other words, the more a child's home acculturation to thinking and language is literacy oriented by virtue of the parents' cultural orientation and experience, the more the likely the child will be to develop independence in learning and metacognitive skills, which, in turn, the child will use within school-based literacy tasks for higher levels of achievement.

Research for Better Teaching (2007) has published a list called "A Proposed Taxonomy of Thinking Skills," developed by Susan Burns, which categorizes fifty-five ways of thinking into five groupings of cognitive skills. To me, these stake out the range of thinking skills a student will need to possess to succeed independently at higher levels in school. Facility with such a wide range of thinking skills is connected to home acculturation in a literacy culture, which, again, means higher levels of metacognitive awareness.

What About You?

If you have your own children, you can do this exercise more easily, but even if you do not, try to remember when you were growing up. It focuses on the type of activities you might do or have done with your child(ren) at around age four or those you did with your parents at that age. Circle the appropriate number for each sample activity, either generally if it is an evening or daily ritual or just in relation to its frequency whenever you do a particular activity. Of course, there are no right answers. Pick the first thing that seems right; don't try to overanalyze.

1 = always 2 = frequently 3 = sometimes 4 = rarely 5 = never					
a. You talk together about the pictures in books.	1	2	3	4	5
b. He/she often watches you work.	1	2	3	4	5
c. He/she "helps" you shop, cook, and so forth, by "reading" a (pretend) recipe or list.	1	2	3	4	5
d. You talk together about a TV show or a movie after you watch it.	1	2	3	4	5
e. He/she uses real knives or tools to help in the kitchen or with other chores.	1	2	3	4	5
f. You "read" "writing" he/she scribbles onto a paper.	1	2	3	4	5
g. You play with him/her as he/she pretend-enacts social or work-related roles.	1	2	3	4	5

It is likely that you circled 1 or 2 for a, c, d, f, and g. These are typical literacy-oriented, middle-class child-rearing activities, as opposed to b and e, which are more typical of watch-and-copy, traditional cultures. We generally parent in ways that fit our particular culture, as do parents everywhere.

Children are apprenticed to become meaningful contributors to society in different ways in different cultures. We can expect that as products of different languages, home communities, and ways of thinking, we have a lot to learn about—and from—the second language learners in our classrooms, and they about us.

Principle 3: Cultures strongly influence patterns of learning (though we must dance lightly with this idea to avoid stereotyping).

Once I asked my three fourth graders in their pullout ELL group to tell me about a field trip their class had been on the previous day. The group consisted of a Sri Lankan boy who came to the United States as a non–English speaker toward the end of first grade and two Cambodian American girls who were born in the United States and English dominant, at least in a school context. Their class had gone to a local pond to collect microorganisms, with the goal of determining the health of the ponds.

I asked Bunthea, "So what did you learn on the field trip?"

"We learned about Gold's Pond."

"Can you tell me what you learned about Gold's Pond? Make an 'I learned that . . .' kind of sentence."

"I learned Gold's Pond is nonhealthy [sic]."

"But how do you know if it is unhealthy?"

"It has trash in it," she said.

"Did you go on the field trip to learn that?" I asked.

"No . . . ," she said pensively.

"I learned that there are invertebrates in Gold's Pond," said Bopha, the other Cambodian American girl.

"That's interesting. Did you learn anything about the invertebrates and the pond? That's why you went on the trip. What's the connection between the invertebrates and the pond water?"

"Aah . . ."

Bunthea added, "We collected invertebrates and looked at them under a microscope."

"That's interesting. But is that what you learned?"

"No . . ."

Achala, the Sri Lankan boy, piped up, "I learned that we can know if the [sic] Gold's Pond water is healthy by looking at the invertebrates."

"Oh, I see."

"Oh yeah!" Bopha and Bunthea chimed in in the background.

I quickly was able to help Achala move to the abstract even more—that we can know if any water system (not just Gold's Pond water) is healthy or not by the kind of invertebrates that live in it—using language that encapsulated the overall lesson the classroom teacher intended the class to get from the trip.

The girls, however, continued to struggle to connect what they learned about invertebrates to water health. They had difficulty stating specifically what it was they had learned and extricating their personal experience out of it. At one point one of them said they learned that Gold's Pond had frogs in it. Each thing they said was certainly true enough and obviously meaningful to them, but without a great deal of repetition, modeling, and support, they could not move their learning into the abstract, to restate the learning they did as being true outside themselves or their direct experience, unlike the Sri Lankan boy, who could do it with almost no support at all. What was going on?

Everybody undoubtedly has the ability to think for him- or herself. Yet it is also true that when we enter a new culture, we experience a great many shared patterns of thinking, valuing, acting, and using language that clearly differ from our own. It is obviously not just a big coincidence of large numbers of individuals just happening to think, feel, believe, value, and act in similar ways!

Think of every human being as having predispositions toward the ways of thinking, feeling, believing, or acting and using language of their parents' discourse community. Predispositions cluster into recognizable patterns and deeply influence us as we internalize our parents' ways of relating to experience. We rarely question them. As teachers, we enact our own acculturation in the way we construct the learning environment, organize learning activities, and expect learning to occur, and we express our predispositions through our use of language.

While children from any culture have the potential for developing any particular array of cognitive skills, the profile and time line of any particular child's cognitive development is strongly shaped by habitual cultural activity, learning tasks, and the language that accompanies them. Even such a "basic" concept as *intelligence* is described differently in different cultures (Healy 2005; Valsiner 1988). So how much can we assume about what understandings we share with our students?

Research has identified a number of continua of cognitive, problem-solving, and learning preference patterns that seem to be influenced by culture. There is also research into the cultural learning styles of various groups, such as African Americans, Native Americans, and Latinos (Shade, Kelly, and Oberg 1997). The following are a few signature examples of general cultural patterns of learning.

Field Independent versus Field Dependent (in Lieberman 1997)[1]

- *Field independent:* comfortable and successful with problem solving alone; problems do not need to be tied closely to present context, can be more abstract

- *Field dependent:* more comfortable and successful with problem solving with others; problems need to be tied closely to present context

Top-Down versus Bottom-Up (Hollins 1996)

- *Top-down:* more comfortable and successful with working with the whole, making connections to discover relevant pieces; reflects more independent orientation to learning

- *Bottom-up:* more comfortable and successful with mastering small pieces, putting the whole together over time; reflects more dependence on adults in learning contexts

Impulsive versus Reflective (in Lieberman 1997)

- *Impulsive:* mistakes and partial answers are expected, seen as integral part of learning (It's important to note that one does not have to *like* mistakes to be considered an impulsive learner.)

- *Reflective:* mistakes are a significant loss of face and are to be avoided

Many people fall somewhere in between the two extremes of each continuum. Having read a brief description of these patterns, you could probably place yourself on the continuum for each (thinking of what is most generally true about you). Try it:

```
Field                                                    Field
Dependent                                            Independent
├──────────────────────────────────────────────────────┤


Bottom-Up                                            Top-Down
├──────────────────────────────────────────────────────┤


Reflective                                           Impulsive
├──────────────────────────────────────────────────────┤
```

It would not be surprising if many dominant-culture readers of this book ended up with relatively similar-looking continua, clustered toward field independent, top-down, and impulsive. These characteristics tend to cluster together, as do their opposites. (Various cultural descriptors can also be clustered into a collectivist versus individualist continuum [Northeast and Islands Regional Educational Laboratory 2002], high context versus low context, and others.) The left side of these continua appears to be more prevalent, among other contexts, in more traditional cultures, while the right side seems to be found more in competitive, literacy-oriented, industrialized societies (Timm 1999; Lieberman 1997).

The point is not to learn these different cultural characterizations, but to recognize the fact that patterns do exist. Because we are all deeply influenced by culture, we may find subtle but profound differences in assumptions about thinking, learning, and problem solving within our classroom community. Becoming sensitized to them and understanding them (while taking care not to reduce them to stereotypes) is part of a reflective practice of inquiry. Learning more about the above patterns and others as well should be a part of any teacher's reflective practice. We just have to find a balance between stereotypically *pre*judging students based on notions of cultural patterns of thinking on the one hand, and being blind to other patterns, or thinking that our way is "right," or the only way, on the other.

Both Bopha and Bunthea from the earlier anecdote seemed to be predominantly field-dependent, bottom-up learners.[2] Their narrative and attempts at restating their learning were centered in their concrete experience, which they could not easily move out of on their own. Achala, on the other hand, although perhaps not from a traditionally field-independent, top-down culture, had adapted quite well to our school's norms. That may be because his home discourse community was very much literacy oriented. He was well positioned to function within the learning task described in the anecdote, and not surprisingly, he was also a much more successful student at our school. James Gee (1990) interestingly defines literacy as the ability to be at home in at least two discourse communities; in that sense as well as the traditional one, Achala was certainly quite literate!

The girls' struggle was not with making sense of what they did or learned on the trip (when asked specific questions about their experience, they mostly gave accurate, pertinent answers). Rather, their difficulty lay in independently organizing the information into a generalized learning statement and knowing that, by extension, they could use what they learned at Gold's Pond to predict the relative health of any water system, anywhere, any time.

I am certainly not negating individuality or advocating that we should reactively assume that all students from culture *x* will think or act in a certain way. Not all the Cambodian American students in our community have the challenge of moving into the abstract, or generalizing, like Bopha and Bunthea. On the other hand, many do struggle in a similar way at our school. As I learned more about the Cambodian community here, I became more sensitized, among other things, to the need to ask questions that probe whether students have independently generalized their learning experiences, and more ready to help scaffold their learning in particular ways if needed. Swimming in that stream of thinking allows me to understand my students more empathetically and knowledgeably.

Academic tasks are cultural tasks, and cultural tasks have a cluster of preferred independent thinking skills that go along with them. Learning tasks in dominant-culture classrooms reflect dominant-culture norms.[3] The more students in the classroom who are from the dominant culture, the more likely this is to be true—especially if the teacher is as well.

We must recognize discourse community difference and actively try to create an equitable learning environment based truly on our students (not on what some pedagogy or other says about best learning). Otherwise, we enhance the empowerment of children from the dominant culture at the expense and disempowerment of our CLD students.

Principle 4: Real student-centered learning is learning centered in who students are, not in a particular way of organizing classroom learning dynamics.

Student-centered learning is generally thought of as a type of natural learning environment where student creativity and individuality are fostered and allowed to flourish, a learning environment where students can construct their own meaning. However, the best learning of CLD students may not naturally be centered in those learning dynamics. In diverse classrooms especially, it is very important to avoid sweeping generalizations about how students learn best. If it is true that students' learning predispositions are rooted in sociocultural apprenticeship in their home community, then best learning is firmly rooted in context. And while it is certainly in the best interests of CLD students to become adept in the dominant discourse community's preferred ways, that is not the same thing as saying that all children are prepared to enact those ways without support and structured efforts to bridge their preferred ways with those of the classroom—or that they will automatically understand those ways to have the same value that we give them.

The very effort to understand ourselves, our students, and our classroom learning environment from linguistic and cultural perspectives, and the knowledge we gain from it, are crucial to creating a more equitable learning environment.

Our field swings from one new pedagogy to the next. Many contemporary pedagogies—whole language, process writing, constructivism, inquiry-based learning, Investigations (a math program)—have been animated and linked by a similar universalist philosophy that claims to represent the best learning of all children, everywhere. Yet the reality has been that each one of these pedagogies has not been as efficacious for many CLD students as it has been for dominant-culture students (see Delpit 1995; Bailey and Pransky 2005). If our thinking is bound by the dictates of pedagogy and not grounded in ourselves and our students, we may perpetuate inequity.

A few years ago, there was a Cambodian student in the first-grade inclusion classroom who loved Cambodian history and was very strong in Khmer, more so than other Cambodian American students his age. The Cambodian paraprofessional told us he was quite unusual in that way. Although the boy was very smart and had these quite mature interests, he didn't listen well and seemed sort of stubborn, even aloof, which was also unusual. The classroom teacher and I raised this issue at the spring conference. The mother laughed in an embarrassed way and said that she knew what we meant. She was very sorry. But because of the boy's precocious interest in Cambodian history—while he was not even in Cambodia—she and in fact the entire Cambodian community were sure that her son was the reincarnation of a famous Cambodian king. He was getting that message both explicitly and implicitly, as the community treated him differently from other children his age. He was developing a privileged personality around it. But the mother did want her child to act more considerate and be aware of others.

I spoke about this with the Cambodian para, and we developed a plan. Amid the true Cambodian stories he read or told to the boy, the para made up short morality tales about King Jaya, a famous, very positive historical figure, when he was young. In these stories, King Jaya showed certain qualities that he became famous for as an adult king—he wisely listened to others, he knew what he knew and what he still needed to learn, and he always did as he was asked (showing respect for his elders). The boy listened with rapt attention to these stories! Then the para, classroom teacher, and I periodically said to him as needed, "I wonder how King Jaya would act now?" or "Be like King Jaya!" Each time, he beamed broadly and did his best to act like King Jaya.

What CLD students need is teaching based in who they are as learners, thinkers, and users of language. Sometimes that may mean teaching in ways that contradict much of we have been trained to think is best and that certainly may not feel right to us instinctively! But to be successful in the classroom curriculum, CLD learners do not need the right pedagogy: they need the right teacher.

Principle 5: Disempowerment is a natural characteristic of diverse classrooms unless and until the teacher takes active steps to combat it.

What is your reaction to this scenario?

> In a sixth-grade classroom, the class has been divided up into heterogeneous groups of three or four for a paper-folding challenge as a part of a unit on Ancient Egypt. They are trying to make a pyramid by folding one piece of paper, a multistep process. As groups work on the project and need further help, the teacher passes out directions slips for each step in mixed-up order but does not tell the groups that the number of each direction has been lightly penciled in on the back of the slip.
>
> One group is composed of Tom, an empowered white student; John, an academically very strong Chinese American student; and Savuth, a disempowered Cambodian American boy (meaning an academically underachieving, poor student who cannot advocate for himself in a classroom of mostly high-achieving, dominant-culture students). As they set to work, Tom takes charge. He engages John directly but does not even glance Savuth's way. He positions the paper to be folded directly in front of his body and tries to fold it, getting frustrated. John is leaning forward in his seat; Savuth leans back in his. From time to time, Tom directs comments John's way, and at those moments, John responds. Meanwhile, the teacher has placed the directions slips quietly at the corner of one of their desks.
>
> Suddenly, Tom pushes back his seat, loudly says, "*I* [emphasis added] can't do this!" and stomps off. Savuth happens to notice the directions slips on the corner of the table and shows them to John. Together they happily begin to lay the strips down and try to make sense of them, chatting and working comfortably together. A little later, Tom returns. He sits down and says loudly, "*I* [emphasis added] got it now!" He pushes the slips to the side and positions the paper in front of his body again. He turns to John and begins to tell him his idea.
>
> At this point, Savuth happens to turn over one of the slips and sees the number. He says in a quiet voice, "There's numbers on the back of these slips."
>
> Tom looks up in annoyance, saying, "Shh! I gotta think!" then goes back to his work. John seems torn about whom to pay attention to, finally deciding to lean toward Tom again. Savuth puts the slip back on the table and leans back in his chair, staring impassively forward for the rest of the time.

In such a well-planned, engaging, and apparently innocent group lesson, the academic pecking order was asserted forcefully—by the students themselves!

Savuth was ignored and devalued, even though he was the one who discovered a key to successfully completing the project. He was disempowered quite blatantly in this scenario, but more often it is a subtle process that insinuates itself into many aspects of classroom life. Think of it this way: not being initiated into the discourse community's implicit norms is, itself, a form of disempowerment for some CLD students.

Groups

Successful grouping strategies are wonderful and can help empower CLD students. Cooperative groups, for example, are an important way to get children to work together and create social cohesion. They are mentioned in almost every book I know about teaching English language learners as a way to further integrate diverse students into classroom activity. And there's no doubt, if done in the right way, they are a wonderful way to integrate children socially and culturally, and therefore we should use them. In fact, field-sensitive (field-dependent) students are understood to prefer learning with others.

On the other hand, groups can just as easily perpetuate disempowerment. What does using groups in the right way mean? It means knowing the following:

- Social and cultural inequities will find their way into children's group work.

- Many disempowered children cannot overcome those inequities on their own, so we must pay attention to group dynamics while they are in process and frequently process or revisit group behaviors and expectations before and after groups.

- Assigning roles in groups does not ensure participation and learning.

- Even when there's a time crunch, we should not drop spending time on group processing.

- Heterogeneous groups are not better than homogeneous groups by definition.

- The most academically empowered students will most likely set the pace of a group's progress in a task or project.

- Weaker students will not necessarily pick things up from discussion and get great student models for their own future work just by being in a group with academically strong students.

Even if children of equal social and academic status are typically able to extend and develop their understanding of things in discussion with one another, all bets are off when children of dissimilar classes, races, cultures, and degrees of academic empowerment are put together. It may work out well, but any assumption that because it is heterogeneous group work it will, disempowers many CLD students. Social inequities and power imbalances can easily color and slant the interactions.

Having CLD students in our classrooms means we must, at least, be very vigilant with group work.

For instance, most Cambodian American students in my school will unfailingly just defer to the opinions of academically empowered students whether they've understood them (or agree with them) or not. This gains them absolutely nothing. If the parameters of learning are set by the most academically empowered student(s) in a group, then the group will probably not serve the academic needs of any underachieving students in it, since it offers little in the way of a trickle-down effect.

Students are either empowered within a classroom discourse community or disempowered. The default setting for many CLD students in classrooms is disempowerment until and unless the teacher actively takes steps to change this dynamic. There is no middle ground, nor can any methodology, technique, or pedagogical philosophy by itself transform this reality. Aside from the obvious, such as disrupting racism, classism, and so on, between students (or in ourselves) when we see it, *active effort* means

✓ trying to understand ourselves, our students, and the learning (and social) dynamics of our classroom through a sociocultural lens

✓ deconstructing assumptions when we realize them

✓ bridging mismatches when they are found

✓ making the tacit explicit

✓ strongly addressing disempowerment issues whenever they surface (Delpit 1995; Gee 1990; Bailey and Pransky 2002–3, 2005)

The act of trying to better understand the assumptions on which we and our schools build our expectations about learning, thinking, and language use is combating disempowerment, as long as we act on the fruits of this process.

Being Empathetic

One necessary way to forge an empathetic relationship with underachieving students, and therefore combat disempowerment, is to try to see schooling from their perspective. A lot of the time school is hard—and, to them, boring! It doesn't connect to the reality of their lives. Why should they put out the extra effort it will take them compared with most of their classmates to read pages 77–82 and answer the questions for homework if they don't see a concrete pay-off, there are no education models among their family members to aspire to, or no one at home can help them? If they have no tangible hopes, dreams, or aspirations for the future, why bother to slog through it? Success in the dominant society can look like an awfully forbidding, impossible—even unattractive—goal to a family beaten down by racism, language chauvinism, and classism.

For sure, many of their empowered classmates will also find that same homework boring, but they most likely have parents who will remind them implicitly if not explicitly of the education goal of college and how that feeds into their adult lives. For them, the future connection to the present moment is always there. Their parents check if they have homework, insist they do it, and more important, can help with it if needed.

Teachers have to fill in these missing pieces at school through empathetic action and understanding conversation with students whose parents do not engage them at home in those ways, explaining that success in school will give them more choices in their future and that they can achieve it. And yes, I also expect them to do the homework, regardless, though I will also help and talk to them about it as much as I need to. These conversations are important, not to browbeat students with, but to help them extend their present into the future and establish relevance where otherwise there may be none.

Speaking of homework, giving homework that requires parent involvement is one of the most disadvantaging and disempowering things a teacher can do in a culturally and linguistically diverse classroom. That automatically favors literacy-oriented, educated parents who know English well. It's like saying to those students, "You were born lucky, so you win a prize!", while saying to other students, "You lose again!" Homework should be practicing what students already have some degree of skill with, and any projects should not value computer-generated work over handmade. School staff should have a dialogue over equitable, reasonable homework policy.

Principle 6: We are most comfortable thinking the norm is what we believe and value, and we base our assumptions about best learning on this norm.

While awaiting another student to arrive in class, I was chatting with a couple of third-grade-age Latino students who had recently moved to our rural western Massachusetts school from New York City. Somehow the topic turned to clothes colors, and I don't recall exactly what had been said, but I remember that I blithely replied, "We don't see many boys wearing pink, do we?"

One of the girls looked at me quizzically and said, "What? We saw boys wearing pink a lot in New York."

Ouch! I was embarrassed. It is so easy to fall into this trap. The idea of this principle was touched on earlier, in the more general sense of looking at popular pedagogical trends. Here the emphasis is on how it plays out in one's classroom expectations.

Focus just on your classroom for a moment. The norms of our classrooms are inextricably bound up with our own beliefs, values, thinking, and ways of using language, which in turn have deep cultural roots. To be effective at teaching CLD students, we need to deconstruct the paradigm of viewing our own ways as normal, culturally neutral, or best for all students.

Read the following statements and rate yourself by circling the appropriate number on a 1–5 scale, with 1 meaning you strongly agree and 5 meaning you strongly disagree.

a. All children are responsible for their own learning.

    1   2   3   4   5

b. The professional training I received was often presented as representing best practices in teaching and learning for all children.

    1   2   3   4   5

c. My belief in equity creates an equitable classroom for all my students.

    1   2   3   4   5

d. Learning is mainly a function of effort and intelligence.

    1   2   3   4   5

e. Learning must be fun for children to be engaged and learn.

    1   2   3   4   5

f. If I present problems or give the big picture to children, and have them explore and grapple with the whole, they will learn much about the relevant parts.

    1   2   3   4   5

How you placed yourself on a continuum regarding these few statements begins to define the discourse community learning norms of your classroom—

A FEW WORDS ABOUT WORKING WITH PARENTS

From dedicated teachers in my own district as well as from teachers I have worked with in a teacher training capacity from other states and districts, I have heard a truism repeated over and over: parents need to be involved with their children's education. Who can deny that this is true? But what does *involved* mean? All too often I hear, and certainly saw this in myself as well, that the meaning of *involved* takes on the norms of the dominant culture's discourse community ways of thinking, believing, valuing, and acting. It becomes "involved in the ways I get involved regarding my own children," "the way the involvement fits into school expectations," or "the way parents *should* get involved if they *really* support their children's education."

When parents are not involved in our preferred ways, it is easy to judge them as being uninvolved. Our schools can feel like forbidding, cold places to people of color, and meetings are often scheduled when parents are working, and so they don't show. Child care and transportation can be huge issues. Parents may not come in when asked for any or all of those reasons, and we make value judgments about them. Relationships with parents from CLD communities can quickly take on a chauvinistic flavor (Carreon, Drake, and Bartob 2005; Ovando, Collier, and Combs 2003; Kermani and Janes 1999)—then it's the student who loses out.

Creating positive, respectful relationships with parents is imperative! In fact, positive parent relationships with their child's teacher can contribute to higher levels of CLD student engagement (Hughes and Kwok 2007). From this perspective, we often see that parents are quite involved in their children's education based on their *own* community's ways, which may look nothing like the school's ways or the teacher's ways. But does that mean it's wrong or not there at all?

I saw this play out with the Cambodian community at our school. As the Cambodian immigrant community expanded and there was a huge influx of Cambodian children into our school, often directly from refugee camps, I and others immersed ourselves in trying to learn as much about the community and their situation as we could. We relied heavily on our new Cambodian staff. We organized bilingual bookmaking days and began significant outreach efforts for parents and families. But interestingly, without consulting with Cambodian cultural informants about this aspect of the relationship, we told the parents at meetings and parent conferences how they should support their children's education, saying things like, "Read to your children. And even if you don't know how to read, you can tell your children lots of stories! Be sure your children do their own homework; don't let older siblings do it for them!" The parents nodded, smiled, and hardly ever said a word. . . .

And we began to get frustrated when we found out that all of the wonderful ideas we'd so generously figured out for them around school involvement turned out not to happen! Then we got annoyed. What was wrong with these parents, anyway? Didn't they even want to get involved with their children's education?

Ah, that silenced dialogue again. Then one year, the first-grade ELL-inclusion classroom teacher and I decided to give our Cambodian students' parents the option of holding conferences in their homes. Several chose to do so, and it was a revelation! We were now on their turf, which naturally moved us to shift the paradigm from what we wanted, expected, and knew to what they wanted. We started asking how Cambodian parents raise their children, how parents relate to schools in Cambodia, what they wanted for their children, and so on. It was one of the most valuable learning experiences I have ever had. We learned that Cambodian parents show support for school by giving their children over to the school and saying, "You are our children's second parents. Do with them as you will." There can't be more respect and trust for school than that! They teach their children to be extremely respectful and never to question a teacher. And if a teacher needs a parent to help him do the job of teaching, well, maybe the teacher shouldn't be getting paid to do that job. We also learned that it is not the parents' job to tell stories to children in that culture; it is the grandparents' job, or the monk might do it. And one way parents support school is by having older children help younger children with homework.

So, it turned out that almost everything we had been telling the parents they should do ran counter to the norms, values, and beliefs of their discourse community! In other words, in our patronizing certainty, we had inadvertently been giving families this message: Your ways are wrong.

One interaction was particularly poignant. When asked how Cambodian children learn from their parents in Cambodia, one parent sighed. "In Cambodia, children watch their parents. Then they do what they do and that is how they learn. Boys watch their fathers and girls watch their mothers. In Cambodia, I was a farmer. My children could watch me and learn. But I can't farm here. I have nothing to do for them to watch." We began to realize that our perspective on the parents' lack of support was our problem, not theirs. The problem was our own blind adherence to our discourse community beliefs and values, which devalued the Cambodian parents (and others) and only emphasized the disempowerment they were already experiencing vis-à-vis the school. We had just expected that they'd be like us because we told them what was best for them, and we subtly signaled our displeasure when they didn't conform.

In retrospect, I find it particularly revealing that around this issue only, we did not feel it necessary to ask for advice from our Cambodian school staff. Rather, we had told them how we were going to do it. They would not have dreamed of telling us we were wrong, and we did not pick up on whatever subtle signals they might have been trying to send us about it. A perfect example of the "silenced dialogue" in action.

the assumptions on which you base your teaching, your expectations of both learning and behavior, and your assumptions about best teaching and learning practices. Those children who share many of those ways of thinking, feeling, believing, acting, and ways you use language are naturally empowered in your classroom (see above); those children who do not, are not. Aside from building this into your own reflective practice, I recommend that you develop a professional dialogue with other teachers around these (and other) belief statements, and engage in the discussion from an empathetic and knowledgeable understanding of your CLD students. That level of philosophical engagement is one way to help a staff see beyond the boundaries of their experience and acculturation.

Naturally, pedagogies in any society (discourse community) are representative of the ways of thinking, believing, and acting of the dominant group(s) in

One cannot separate cultural values and assumptions from pedagogy, because no teaching can possibly be without a cultural context.

that society. Table 1–1 deconstructs some dominant-culture values and assumptions about learning that underlie the popular and very influential pedagogy of constructivism, developed by Brooks and Brooks (1999). It compares them with those held by the Cambodian American community in my town, as learned through conversations with parents and Cambodian professionals and paraprofessionals in our building as well as working with students over many years.

The reflective process helps us deconstruct our teaching and the learning dynamics in our classrooms in terms of discourse community norms, values, and expectations. By engaging in reflection, we begin a slow transformation of our teaching. We do not need to abandon our previous ways of doing things wholesale. Rather, as our perspective on teaching, learning, ourselves, and our students matures and deepens, how we teach becomes more considered and successful for all children. However we teach then is good.

Principle 7: Successful teachers of CLD students form genuine, interested relationships with them on the students' own terms, both personally and as learners.

The Minority Student Achievement Network (MSAN) is an affiliation of basically affluent districts in which students of color, while generally outperforming students of color nationally, still underachieve relative to the dominant communities in those districts. It was formed to find out the causes of this dynamic and how it could be changed. One way MSAN set about this task was by interviewing middle and high school students from participating districts about their experiences and attitudes toward school.

One of their findings is that students from similar racial and cultural backgrounds across the country answer many questions about education in strikingly similar ways. In particular, there is a significantly stronger correlation for African American and Latino students between their effort in a classroom and positive relationships with their teachers than there is for white students (Ferguson 2008).[4] This truth can be found in any book on working with multiculturally diverse populations. Clearly, this holds a lesson for all of us regarding the need for empathy in our teaching.

When children from nondominant communities come to our classrooms, they are not primarily looking for methodologies, techniques, or what research says are the best ways to teach. They are looking for genuine caring. When children from historically subordinated groups enter the dominant culture, we

CONTRASTING CULTURAL ASSUMPTIONS

Cultural Beliefs That Support Constructivism	Contrasting Cultural Beliefs of the Local Cambodian American Community
Children should develop a personal point of view about the world. This prepares them for a society in which individuality is prized and democracy is the ideal.	Personal views are less important than the culture's accepted views. In particular, children's personal views are not culturally valued until they reach maturity.
Questioning (and even challenging) the teacher's ideas play a vital role in learning.	Children should not question what adults tell them (even if they do not understand it well).
Learning proceeds from *whole to part*. Children need to see the big picture; then they can analyze the whole to discover the relevant parts and make connections.	Learning proceeds from *part to whole*. Children need to learn the parts; then they can synthesize them into a coherent whole as they mature *over time*.
Children are naturally curious and want to learn; motivation is inherent in the individual.	Children are curious and want to learn; in learning of cultural importance, a child's motivation is subordinate to cultural expectations and adult authority.
Mistakes are a natural part of learning and should be integrated into the classroom experience.	Making mistakes in front of others causes one to lose face.
Children develop metacognitive understanding *simultaneously* with core subject matter.	Children develop metacognitive understanding *over time* as they mature and gain experience.
The student is expected to be an active, independent learning: questioning, making connections, and articulating her evolving understandings.	The student is expected to conform to the pace and structure of learning as orchestrated by adults.

TABLE 1–1. *From Bailey and Pransky (2005). Reprinted with permission.*

who are representatives of the dominant culture first have to prove our genuine caring and interest to them. Students from differing cultural backgrounds will be looking for proof in different ways. The first step of proving we care is by showing a sincere interest in what different students are looking for!

I conducted a teacher training recently for a mixed Latino and Anglo audience in a district with a large percentage of underachieving Latino students. I asked the Latino teachers at one point to put together a poster that they could show the rest of us that would communicate the three most important things they felt non-Latino teachers needed to understand about working successfully with Latino students in that district. First and foremost, they named forming positive relationships. One of them surprised us by saying, "On the first day, if you have a Latino student and you smile and say, 'Hello, nice to meet you and have you in our class,' and then tell them where their desk is, you've lost them for the rest of the year!" Though she may have been exaggerating a bit, her point was very clear. The group then went on to explain if teachers show a lot more clear interest in that student—"I want to meet your family, I bet you have so much to teach us this year about yourself, I can't wait to learn all the wonderful things you can do"—then that student will happily try hard.

> *High expectations without a strong relationship is browbeating for many CLD students. Conversely, caring without high expectations is not genuine caring.*

Principle 8: Equity does not necessarily mean equal.

How do you balance the many competing needs of your students? Do you think fairness is giving students equal time and attention, or is it to give each student what he needs in terms of your time and attention to be successful? I could even ask, Do we think fairness is starting with what the students bring into our classrooms and going from there, or is trying to redress imbalances that exist outside the walls of our classrooms?

These are difficult questions that go right to the core of what we believe as teachers and human beings. Both sides of the argument have a certain logic to them. However one comes down in one's heart regarding these questions, this fact remains: we can most likely not be successful teachers of CLD students if we think that fairness means *equal* and that its calculus starts within the walls of the classroom.

Picture a marathon in which most runners start at mile 0, though some start at mile 10, while others are 15 miles behind the starting line. In addition, some racers come from families that have run marathons for generations, while others have only been taught to sprint. Even though racers are told that it's good whenever they finish, there is a preferred finish time, too, and if you come in after that time, your race doesn't really count, or at least not so much. If you finish within that time, you get a prize, and the faster the finish, the better the prize.

Obviously some runners will have big built-in advantage before the race even starts. Of course, that's the way it is in racing; not every runner starts equally able to win. That's life. If the race is a race of choice, then this logic is palatable, even inevitable. But what if the race is a race that everyone *has* to run, and not only that, but the families of the runners who have the most advantages to start with are the ones who set the course and parameters of the race? It's likely that without some extra intervention on behalf of the disadvantaged runners, without extraordinary circumstances or incredible luck, the most advantaged runners will win the prizes. What does fairness mean within the context of such imbalance, when *all* students deserve our attention? Each of us must decide for ourselves—but if we avoid the question, we are further disempowering our underachieving students.

How do we allocate our attention in the class? How will we construct the learning environment? How will we balance competing interests? How do we deal with the fact that institutional policies and practices generally favor the already empowered? How do we account for differing levels of material availability in the home? There is no one answer to these questions. It depends on our students and their needs. I know I probably spend more time with the needier students (ESL or not) in the ESL-inclusion classrooms I work in, even as I try to design engaging lessons for the entire class. Of course, I always construct the learning environment with the principles of the sociocultural framework laid out in these first three chapters in the front of my mind. At times I design materials (e.g., math problems) at different levels of ability so students are challenged as they need to be. I never give more credit for work done on the computer at home, and I sometimes send the same materials home for homework projects to all students, saying that everyone has to use only what they've been given. There are lots of ways I try to act on what I understand an equitable classroom environment to mean.

But that's me. Each of us has to first think consciously about what equity means to us based on whom we teach and then act on that awareness accordingly. One gift of working with CLD students is that these questions are never allowed to fade into the background.

Notes

1. This comparison is sometimes referred to as field sensitive versus field dependent. Whether this cultural pattern actually exists or not is also a matter of some dispute in the field (Irvine and York 1995). However, I include it because I am convinced I see it within the shared ways of thinking, believing, acting, and using language of some groups of CLD students at my school, and it is at times an important guidepost for me as I think about working with them.

2. There appears to be a strong correlation between field dependence/independence, bottom-up/top-down learning preferences and the type of primary language organization.

3. I find it very interesting that Vygotsky considered "scientific" (i.e., formal school) learning to be by nature a top-down phenomenon, requiring logical reasoning skills in language. I see a direct connection between Vygotsky's view of the nature of education and school learning—which is, after all, the end result of literacy acquisition—and the way literacy-oriented communities apprentice children to thinking and language.

4. For more on the Minority Student Achievement network and its projects, visit the *Tripod Project* website at www.tripodproject.org.

Learning English

Hassan is a fourth-grade student who came to this country a little over a year ago as a non–English speaker. He's out on the playground at recess and happily engaged in a basketball game. Although he makes grammatical errors, he fluidly responds to and initiates language during the game, and he horses around with English-speaking friends, talking about video games afterward until the bell sounds to go back in.

Back in the classroom, Hassan seems to struggle with learning the curriculum. The teacher wonders, "What's with Hassan? He seems to have no problem talking to his friends, so what's his problem in class?"

In a neighboring classroom, Sothy is chatting with a friend. If you closed your eyes and just listened, you would be hard-pressed to identify Sothy as a second language learner. There is no perceptible accent; he sounds just like his friend. In fact, he was born in this country. Yet Sothy struggles to learn in the classroom. The teacher thinks, "If he knows English so well, does that mean he has a learning disability?"

IN CHAPTER 1, we tied the development of language in young children directly to the parallel development of cognition through meaningful interactions with parents and other significant adults in a familiar cultural context. In this chapter, we'll focus on language itself. The anecdotes may make teachers wonder:

- What is the process by which children learn a second language?

- Are there different kinds of English? And if so, what are they?

- What are the issues involved in learning a new language?

- Are the only language issues that impact school learning that a child is learning English as a second language or has a special language need (such as a communication disorder, etc.)?

The following principles covered in this chapter address these questions:

1. There is a predictable and supportable process to beginning second language learning.

2. Language can be characterized as having a domain of communicative proficiency as well as a domain of academic proficiency; proficiency in one does not guarantee proficiency in the other.

3. The development of language is directly tied to sociocultural development.

4. Dominant-culture, standard dialect, formal register English is the favored language of schooling in most public schools. It is the language of power in this society.

5. The organization of memory and the organization of language are mutually supportive.

6. A rich vocabulary plays an *essential* role in academic competence.

Let's explore each principle further.

Principle 1: There is a predictable and supportable process to beginning second language learning.

Although this is not a book on ESL per se, it is important to touch on basic ESL information because ESL is included in the CLD continuum. Steve Krashen (Krashen and Terrell 1983), a prominent theorist in the field of second language acquisition, has described several basic factors involved in learning a new language. Within the ELL field, there is much debate over whether they are universally applicable to second language acquisition, and certainly language acquisition does not occur with lockstep predictability in all children. There are many competing models that try to grab hold of the complex process of language acquisition. However, a lot of that discussion is more germane to the ESL field per se. Some of Krashen's basic concepts are valuable for classroom teachers in the role they can play facilitating language acquisition for non–English or very limited English speakers.

Learning versus Acquisition

We learn another language most easily through meaningful participation in activities that we enjoy or are important for our daily lives. Language *acquisition* means learning new language through using it and/or hearing it in meaningful experiences, and having it available for use in future communicative contexts. This is how we learn our first language. Children typically acquire language from significant adults, peers at play, and in social situations more quickly than they learn it in formal classroom language lessons or from instructional language. What one has learned *formally* is not necessarily available for use in natural, communicative contexts. Whatever the context, the key is participation in meaningful activity, with a moderated language environment.

Comprehensible Input

Our progress in acquiring a new language is furthered when we are exposed to (and interact with) language input that is at our level of understanding: too easy or too hard, and we don't understand. When comprehensible input occurs within meaningful activity, we acquire language more easily, and providing comprehensible input is essential for teaching subject matter to ELLs. It is the jumping-off point ESL teachers use to slightly stretch a language learner into more unfamiliar aspects of language. Following are some ways you can provide comprehensible input for beginner and early intermediate students:

- Slow speech down to about 85 percent speed. Go too fast and it is not comprehensible; go too slow and it becomes distorted. Loudness has nothing to do with it.

- Simplify your sentence structure and vocabulary apart from the target vocabulary, but be careful not to confuse simplified vocabulary with baby talk—leaving out words and distorting inflection. For example, for an early intermediate ESL student I might change "I'll explain it to you after your work is completed" to "Finish your work. Then I'll talk to you about it."

- Repeat and rephrase often.

- Pause *slightly more* at phrase or meaning breaks than you otherwise might (so . . . you might break . . . your speech up . . . like this), and longer as needed if the language involved is complex for the student; this enables the listener to catch up to, and process, the flow of speech.

- Use gestures and inflection to enhance meaning.

- Use objects (referred to as *realia*) and pictures.

- If possible, allow students to process together in their first language as needed.

One methodology ESL teachers employ with beginning language learners is called *total physical response*, or TPR (Asher 1979). In TPR, comprehension is initially stressed over oral production—children are initially just asked to physically respond to commands that focus on acquiring useful verbs (e.g., *sit, stand, walk, put, take, point*), which in turn aids the acquisition of useful nouns, adjectives, and prepositions. You can integrate beginning ESL students into the classroom community and further the acquisition process by asking them to help out when possible—"Juan, turn off the lights, please" or "Khmeri, please get me twenty pieces of yellow paper"—after they have built up even a small store of such vocabulary.

Silent Period

Some young beginning language learners may begin to speak right away, often in single words first, then in longer phrases and sentences, often with many mistakes. But others may choose not to speak until they can produce fairly correct sentences. This may take a long while, especially in younger children. It's important to respect a student's wish to be silent, especially early in her language learning experience; otherwise she may become even more inhibited about speaking and shut down further.

A small number of beginning speakers may exhibit an early period of abnormal behavior. For example, they may act very silly, act out, or be very loud. The tension of being in an unfamiliar environment with people prattling on all around you in an unfamiliar language and laughing together, while you are totally lost and even embarrassed, can be too much. As children learn beginning language skills and integrate more into the classroom community, they settle into more normal behavioral rhythms.

Affective Filter

The affective filter concept is related to motivation. If we feel disempowered or have negative feelings toward our environment or people around us, we build a higher wall, we are less motivated, and we are less open to the acquisition of language. When we engage in comfortable, enjoyable social interaction, we learn more deeply, are more open to the natural process of language acquisition, and are less concerned with making errors or monitoring what we say. Our wall, or *affective filter*, is lowered. A student's affective filter is either high or low; there is no neutral. Therefore, we should *actively* work toward creating as accessible and comfortable a classroom environment as possible.

A few years ago, I had a charming set of first-grade-age Iranian twins, a brother and a sister. The girl acculturated to the new environment relatively easily, and her English skills developed quickly. But the boy, although clearly an extremely intelligent and perceptive child, had a much more difficult time learning English. He also acted out a lot. I finally spoke with the father about it. He said his son was quite gifted in Farsi, and he loved his culture and language. The father could not understand why he was having such a hard time. I wondered if it might be because he loved being Iranian so much that he felt ambivalent about committing to this new language and culture, even at that young age. The father agreed to speak to the boy about it, and sure enough, the boy said that if he felt OK about learning English, he would be betraying (my take on it, not the boy's exact words) his culture, his family, and his language. Once we spoke openly with him about that—that nothing would be lost, and in fact, something would be gained—he gradually grew more comfortable, learned English more quickly, and improved his behavior.

It's important to note that there are no significant differences in the ability to learn a new language (other than the ability to attain native-speaker pronunciation) between young and old children, and even adults; however, a strong affective filter and issues of motivation are more likely to affect learning (depending on the circumstances) as we get older.

Mistakes

In addition to receiving comprehensible input, using language—that is, speaking, called *production* in the ESL field—is also important to second language acquisition because it focuses the learner's attention on the details of language. But by speaking more, students are bound to make more mistakes. We need to take great care not to stifle their desire to communicate, which is certainly a danger if we focus on error correction. When children begin to more comfortably use language, we should nurture that process by balancing the understanding of how error correction may inhibit learning with the knowledge that helping students focus on appropriate details in their output is useful.

Language structure mistakes may be caused by a number of factors. They may be self-correctable slipups. Or they may be caused by first language inter-

As a rule of thumb for those of you who are not ESL teachers, don't correct grammar errors unless communication has been impaired, especially at earlier stages in language learning. If possible and appropriate, rephrase the student's speech correctly in your reply.

ference, by overgeneralizing grammatical rules, by needing to talk around something because one does not have the appropriate language structure, and other factors. As a new language learner is exposed to more comprehensible input and uses language in a wider variety of meaningful contexts, the brain seems to internalize new language structures in a generally sequential way; some errors phase out while new ones phase in as attempts are made to use more complex language. But until they have complete mastery of the target language, ESL students will make errors as a natural extension of their attempts to use the new language.

Of course, pronunciation errors will occur. The same correction advice holds true here. Correct pronunciation mostly takes care of itself over time based on the amount of comprehensible input and meaningful production time children have (especially in young learners), the sound system of child's first language versus that of English, and aptitude. We must also remember that if students are *reflective* learners (see Chapter 1), overt error correction in public may inhibit their desire to speak. If you still really want to work with a student's errors, be they

LANGUAGE TRANSFER

One of the most important voices in the field of language learning and bilingual education, Jim Cummins (1986), draws important parallels between the development of L$_1$ and L$_2$. He identifies what he calls *underlying language proficiency*, namely, concepts that transfer across languages, such as the ability to read. Second language learning parallels the process of first language learning and is built upon one's first language strengths. So if a child is a proficient reader in L$_1$, it is likely the child will become a proficient reader in the second language as well.

Children who are dominant or monolingual in their parents' first language naturally acquire a second language based on meaningful activity, motivation, and comprehensible input, which we can foster in our classrooms. Students will naturally make many kinds of mistakes, but eliminating them is most often *not* a function of formal language lessons or correction. Rather, it is a matter of time, a lowered affective filter, and sufficient comprehensible input.

structural, idiomatic, or related to pronunciation, consult your school's ESL teacher, so you get his or her insights into the student as a language learner and can piggyback on that teacher's methods of working with errors. Identifying and working with language acquisition errors is obviously one of the central aspects of the ESL teacher's job and experience.

This first principle has been directly linked to ESL. I encourage anyone with ESL students in their class to:

1. collaborate closely with your building's ESL teacher(s);

2. learn more about structuring the learning environment for *sheltering English*, techniques for regulating language and generally creating a more "learning friendly" classroom environment for second language learners and others (e.g., the SIOP model: Echevarria, Vogt, and Short 2008);

3. find resources that show how to enhance reading and writing for ELLs in classrooms (as in Peregoy and Boyle 2005; Ovando, Collier, and Combs 2003); and

4. learn to foster more inclusive classroom learning communities (e.g., Faltis 2006).

However, although very helpful, even those wonderful resources and ideas are not enough to fully support the successful, independent learning of non-literacy-oriented CLD students. The process of helping non-literacy-oriented CLD students (dominant in whatever language, ESL student or not) develop classroom English needs to be explicit, systematic, and knowledgeable. This idea is examined in the remaining principles in this chapter.

What a child can do academically in his dominant language is the ceiling of what he can do in his second language.

Principle 2: Language can be characterized as having a domain of communicative proficiency as well as a domain of academic proficiency; proficiency in one does not guarantee proficiency in the other.

There are distinct differences between communicative, everyday English and the English of the classroom and formal study. These two varieties of English can sometimes feel like different languages to students. Issues of *academic language* underlie many CLD students' academic difficulties and struggles in the classroom. Although this concept also starts as ESL theory, it is used as a jumping-off point to explore ideas that lie beyond it.

Exercise

The following exercise will help clarify these two domains of English, the communicative and the academic. There are two short passages to read. The first is from a novel. It uses language in a similar way to how you might write about your own daily life in a letter or journal or how you might talk with friends and family.

The second is from an academic text. It is more similar to how you might write in your professional life or how you had to write in college. It is language you use professionally, in formal letters, and so on.

The chart that follows the two passages will compare them in different ways:

- the average total number of words in each sentence

- the number of words that have three or more syllables

- the number of sophisticated one- or two-syllable words

- how many different connecting words are used (e.g., *afterward, however, therefore,* but not *and, but, when,* or *then*)

- variety in sentence structure, such as passive constructions (e.g., *is found* as opposed to *find*), more complex sentences, or the conditional tense

Passage 1

I thought about the tire iron. It'd be really satisfying to clonk Morelli on the head with it. "Is that why you invited me?"

Morelli grinned.

Yep, he definitely deserved to get smacked with the tire iron. Then after I'd smacked him, I'd kiss him. . . .

Grandma materialized at my elbow. "How nice to see you," she said to Morelli. "Hope this means you're going to start paying attention to my granddaughter again. Things are pretty dull since you got cut out of the scene." (Evanovich 1999, 129)

Passage 2

It seems clear from the foregoing discussion that human beings have the capacity to control much of their own behavior, mental as well as physical, not on the basis of their biological urges that arise from the inside, but from the outside through the creation and use of material and symbolic artifacts. Many of the artifacts we use to construct our worlds and mediate our relationships to these worlds are often created by other individuals; some are contemporaries, but importantly there are also some who preceded us in time and space. (Lantolf 2000, 171)

Writing Type	Average Sentence Length	Number of Multisyllabic Words (Three or More Syllables)	Sophisticated One- and Two-Syllable Words	Connecting Words	Notes on Sentence Construction
informal English (passage 1– 83 words)	+/– 7 words	6	*smacked*	*since*	short, informal
formal English (passage 2– 91 words)	+/– 50 words	15	*basis, urges, arise, mental, construct, precede*	*not . . . but*	use of semicolon, several phrases set off by commas

I encourage you try this out yourself, writing for three to five minutes about your daily life and then another three to five about an issue in your professional life. Another way to look at this difference is to randomly open beach novels to different pages and compare them with college textbooks. Then analyze them as in the chart. I think you will find that the patterns hold.

Both Hassan and Sothy from the opening anecdotes are struggling with the same issue: the English Sothy knows so well and that Hassan is learning so quickly is mostly *not* the English of their classroom learning. The difference between Hassan and Sothy is that Hassan will overcome this temporary language obstacle to his classroom learning sooner—given continued motivation, comprehensible input, and a lowered affective filter—because his first language is school matched (literacy oriented), whereas Sothy will most likely continue to struggle even though he operates from a much more fluent communicative base in English.

Jim Cummins (1986, 2000) has described two different aspects of English. The first he terms *BICS*, for basic interpersonal communication skills. ELL students are exposed to BICS English on the playground, in the lunchroom, when interacting socially, and so on. Even if their home and community language is not English, they often are surrounded by English when they turn on the TV, listen to music, play video games, interact with friends, and go into the broader community. Children learn BICS quite quickly, as it is embedded in the direct physical and social activity they enjoy doing most. Beyond its communicative nature, BICS generates the *basic* language structures that allow us to organize and express our thinking.

BICS draws mainly on the Anglo-Saxon side of English. The language most young children use with each other consists mainly of one- and two-syllable words, such as *see*, *show*, and *good*. The grammar of BICS English most often includes simple sentences and sentences strung together with common connecting words. It might be said that BICS is what people mostly think of when they first think of learning another language.

Cummins calls the second English *CALP*, for cognitive academic language proficiency. It is the English of instruction, academic texts, for understanding content, of learning. CALP is described both by its language features and by the particular contexts in which it is used. CALP is characterized by more complex sentence structures and a very rich, often multisyllabic vocabulary, which in English is heavily drawn from our Romance language antecedents, such as *observe*, *demonstrate*, and *delicate*. It is embedded in the language of literacy-oriented homes. While there are certainly many elements of BICS in classroom language, they are overshadowed in importance by CALP.

> For CLD students without strong, literacy-oriented first language skills, the process of moving from BICS to CALP English is not necessarily systematically *developed* by the school environment.

Research shows that BICS takes between one and three years to learn proficiently, while CALP typically takes five to seven years or even more (e.g., Ramirez 1991).[1] Teachers may misperceive CLD students' academic ability or effort because they do not discriminate between BICS and CALP. ELL program levels (beginning, intermediate, advanced) typically emphasize BICS at the lower levels and CALP at the higher levels, and for program exit criteria.

In sum, BICS is *acquired* (in Krashen's sense) because all children have BICS, while CALP must be explicitly *developed*, especially if a child does not have school-appropriate CALP in L_1 to transfer to L_2. If students don't have developed CALP in any language, it must be the focus of their academic program. It is not even a given that ELL programs assist students specifically in the systematic *development* of CALP skills if they need it, as opposed to merely supporting the *transferral* of CALP from the students' L_1 to English if it is there to begin with, because second language acquisition theory has not yet caught up with the issue of literacy orientation. Really focusing on systematic CALP *development* drastically changes the face of our instruction!

So the question becomes What are CALP skills and how can we help students develop them? The remaining principles in this chapter are devoted to the answer.

Principle 3: The development of language is directly tied to sociocultural development.

This principle restates Principle 2 from Chapter 1, just more directly centered in language. In particular, I want to highlight the role that subvocalized, organizational (or planning) speech plays in learning, and its roots in children's home apprenticeship to language and learning. By that I mean the language we access to talk ourselves through problem-solving situations and learning tasks. It is a very important but underappreciated element of the language leg of the *language–thinking skills–problem-solving style* tripod introduced in Chapter 1 (Figure 1–3).

Although I hardly hear educators talk about organizational speech, the more I learn about it, the more important I realize it is. For example, in her fascinating book, *The Social Context of Cognitive Development* (2001), Mary Gauvain cites a study that correlates successful problem solvers to the quantity and quality of talk they use, both with peers and self-talk. As self-talk is a vital link between past, present, and future learning experiences, it behooves us to understand this concept and the role it plays in learning better.

INSIDE OUT, OR OUTSIDE IN, THAT IS THE QUESTION . . .

There are two schools of thought about subvocalized speech. One was developed by the noted childhood expert Jean Piaget (discussed in Power and Hubbard 1996), who focused primarily on the *internal* landscape of childhood development. He concluded that when young children speak aloud during play or some activity, it is *egocentric* (self-centered) speech that may or may not have anything to do with the activity at hand. He proposed that as children grow and become more socialized, their oral, egocentric speech gradually *fades away*. He viewed it as a temporary developmental phase of an inside-out process: the stage of purely self-centered, self-aware speech disappears and is *replaced* by internal speech that is more sophisticated and socially aware. Therefore, it would *not* be an issue affecting the learning of elementary school students.

In contrast, the Russian psychologist Lev Vygotsky (1978, 1986), focused primarily on how the *external* (social and cultural) landscape helps shape the internal. He proposed that a child's egocentric speech actually involves planning and problem solving, that it is *not* just parallel to play or activity. Further, he asserted that oral, egocentric speech *evolves into* internal speech. He viewed it as an outside-in process: egocentric speech is really the *internalization* of the social speech of parents and significant adults. Moreover, he accorded internal speech great importance in learning, since we use it to organize a task and point ourselves in the right direction in thinking and problem solving. Therefore, it would be an *important* issue affecting the learning of some elementary school students.

Research has since confirmed that Vygotsky is correct (Reiber and Robinson 2004; Kozulin 1998).

An important researcher on language and memory, Katherine Nelson (in Cole 1996) buttresses the outside-in perspective by asserting that adults provide children with culturally appropriate scripts that eventually enable them to integrate meaningfully into adult activity. With dominant-culture, literacy-oriented students who are matched in this way to the expectations of formal school learning, the issue of subvocalized, organizational speech is invisible to us. However, we need to understand that many CLD students come to school with organizational speech that mirrors the language use and problem-solving style of homes where the sociocultural training of children does *not* match our own or those of their dominant-culture classmates. The subvocalized, organizational speech of our students will reflect

- how their parents have structured culturally significant types of learning tasks for them;

- how their parents have trained them to orient to such tasks and position themselves within the learning dynamics of those tasks; and

- the independent cognitive skills they have developed to successfully and appropriately perform those types of tasks.

School-matched subvocalized, organizational speech is directly tied to higher levels of metacognitive awareness.

In one intriguing study that illustrates this (in Rogoff and Lave 1999), middle-class Brazilian city mothers and poor mothers in a small Amazon village were given puzzles to work on with their young children. The middle-class city mothers engaged in practices we would all be quite familiar with—they asked the children what pieces they would use, what they might do next, and so on. They acted as coaches and facilitators while the children primarily put the puzzles together. The mothers used the children's mistakes as learning opportunities. The village mothers, however, were quite different! They directed the children as to what pieces to put where and how. They made sure the puzzle was done correctly, with no errors. The children merely did as they were told. Clearly, the planning speech, thinking skills cluster, and task familiarity fostered by those two situations are very different. The children from those two communities will take their particular language socialization with them into the next learning situation, and it will be reflected in their subvocalized, organizational speech. There are many studies linking children's problem-solving strategies to maternal scaffolding (such as in Meadows 2006; Portes et al. 1994; Kermani and Janes 1999; and Solomon and Rhodes 1995), and organizational self-talk is part and parcel of problem-solving strategies.

Let's say I am a top-down, field-independent, impulsive, literacy-oriented student confronted with an open-ended math problem. I have a highly developed sense of independence in learning and a pretty sophisticated metacognitive awareness. I might generate the following subvocalized speech: "OK, I have to figure out what the important numbers are. . . . Oh, this is kind of like the problem we did last month; let's see, how did we do that one? . . . I remember, I saved a paper that can help me. . . . Let me try some different things here and see if they work. . . . I need to remember to keep checking to see if my thinking makes sense. . . ." With that subvocalized speech, I would launch myself into the task.

If I am a bottom-up, reflective learner who has been primarily trained in my home community to be guided by adult direction, however, I might generate this subvocalized speech: "How do I start? Where is the teacher?" Without the appropriate subvocalized speech for school tasks and expectations, I may freeze. It is not a matter of knowing the subject or of intelligence, but rather one of *acculturation*. And what a huge difference it makes!

The organizational speech needed for classroom academic tasks must be a practiced activity for mismatched CLD students. They can explicitly practice it by writing down the speech that they will find helpful as subvocalized speech to orient themselves to similar activities in the future. Learning logs or journals are a good way for students to practice organizational speech: "Next time I see this type of problem, I will . . ." Or, students can rehearse organizational speech aloud in a safe place with teacher support. Then when a familiar problem or task arises, the student should have the opportunity to refer back to her journal, or say how she is going to proceed, what she is going to look for, and so on, before she starts working.

In sum, as young children are developing problem-solving skills through interactions in the home, they are simultaneously internalizing the adult speech that accompanies those interactions as their own future subvocalized speech (self-talk). This is intimately connected to levels of independence in learning, as well as accessing the cluster of thinking skills needed for successfully interacting with those types of tasks. However, some students' subvocalized speech may not match the learning or problem-solving tasks of the classroom, the degrees of independence they demand, etc. Then we have to make explicit, focused, and systematic attempts to help them develop the problem-solving skills, thinking skills, and subvocalized speech they need to successfully perform school tasks *independently*; without the latter, independent performance with the first two is problematic.

Sociocultural Development and Instructional Language

A different application of this principle is that our *own* socioculturally (and professionally) developed language use patterns are reflected in how we teach (see "Discourse Community" sidebar in Chapter 1, page 6). For example, take the word *so*. In a top-down classroom that expects students to be active learners—making connections, drawing conclusions, and being metacognitively aware—*so* is often used as an instructional link. We may give an example, refer back to previous learning, or launch our instruction with an anecdote, then say, "So," and switch to the new topic or teaching. The implication is that the *so* will inform students that they must (1) make the link and (2) use it to inform their new learning.

However, bottom-up learners who are waiting to *explicitly* be told, "Learn this, now learn that," often misperceive the instructional format and how the use of the word *so* should trigger a certain internal thinking process. Of course, they may easily produce singular BICS sentences with *so*, such as "I have a cold today, so my mom said I couldn't go out for recess." However, BICS and CALP contexts are often quite distinct.

> When *so* is used to transition between ideas and concepts (especially if abstract), and is used as a sociocultural link to stimulate a certain type of thinking, school-mismatched students can easily get lost.

Recently I have tried training some very academically at-risk third- and fourth-grade students to hook their fingers together (like a chain) to symbolize that a connection has to be made when they hear me say, "So . . . ," during instruction. This has at least gotten them to focus more on the word and their job as listeners and learners. Now we have to work on creating a stronger, continuously active focus, because if they have not listened carefully to the previous instructional speech, recognizing *so* will still not be enough!

CLD students may be socioculturally mismatched in their own organizational speech as well as to our instructional language. We have to find ways to explicitly help them practice school-matched skills in both.

Principle 4: Dominant-culture, standard dialect, formal register English is the favored language of schooling in most public schools.

As we begin to deconstruct classroom language, we see two other important factors of language whose impact on learning we understand less clearly. Yet they are deeply intertwined with issues of culture and characterize the language of many less successful CLD students. They are *dialect* and *register*.

Dialect

Dialect is a variety of language distinguishable by pronunciation, vocabulary, or grammar. It may be regional, national, occupational, or social. This includes the mainstream use of language, which is called *standard dialect*. It is important for those of us who are standard dialect speakers to understand that it is only standard in the sense that it is the dialect used by the dominant groups in society. The *language of power* (Delpit 1995) in our classrooms and in our society is definitely standard English dialect. The relevance of dialect to this discussion has five dimensions.

First, CLD students who speak a dialectically different English do not seem to develop all the language structures of standard dialect merely by exposure to comprehensible input, as do classic ESL learners. This is especially the case for those students whose parents no longer use their own first language in the home, or at least not predominantly, and instead use their own English as a second language as the home language. In other words, their children speak English as a second language as their first or dominant language, which in essence is a dialectically different English (and very mismatched to school English).

As a small example, many of my English-dominant, non-literacy-oriented CLD students continue to say and write, "That's mines," even after it has been modeled in standard dialect and students have had their attention repeatedly focused on the difference between their language and the form we use at school. In contrast, my classic ELL students almost never use that nonstandard form, or if they do, it quickly disappears from their language with exposure to sufficient comprehensible input. A variety of pronunciation and grammar forms that are standard in one dialect are considered mistakes by standard dialect speakers.

In my experience, more academically struggling students exhibit plateauing (when one's language levels off and does not develop further) in their linguistic development than do literacy-oriented ESL students (although plateauing can be a feature of second language acquisition at advanced ESL levels). For my non-literacy-oriented CLD students, this means they do not easily acquire standard dialect forms, stay within a limited range of sentence structures, and employ nonstandard usages in both their speaking and their writing. It's not that their different dialect forms are objectively worse, but those differences will continue to be marked as mistakes at school, work against others' perceptions of their academic competence, cause less sensitive teachers to devalue what they produce, and interfere with their ability to process text meaning fluently and completely.

Speakers of nonstandard English dialects must be taught standard dialect forms sensitively, but deliberately and explicitly.

The second dimension is related to the first, in that we tend to react in strong, stereotyped ways to different dialects. For example, standard dialect speakers tend to value or devalue a person's intelligence and social standing based just on hearing what they consider to be an inferior dialect, such as

REFLECTION TASK

Think for a moment about this scenario: In a guided reading group, a student misreads a sentence. She reads, "The girl see the ball," instead of "The girl sees the ball." Are you going to correct it? If so, why? If not, why not?

There is no mechanical right answer. If we think we should correct any misreading of text, then we might consider that in that child's dialect, the third person -s might habitually be dropped (this is also quite a common beginner and intermediate ESL error). So telling her that she's reading incorrectly is telling

her that she (and by extension, her family) speaks incorrectly. Is that likely to foster a sense of belonging and empowerment? Conversely, if we think that we should not correct dialect differences when reading because it is insensitive, then we might consider that it is in the child's best long-term academic interests to learn to be fully conversant and comfortable with standard dialect as used in text as well as in the classroom. Whatever we decide to do, we need to have our *why* and *how* centered in our students, in that moment.

Ebonics. Reacting negatively to dialect differences as mistakes can be tantamount to chauvinistically insulting a child, her family, and her community. We have to be on our guard to not let our dominant-culture privilege color the way we perceive a child's language.

Research with African American, Hawaiian, Native American, Latino, and other populations (Delpit 1995; Cazden 1988; Heath 1983; and Au 1980) clearly shows that when the language *and dialect* of the classroom discourse community match that of the students' home community, young children's learning is enhanced. Conversely, these factors detract from learning when they do not match. It is certainly challenging to incorporate dialect difference into the standard dialect, predominantly mainstream culture classroom community (like at my school), though we need to try. Finally, we must always be on guard to not misconstrue dialect difference as a special need.[2]

The third dimension is that dialect is connected to narrative. By *narrative*, I mean the macrostructures of language we use to organize our thinking (Bruner 1985; Nelson 1998; Hughes 1997; Olson and Torrance 1996; Engel 1995). There are two issues with narrative: there are culturally different narrative forms, and there can be underdevelopment of a child's personal narrative in English (vis-à-vis dominant culture norms). Here, I refer to the latter. The issue of narrative is revisited in Chapter 5 vis-à-vis its importance to the reading process.

Children process text, retell stories, produce speech, and write according to their present narrative stage. Their independent skill level is capped by this stage.

PERSONAL NARRATIVE

A longtime educator, Maryellen Moreau (2005, 2007) has created an important developmental curriculum for (standard dialect, formal register) English narrative based on important research in the field. There are different ways to categorize narrative development, but the developmental stages of narrative according to this school of thought evolve from the simplest constructions—simple descriptions or lists of actions, what preschool-age children produce independently—to the complete, complex episodic structures of adolescents and adults. Narratives help organize and give meaning to the world, and even a person's sense of self. As narratives develop, they incorporate recognizing and using culturally relevant themes, sequencing events and placing them in time, perspective taking, linking meaning with a variety of cohesive ties (connecting words like *and*, *then*, *after*, *if*, *because*, and *so*), character development, and problem resolution.

I propose that literacy culture hyperaccelerates the development of narrative stages as it does with other elements of language and thinking, and therefore many literacy-oriented students are not affected by the expectations of the high level of narrative skill implied in formal schooling. However, other children may not have developed their narrative stage to the age-appropriate English narrative level suggested by this research. How many of us have students who, in writing or speaking,

primarily link ideas or events with *and . . . and then . . . and then . . .* ? That linking device corresponds to a preschool-age stage ("action sequence") of narrative—yet I have had (and continue to have) fifth graders who produce that level of narrative.

Students without the development of an age-matched narrative are way behind the narrative level of text and classroom instruction, and specific practice developing their personal narrative ability is *crucial* to their long-term independent academic success. Of course, students who use a different English dialect or register may also have a different narrative form or a different timetable for evolving through the various developmental stages of English narrative. However, although their language strengths can be used to analyze the characteristics of a school-matched narrative, they also need to develop school-matched narrative skills in order to develop independent, grade-level academic skills.

All of us need to learn more about the impact of personal narrative on learning, as it is a crucial yet little understood aspect of reading and writing ability (see also Chapter 5). I *highly* recommend that anyone who works with non-literacy-oriented students visit Moreau's website, www.mindwingconcepts.com, to learn more about narrative, its implications for classroom literacy and instruction, and to see materials developed for working with it.

The fourth issue about dialect is that it is closely tied to vocabulary. Recently, a Dominican family of English-dominant, different dialect speakers from New York moved to our school community. The students initially said things like, "Last night we went to the pizza store." Their level of vocabulary overall continues to be very limited, and this significantly impacts their ability to work at grade level. Instead of referring to things with specific descriptive labels, they point a lot and say "that thing," a common characteristic of many of my underachieving, English-dominant CLD students.

One year I experienced a surprising dialect-related vocabulary difference. I had been working with two Cambodian American girls in the Feuerstein Instrumental Enrichment (FIE) program, a program composed of fourteen instruments that systematically target a range of thinking skills. We were beginning the "Comparisons" section of the program, one purpose of which is to further facility with *attribute categories* (terms that organize language semantically, such as *size, shape, distance,* and *feeling*). Overall, this proved to be a difficult unit for them as they grappled with organizing language semantically as well as using language to show varying degrees of certainty (e.g., *I know, I think, it could be, it probably is,* etc.) to express their ideas and compare items in a variety of different ways.

We had just done the exercise shown in Figure 2–1, which first just asked them to simply compare two different-sized apples.

I next asked *why* they thought one was big and one was small—one of the main points of the exercise is to determine how a student chose to phrase her response and discuss why she chose to phrase it in that particular way—and the following conversation ensued. I've underlined the words that caught my ear and italicized words I emphasized in my response:

LOKANA: It <u>is</u> a different kind of apple.

ME: It *is*? How do you know?

SOKNA: Oh, it's <u>probably</u> just far away.

ME: It *probably* is? Why do you think so?

LOKANA: Aah . . . it <u>could be</u> on a tree far away.

Suddenly my antenna went up! I had heard the girls—and many of the Cambodian students, as I thought about it—frequently using *probably* and *maybe* almost as throwaway words, which would briefly lead me to wonder why

FIGURE 2–1. *Apple Comparison*

they had used those particular words in those contexts. But after all, these girls were English dominant—Lokana was practically a monolingual English speaker and Sokna had been speaking English for more than six years—and I had assumed (ouch!) that they would have no confusion about the meanings of those two words. And yet what a coincidence that the girls were now clearly using *probably* in a way that did not seem to match the accepted standard dialect meaning.

I wrote *probably* on a sticky note and asked Lokana to stick it on our "Being Sure" chart (see Figure 2–2), which helps students see how to express the degree of surety they intend in standard dialect English.

She first stuck it down around 25 percent, next to "wondering." Then I asked Sokna to do the same thing, and she stuck it at about 40 percent. We did the same thing with *maybe,* and to my surprise, they both stuck it at about 75 percent, near "pretty sure about"! Those were common words in their functional vocabularies, yet they apparently used these words to routinely convey the *opposite* meaning from standard dialect usage. Put another way, these must have been the commonly accepted meanings of those words in their primary discourse community, in which English played a very significant role. Recently, I heard the Cambodian paraprofessional in our school use *probably* in a way that made me reflect back to this very issue. I found myself thinking that I would have used *possibly* or *maybe.* This confirmed my thinking that the girls' language usage must have been a dialect-related difference, as opposed to just a mistake.

The fifth aspect of dialect is that the ability to employ good sentence fluency in writing—combining sentences in a variety of ways, altering sentence structures, and so forth—is predicated on facility with standard dialect, formal register (see next section) structures. This is typically a weak area of ESL students in general and low-literacy CLD students in particular. But it is difficult for young students to employ language in writing that is not *also* a part of their oral language (narrative) repertoire.

Register

Register is the use of language appropriate to social settings (Joos 1967, in Payne 1998; Halliday 1987). There are five main registers in English:

- *formal* (the discourse of work and academia)
- *casual* (the discourse of friends)
- *frozen* (e.g., religious prayer)
- *consultative* (the formal register used socially)
- *intimate* (the language of lovers)

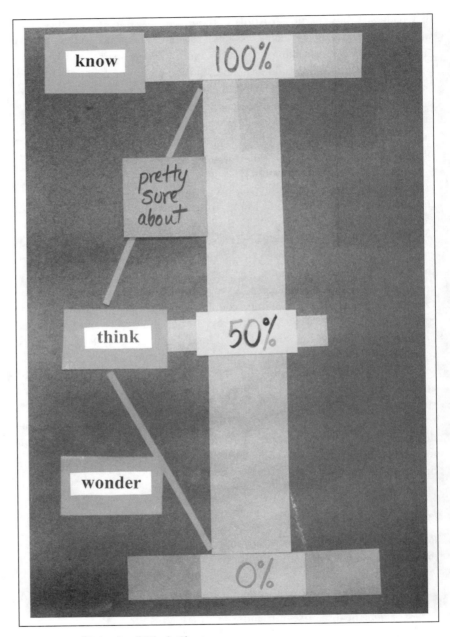

FIGURE 2–2. *"Being Sure" Words Chart*

The register of the classroom is the formal register. The formal register is in some sense synonymous with CALP. It is characterized by a strong vocabulary (see also the discussion of Principle 6 on page 62 for facts on the average vocabulary bases of children from different socioeconomic classes), abstract referents, and linearity. Standard dialect, formal register English is the language of nonfiction and much fiction, the language of instruction, and the language of testing. The formal register is also the predominant register of middle-class and affluent literacy-oriented homes (Montano-Harmon 1991; Payne 1998). Therefore, the language register of school and home are closely matched for many mainstream children, but not necessarily for all children. To reiterate, there is nothing objectively better about formal register English, nor deficit-oriented about using the informal register more. It's just that at school, they often clash, and to the disadvantage of those who are not fluent with the formal register.

Put on your teacher hat and read these two versions of the beginning of the fable "The Ant and the Grasshopper." The first version is told in the formal register.

> It was summer, and Grasshopper was merrily playing a tune and lying in the warm sun when he saw his friend Ant. Ant was lugging some heavy food back to his home.
>
> "Hey there, Friend!" called Grasshopper. "Why are you working so hard on this lovely day? Why not play with me instead?"
>
> Ant wiped some sweat off his brow and said, "I have to get ready for winter, when there will be no food." Grasshopper just stared at Ant in amused disbelief.

This version probably feels very familiar. It is book language we are all familiar with. Now read the following different register version (which also shows elements of narrative underdevelopment):

> There was this grasshopper, you know, and he, like, didn't work much. And this ant, he worked a lot and stuff, and then the grasshopper wanted to play with him and then Ant said no and then the grasshopper was, you know, like . . . he wanted to play with Ant but Ant didn't want to play with him.

This is quite evocative of the way many of my academically struggling CLD students use language and structure narrative, and I imagine it's evocative of students you have worked with, too. We might wonder why students who use a different register and dialect do not just quickly learn standard dialect, formal register forms. Even if students hear a difference, since their language is English, too, they are not likely to think through the implications, especially at an elementary school age. Plus, why would they be anxious to change *their own* language?

Therefore, the process of learning a different dialect and register requires much more systematic instruction and direct focus—and especially empathy and knowledge—from us.

One idea for working with dialect and register is to have the class make a school-English version of a popular song, or of the way kids talk on the playground, or conversely, a playground-English version of a page from a chapter book or textbook. Explicitly focusing student attention on register and dialect difference—*as this and that* as opposed to *right and wrong*—in a positive, respectful way helps demystify the differences and make them clearer.

Questions

There is little in language more fundamental to the formal learning process than the use of questions. Yet questioning practices vary across discourse communities (and thus, dialects), and therefore it is quite possible that question mismatches may arise in a diverse classroom between teacher and students.

In a landmark study, Heath (1983) shows how the type of "innocent" naming questions typical of a middle-class, literacy-oriented community convey a negative message to children from a working-class and poor African American community. For example, if a white kindergarten or first-grade teacher asks, "What is that?" while pointing to a picture of a clock in a book, the message conveyed to the African American children may well be "You're black, so I want to see if you're smart enough to know such a simple thing." In that child's discourse community, no one would ask anyone to identify a familiar object that both could clearly see! So the student might refuse to answer based on perceived racism in the question, which might cause the teacher to think, "This child doesn't even know what this is called!" or "What a rude child; she won't even answer me!"

Delpit (1995) similarly shows a mismatched use of questions between African American children and dominant-culture discourse. A dominant-culture teacher or parent might "ask a command." Power-holding groups in our society think the command-as-question appropriately softens the adult's power, though there is no doubt that the child must take it as a command and not as a question to answer. For example, a teacher sees a student continuing to walk around the room after she has said, "Everyone please take your seats." She asks the student, "Marcus, are you ready to sit down yet?" If the student is from a discourse community similar to the teacher's, he understands that that question really means "Sit down now." In a different discourse community, however, it is quite possible that questions are asked only if one is genuinely seeking unknown information or wants the other person's opinion; in this case, a child from such a community might think that if the adult really wanted him to sit, she'd tell him so! So he might answer, "No, not yet." If you were that teacher, what would your reaction be to such an "obvious challenge" and "rudeness"? Especially if the child were a student of color?

The first time I was aware of the phenomenon of question mismatch was when I was working with the first immigrant Cambodian children at our school many years ago. A child might have come up with some interesting answer, and I or another teacher would say, "That's interesting. Why did you come up with that answer?" The response of many Cambodian students was to look down and mumble, "I forgot," in obvious discomfort. Yet that type of question is typical of our discourse community and is a positive thing. I wondered where the discomfort came from—embarrassment, confusion? Then I learned that in their home discourse community, an adult's use of *why* questions about a child's action or behavior almost always conveyed *displeasure*; for example, "Why haven't you cleaned that up yet?" or "Why did you hit your baby brother?" So the message we were unintentionally giving the students was "Your answer is bad"!

There are profound differences in the use of questions, who is responsible for them, and when to use them between cultures, across discourse communities, even between different communities of English speakers. Yet questions are one of our primary teaching tools, so we must be sensitive to the various nuances questions have within the classroom community and the different ways our CLD students may respond to them. (The issue of dialect comes up again in Chapters 4, 5, and 6, which look at reading and math instruction in more depth.)

By raising issues about dialect and register, I do *not* mean to imply that

- a different dialect or register by definition means academic difficulty
- dialect and register by themselves are problems for CLD students
- no issues of dialect or register can be accommodated in the course of regular classroom instruction

I *do* mean to imply that

- if a CLD student with a different dialect or register is also having academic difficulties, then dialect and register may help point us in the right direction if other modifications to teaching content do not sufficiently help the child
- differences in dialect or register in an English-dominant or monolingual English student whose parents are not native English speakers may well be a sign of long-term academic difficulty
- we all need to learn more about dialect and register

Principle 5: The organization of memory and the organization of language are mutually supportive.

Children develop ways of using language, understanding the world, and orienting to problem-solving experiences based on meaningful, culturally familiar interactions with their parents. Those three aspects of the interaction of our psychological and cultural tools come as a package. Added to that is *memory*.

Culture strongly influences memory!

At first, this may seem odd. Doesn't everyone's brain process memory in the same way neurologically and physiologically? And isn't memory from a person's own direct experience? The answer to those questions is yes. However, as memory takes shape within language, meaning and organization become more paramount.

Young children often construct their memory of events through language interactions with their parents. These emphasize recalling the details of experience; it is classic talk about talk used in middle-class homes (of course, I do not mean to say it is restricted to dominant-culture, middle-class discourse, but that it is more typical of it). Over time, a child's memory gets shaped in a particular way through these interactions. Nelson (1998) calls these *elaborative* memory interactions.

For example, a child goes to the zoo with her family. The child's memory of that experience is in large part reconstructed based on how the parents reshare that experience via language after the trip, including the questions they ask. The child's future recall of that event will be strongly colored by how she initially coconstructed her memory of it with her parents.

Memory is to some degree socially constructed, and certain memory practices appear to enhance formal classroom learning.[3]

Parents in all cultures do not use an elaborative memory interaction style. Although there is no better or worse among the various cultural memory styles, research does show that elaborative memory interactions lead to greater *independent* recall of event detail. And interestingly, Nelson (1998) ties elaborative memory acculturation to the types of skills that schooling demands.

The school curriculum draws heavily on facility with *semantic memory*, which refers to words and concepts ordered hierarchically and taxonomically into super- and subordinate categories (Cole, Griffin, and Newman 1989; Feuerstein et al. 1980). Semantic memory relates us to the world based on the abstracted qualities and characteristics of objects, events, and so on, whose semantic "reality" exists in language, and not in the physical world. In other words, developing a predisposition for accessing semantic memory when young is a form of language socialization, particularly in literacy culture.

How does this impact schooling? Let's say you're a fourth grader, and your teacher brings up dogs as a segue into a lesson about mammals. She is expecting you to associate dog *on your own* with superordinate categories such as animal and subordinate categories like fur, types of dogs, wolf, bark, and pets. Although you might first think of your own dog if you have one, you'll quickly access the salient semantic aspects of the word. Unless it is about a creative writing piece, the discussion will be more concerned with the characteristics of dogs than the games you might play with your pet dog, the fact that a dog barked at you near the mall and scared you, or other personal experiences. You position yourself well to understand the qualities of mammals by what you pull up in your mind about dogs.

What about the student, though, who when he hears "dog" draws primarily on episodic (relating to personal experience) or autobiographical memory? He might think, "My neighbor has one; it barks at me and I get scared; I want a pet; once I played ball with a dog. . . ." This student is accessing personally meaningful information, but not the type of super- and subordinately organized information needed for that lesson. If we asked that student direct questions about the characteristics of dogs, we would probably find that much if not all of the expected information about dogs was there. It is just not linked up and organized in the same way, so it is not independently accessed as quickly. It's like the student pulls the wrong files for "dog" and has to go back to find the right ones. But meanwhile, the class has moved on, grounded in the semantic schema it will need to draw on for the mammals lesson.

> *Memory structure directly impacts classroom learning.*

> *It may be that memory organization has some of the greatest impact on classroom underperformance, and yet we understand so little about it! It's the difference between floating downstream with the current, or fighting it going upstream.*

Amplification

A wide array of cultural, linguistic, and cognitive *amplifiers* is hidden in classrooms that privilege the home acculturation of children from literacy-oriented discourse communities. When students with a mismatched cultural learning style or problem-solving preference participate in learning activities that rely heavily on independence and require top-down (whole to part) types of cognitive skills, differences in memory organization may complicate the students' ability to engage meaningfully in them.

One important feature of semantic memory that connects directly to language use (CALP) is the wide array of attribute categories it generates. However, a wide variety of attribute category words is not a generic feature of all students' language. One common attribute word that many of my underachieving CLD

DISCOVERING *AMPLIFICATION*

Michael Cole (Cole, Griffin, and Newman 1989) discovered that the organization of language and memory in dominant-culture students enhances the learning of the school curriculum, and that in turn, the organization of the school curriculum reinforces those students' language and memory organization. Cole refers to this mutually resonating dynamic as *amplification*. Conversely, he realized that students whose language and memory systems are *not* similarly organized have extra work to do. They must learn not only the information curriculum but also the hidden language and memory organization of the curriculum.

Cole arrived at this realization during a field experiment he conducted in a culturally and linguistically diverse fourth-grade classroom in one California school district. Cole set out to prove that higher achievers achieve more highly because they know more about the subject to begin with. What he found, however, did not correlate to his hypothesis at all—the highest achievers on the unit posttest were actually, in the aggregate, slightly *lower* achievers on the unit pretest (given at the conclusion of the first unit lesson, which introduced the major vocabulary and concepts)! In trying to understand how this could be, he found that the higher achievers' *wrong* answers on that first test were qualitatively different than the lower achievers': they were semantically closer to the right answers than those of the lower achievers, whose wrong answers were generally random. (I highly recommend reading the chapter that describes this study in Cole's [1989] book *The Construction Zone*.)

This is landmark research that has not received enough attention. Cole realized that the higher achievers had learned more during the first lesson, and throughout the entire unit, because their *internal language and memory organization mirrored*—and therefore enhanced, or *amplified*—the organization of the academic curriculum and lesson delivery, and vice versa. Their memory organization resonated within the curriculum, and the organization of the curriculum resonated within them.

In Cole's words, because of amplification, the rich still got richer, even though the classes he observed were very well planned, the learning was active, and the teacher accessed a number of different learning channels in her lesson delivery, all things that our field tells us should "level the playing field" for all students.

As another example of semantic memory, an anecdote in Timm (1999) describes a Hmong student who, when faced with an item on a sorting test about which item did *not* belong—between *hammer, saw, fire, hatchet*—he chose *hammer* instead of the expected, semantically organized answer *fire* (i.e., it's not a tool). When asked why he chose *hammer*, he explained that you don't use a hammer to cut wood for a fire like you do with a hatchet and saw. In other words, he created a concrete, functional interrelationship between the items instead of relying on an abstract semantic categorization, the type of memory practice privileged by school (and literacy culture) by being embedded in the curriculum, in learning tasks, and in our instruction.

students do not initially understand in its (abstract) categorizing role is size. They connect it to shopping (the concrete)—for example, their mom shops for a certain size shirt for them. If a teacher says "size" during instruction, he expects students to open the "size" file, which should be filled with descriptive adjectives like *big, small, short, tall*, and all their synonyms. But what if some students are just connecting it with particular items?

Of course, a student may know some of the adjectives that populate the "size" category but not independently *organize* them that way. Certainly the seed of understanding "size" as an abstract attribute category word lies in the image and the experience of shopping, but for students who are not semantically oriented, it requires teachers to take further steps: (1) realize the student may not know the attribute category function of the word, (2) allow time to help the student see how his image can translate into an attribute category, (3) help him reorganize their semantic memory accordingly, and (4) help him apply that new learning to the task at hand. The instructional language in dominant-culture learning spaces often relies on familiarity with abstract attribute category terms and semantic memory organization.

During my work with attribute categories involving the two fourth-grade Cambodian American girls mentioned in the earlier anecdote about the apples, I was suddenly struck by something I'd had only a vague glimmering of previously: the predilection of the girls to *enter into learning at the level of detail*. For example, when looking at the drawing of two apples and asked what was different about them, they said, "One apple is big and one apple is small." My instinct would have been to say, "They are not the same size." In other words, I'm sure I'd have instinctively chosen an abstract attribute category to frame my answer (via the hierarchical structure of semantic memory), and I imagine many of my readers would have also. It is not that the students were wrong. It's that they went at it from the bottom up, and our assumption is often that students approach learning from the top down.

So we began to keep track of attribute words. We initially generated from their own thinking and the "Comparisons" unit the following:

> Some attribute words they knew mainly as concrete nouns: *color, height, dimension, number, shape, size, length, place, time, space, orientation* (from a previous unit in the thinking skills program), *number*[4]
>
> Unfamiliar attribute words: *location, gender, width, characteristic, texture*

As we explored these words in more detail, what was illuminating to me was the girls' lack of familiarity with many of the words' function as abstract categorizing concepts, again *in spite of* the fact that the words are used in that way quite frequently in our school's (and probably in most schools') discourse community. Reflecting on this, I wondered what the impact of a lack of fluency with general semantic categories had been on their formal school learning, how often they were out of synch with classroom learning assumptions. Like the less successful students in Cole's study, they must have often missed the implied meaning of the way the curriculum, and the language used to encode and convey it, was organized. (I see this also as looping back to narrative, further illustrating the mutually connecting nature of amplifiers.)

Moreover, the development of a rich system of attribute categories logically demands a rich vocabulary to populate them. In contrast, these two girls and many other of my academically underachieving CLD students function within a very simple *mean/nice, good/bad, happy/sad,* and *big/small* realm of vocabulary. I see a strong connection between CALP language, certain thinking practices, certain organizational speech, standard dialect, a strong vocabulary, and semantic memory.

The simplified graphics in Figures 2–3 and 2–4 sketch out hypothetical differences between a predominantly semantic versus a nonsemantic memory system. They illustrate how two children might organize their McDonald's memories and experiences. (Of course, these are very shorthand versions):

Figure 2–3 represents a hypothetical hierarchically and taxonomically organized semantic memory about McDonald's, while Figure 2–4 represents the same general experiences organized autobiographically. Note that the "personal feelings" link in Figure 2–3 has been boldfaced to show that it is really not in-

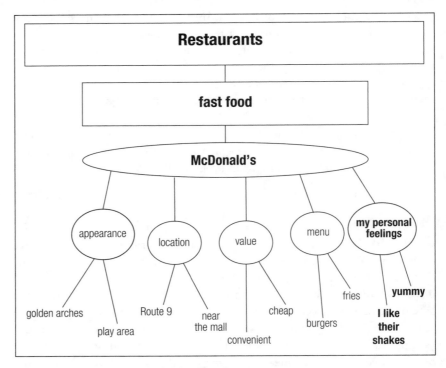

Figure 2–3. *Restaurant Organization Flowchart*

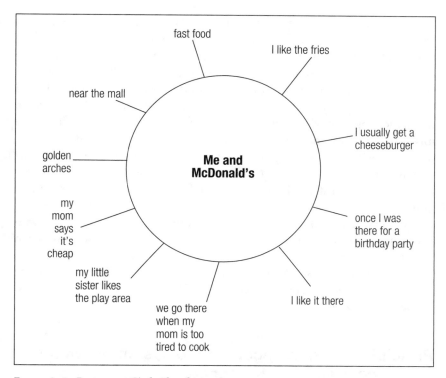

FIGURE 2–4. *Restaurant Circle Flowchart*

formation about McDonald's per se and is characterized accordingly, whereas there is no such distinction in Figure 2–4. Note also that the child represented in Figure 2–3 can easily link up McDonald's for comparison with other places via the attribute categories and also can more easily talk about McDonald's *in general* than the student represented in Figure 2–4 can. If a teacher asked, "What do *you* like about McDonald's?" both children would have easy access to those memories and preferences. However, if asked, "What do *people* like about McDonald's?" the semantically oriented child would have a much readier access to language already stored as abstraction (e.g., cheap, convenient); although the second child has all the same information (but not necessarily the same vocabulary) available to her (e.g., "My mother likes it because it's cheap."), she has mostly *not* stored it as abstract concepts *divorced from self*, nor chunked them categorically (at least not to as great an extent). Another way to look at it is that both students will be able to easily write about their own personal trip to McDonald's, but only the first student will readily be able to apply his experience to enhance the writing of an expository piece about McDonald's or other fast-food restaurants without significant support.

I do not claim to be an expert in this area by any means. All I know is that most school discourse is very top-down and semantically organized and that children from the dominant culture apparently match that model in their own language and memories, whereas my academically struggling CLD students do not. (This is one reason why *wait time* is so important, albeit a reason that may not be readily apparent to many teachers.) I just try to be much more open to what it may mean for my students, how to notice when a mismatch in this arena may be occurring, and how to try to address it. The more I try to be open to it, the more I might see its impact, on both the content and the *pace* of learning. Cultivating a reflective practice is so important, because even if we do not get all the answers, we discover more and more questions to ask.

Mel Levine (2002) has many suggestions for working with children who have some difficulty with various aspects of the memory process. Although CLD students do not have neurological dysfunction that impairs memory in the way that Levine frames the subject, the suggestions he gives for working with children who do are also helpful for CLD students with mismatched memory organization.

Principle 6: A rich vocabulary plays an *essential* role in academic competence.

Think about the following troubling statistics that I heard presented by Beck and McKeown, two of the leading researchers in vocabulary development, at the AERA (American Educational Research Association) in Montreal, Canada, in 2005:

- Academically struggling twelfth graders were once found to have the vocabulary of academically successful third graders (Smith 1941).

- In a professional household, the average four-year-old has a vocabulary of 1,100 words; in a working-class home, it is 700; and in a family on public assistance, it is 500 (Hart and Risley 1995).

- The average four-year-old in a professional household has heard about thirty million words; in working-class home, twenty million; and in a family on public assistance, ten million (Hart and Risley 1995).

- "Low knowledge" first graders knew about five thousand words while "high knowledge" first graders knew about twenty thousand (Moats 2001).

These statistics should concern every educator. Every aspect of classroom learning and teaching—and certainly literacy—is *strongly* colored by vocabulary. Larger vocabularies contribute to better reading skills and support academic performance throughout the curriculum. Weak vocabularies directly contribute to academic underperformance.

> *Non-literacy-oriented CLD students are particularly at risk for the effects of the vocabulary gap.*

Too often, when vocabulary is made the object of study, it is synonymous with dictionary work or studying word lists. There is little more boring and fruitless for students to do in the service of vocabulary building! Sometimes it is matched with spelling lists, but in that case, the words are learned because of their spelling, not their importance to students (especially CLD students). Vocabulary must be acquired contextually and practiced enjoyably, meaningfully, and frequently. The vocabulary gap has to be closed. Then two questions arise:

- What words over and above the important vocabulary of curriculum or literature study does one choose to help close this gap?

- What types of activities aid the learning and retention of vocabulary?

What Words to Study?

One helpful way to think about vocabulary in regard to CLD students is that it has *three tiers* (Beck, McKeown, and Kucan 2002):

- *Tier 1:* everyday words

- *Tier 2:* general academic vocabulary and sophisticated synonyms for tier 1 words

- *Tier 3:* specialized academic vocabulary and very sophisticated, low-frequency words

In the context of this chapter, the first tier can be thought of as common, everyday BICS-related words like *clock, lunch, play, see, throw,* and *ball.* These are learned and used often enough in natural acquisition contexts that we do not need to focus on them. Jumping to the third tier, these are obviously CALP: usually multisyllabic words tied to content study, like *polygon* and *metamorphic,* or found in more sophisticated literature, like *serendipity.* We can characterize these words as either being highlighted for the whole class to know based on content study or words that children come across in novels that they are unlikely to experience or use enough to bother focusing on. So we do not really need to think specifically about this category for vocabulary-needy students, either (other than having clear lessons for the academic terms).

That leaves tier 2 words, sophisticated synonyms for tier 1 words, which are very useful for students to know. One way to think of them is the array of words that flesh out semantic attribute categories. Some tier 2 synonyms for *happy* would be *pleased*, *enthusiastic*, *satisfied*, and *joyful*. These words are not typically focused on in dominant-culture classrooms, at least not in a systematic way, as we assume students must know them (because *our own* children do, or we, ourselves, did at that age). But helping CLD students increase their store of tier 2 words is a key to their academic success.

An example of tier 2 words in text was illustrated in a fifth-grade ELL pullout reading group of mine. We were reading about the huge forest fires in Yellowstone National Park in 1988. There were two CLD students born in the United States in the group, both English dominant, though one had more first language ability (in Khmer) than the other (in Spanish). In addition to important tier 3 words like *controversy*, *ecology*, and *drought*, which I highlighted for them from the back cover before we read the text, they did not know the following words from the book after reading just three (relatively short) pages: *abundant*, *vivid*, *little* (in the sense of "not much"), *despite*, *vital*, *bleak*, *blaze*, and *lack*. I placed their learning of those tier 2 words above the reading of that particular book in importance.

Figure 2–5 shows one of those two student's lists of guessed words from a novel they read later in the year (*The Forgotten Door* by Alexander Key [1965]). The checkmarks are words he and I chose as being important for him to learn.

These fifteen words and phrases were from just five pages of the novel, and many of them are very useful tier 2 words. I was quite surprised at some of the words he was not sure about or did not know at all as a dominant English-speaking fifth grader—*relief*, *speech*, *startled*, *pleasant*, *interrupted*, *doubtfully*, *ashamed*, *recalled*. I had already given the students a list of a few idiomatic language usages in that chapter, which if added to his list would have totaled about twenty-five unknown expressions and words for those five pages, not including a couple of other unfamiliar words that the student missed noting.

One example from the student's list is particularly illustrative of the difficulties CLD students can face in English: *point* (to say). In this case, it does not have either of the BICS meanings the student was familiar with ("pencil point" or "point to [something]"). *Point* both has idiomatic usages (as in this particular case) as well as being a word with multiple meanings.

Idioms are one area of vocabulary with which CLD students need to become more fluent, as English is *filled* with idiomatic usage, both at the BICS level and the CALP level. There are two kinds of idioms. The first are two-word

Word or Idiom	page & ¶	your guess about meaning
✓ Clutching	Page 45 #2	felling
quilt	Page 45 #2	rug
✓ relief	Page 45 #4	To be free
Speech	Page 45 #4	talking for a long tim
Point to say	Page 46 #2	Big reason
✓ startled folks	Page 46 #2	Same folks
Pleasant	Page 46 #2	happy
Reassuring	Page 46 #2	Saying No
✓ interrupted	Page 46 #5	Said Something
Jabbering	Page 47 #1	talking
Pupils	Page 47 #1	People
✓ doubtfully	Page 48 #5	trutefully
herded	Page 49 #1	ran
ashamed	Page 49 #5	fell bad
✓ recalled	Page 49 #7	Said clearly

FIGURE 2–5. *Vocabulary List*

(or phrasal) verbs such as *put on, put off, put in, put up,* and *put through.* A second kind are idiomatic expressions like *rise and shine, shake out the cobwebs,* and *a piece of cake,* which often demand a certain degree of cultural expertise beyond language to know. We should be aware that both our oral language and the language of text are riddled with both kinds of idioms that can throw off a CLD student's comprehension. Related to idioms, sometimes English uses different phrases to stand for one meaning as sentence headers: for example, *Be that as it may* and *Having said that* both sort of mean "Yeah, but . . ." Familiarity with sentence headers is particularly useful in nonfiction reading and writing. We need to understand many idioms as tier 2 words for students to learn.

The other aspect of English vocabulary illustrated by *point* are the multiple, unrelated meanings a single word can have. The student already knew two meanings of *point*; it just happened to have a third! Take the word *bar*, which as a noun could mean "pub," "soap," "a sandy area," "steel," or "thick line" and can also be a tier 2 verb, meaning "keep out." Unfortunately for CLD students, English is filled with such words. (One reason English lends itself so readily to puns is because of this phenomenon.)

> We have to increase our own understanding and awareness of the English language to be successful teachers of CLD students.

As a side note, given all this, just keeping that student specifically (or underachieving, non-literacy-oriented CLD students in general) reading chapter books one or two years below his grade level would not be in his best long-term interest, as *vocabulary* in its myriad forms is the issue, and just reading simpler books will *not* address the vocabulary need. A balance needs to be struck between easier books to develop fluency and other reading skills, and working with more challenging text to develop facility interacting with more complex plots and characterizations. At the same time, students need to develop a stronger vocabulary base. We have to figure out how to support students' vocabulary growth while balancing the competing needs of a range of reading skills. (Also see Chapters 4 and 5 for more on reading.)

Instructional Vocabulary

An *especially* important category of tier 2 CALP words is *instructional vocabulary*. If students do not understand our instruction, how can they learn? Notice that the following terms are typical CALP words in that they are almost all two-plus-syllable synonyms for their BICS counterparts and that the shorter words (*scan, note, prove*) are not that common in social speech. These are some tier 2 instructional verbs listed under their simple synonyms:

Think	**Show**	**Look**
consider	demonstrate	examine
predict	illustrate	explore
draw conclusions	indicate	scan
make a hypothesis	prove	preview
infer	exhibit	observe
synthesize	present	notice
imagine	point out/to	note
reflect		

These lists are not meant to be complete, nor do they represent all the semantic categories of instructional words that are commonly used in classrooms. They are here just to kick-start your thinking. Ultimately, we must learn to monitor ourselves as we use them and list them (for example, on a wall chart) or group them by semantic mapping charts, highlighting and referring to them frequently during instruction, because they pertain to all the different content areas of the curriculum.

The noted African American educator and inspirational speaker Larry Bell has compiled a list of twelve instructional words, the mastery of which, he claims, contributes to better standardized test performance (see www.larry-bell.com). He rightly asserts that what often throws students off or prevents them from answering a test question is the verb that defines what they must *do* with the information. Larry Bell's twelve words are

trace	analyze
infer	evaluate
formulate	describe
support	explain
summarize	compare
contrast	predict

Bell advocates working with these words from early in elementary school, teaching them through simple definitions, songs, and hand gestures to young children when first introduced and then using them appropriately in instructional settings. Of course, these are not the only important words students must learn, and they will naturally be subsumed within any systematic, global attempt to familiarize students with instructional and other CALP vocabulary. A wonderful way to get young children thinking about and learning important instructional verbs is to use a CD of nursery rhyme karaoke tunes and create simple songs about the target words.

Bloom's Taxonomy is another source of very useful vocabulary that traces the development of cognition as we do increasingly complex things with information. Research for Better Teaching has published a list of 146(!) "performance verbs and question cues" that flesh out the instructional language of a classroom discourse community (as well as the "Proposed Taxonomy of Thinking Skills" mentioned in Chapter 1). Students need to become familiar with the tiers 2 and 3 instructional vocabulary of our classrooms, as well as the thinking skills they describe.

Vocabulary Activities

The key is having a multifaceted, enjoyable repertoire of vocabulary activities and a frame for understanding vocabulary development. Marzano and Pickering (2005) have some useful lists of vocabulary by grade level in each major subject area. Combining an expanded understanding of the importance of tier 2 words with a more clear awareness of the need to highlight tier 3 (academic) words during content area study is in the best interests of CLD students. Whatever lists we use, though, we need to create activities that actually further vocabulary acquisition.

An excellent frame for vocabulary instruction is *present-practice-use* (Moran 1984). It's how we learn words in a new language: we have to be exposed to it, we must have chances to use it, and we must either need or want to use it. Just presenting vocabulary (e.g., using sophisticated words during instruction or having a glossary to help read academic text) does not further a CLD student's vocabulary *acquisition*, nor does a direct jump from presentation to an expectation of use. It's *practice* that's most needed, along with multiple opportunities for use. The process should be meaningful, useful, and fun and deepen the semantic connections between words and concepts.

Card games are a great vocabulary learning tool. Tier 2 words or targeted academic (tier 3) vocabulary can be written on index cards of one color, with simple tier 1 (if possible) definitions on index cards of another color. All kinds of practice and use games are readily possible (fish, concentration, sorting activities, etc.). Vocabulary-weak students can be asked to write out multiple sets of such cards, and the act of repetitively writing the words and their definitions is a first presentation step that quickly becomes a kind of practice. Other games for vocabulary can be taken from TV game shows like *Jeopardy*, *Password*, and *The $20,000 Pyramid*. Bingo is another great game to adapt to vocabulary development (as a practice activity).

Venn diagrams are a good use activity. They require students to compare two words that are close in meaning. For example, the Venn in Figure 2–6 compares *relieved* and *satisfied*.

Open-sort activities are another good use activity. Students have to group words according to their *own* categorizations and justify their choices (as opposed to closed sorts, when students group words into predefined categories and there is just one right answer). Other graphic organizers require students to organize words in other ways.

Finally, especially for tier 3 academic words, focusing on frequently occurring *prefixes*, *suffixes*, and *roots* (when obvious) is important. All prefixes or suffixes are not equally important, and roots can be confusing, but when they illuminate meaning (e.g., words with the root *cycle*), it is important to draw stu-

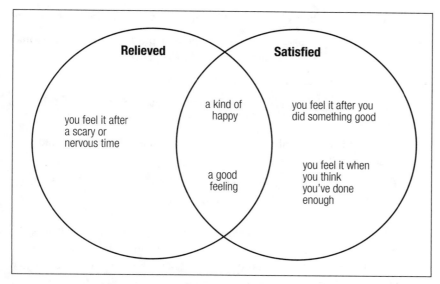

FIGURE 2–6. *Venn Diagram*—Relieved *and* Satisfied

dents' attention to them. Upper-elementary students should also learn the difference between the roles of prefixes and suffixes: prefixes change a word's meaning, while suffixes change their part of speech. So if the root is *pleasant*, adding *un-* to it means *not* pleasant, while adding *-ly* to the end changes the adjective to an adverb. But again, just dropping lists on students to learn only makes it boring and meaningless, the opposite of what we want, which is more engaging and meaningful.

Vocabulary development—both tier 2 for vocabulary-needy students and tier 3 for all students—must be intentional, or only students with strong vocabularies are empowered. I encourage all teachers to seek out interesting, creative ideas for vocabulary development, and I strongly encourage schools to create a systematic tier 2 vocabulary program across grades for vocabulary-needy students.

Summary

Following are some of the various language issues that affect a CLD student's academic progress:

- ways to nurture beginning language learning

- BICS versus CALP language

- the connection between memory, language, and learning in the classroom
- the crucial role dialect and register play in the formation of personal narrative, and how that shapes the way we organize our thoughts
- the role of language in shaping identity
- the connection between ways of using language and ways of thinking and learning
- the nurturing of vocabulary development, which is key for the academic success of CLD students
- how school questions may be mismatched to the way questions are used in some students' home discourse communities

Without clearly defining the characteristics of the English that is used in the classroom (for ourselves and our students), it is unlikely that we can help CLD students work on those areas of language that must be developed further to become school matched. However, we must do this in a way that (1) builds on the child's own language strengths even if they are not, at first glance, school matched and (2) honors and values the language that the child brings to the classroom. After all, that language directly connects to the child's home community and family.

Some studies show that higher verbal IQs are correlated to higher socioeconomic status (such as Morgan, Alwin, and Griffin 1979), and what is being measured there are the literacy skills of language described in this chapter. It's no big deal for many dominant-culture, literacy-oriented students to score so highly in that type of measure—after all, we should not be surprised if we squeeze oranges and orange juice comes out! That does not mean, however, that just because we happen to like orange juice better, apple juice is inferior. It's only how we analyze this information and what we take from it that can point us in the right direction.

So why do so many children from the dominant culture seem to enter school as academic successes waiting to happen? As we explored in Chapter 1, their school culture and home culture mirror each other. Now we see those elements of their language that culture gives rise to (i.e., amplifiers) that are privileged in school. As the classroom discourse community is usually predicated on dominant-culture interaction and learning norms, and uses the types of thinking valued in those communities (which accelerates the development of metacognition), its language is most often the language of the dominant culture as well, that is to say, standard dialect, CALP-oriented, vocabulary-rich, formal register English. Added to that is a certain level of narrative development to encode thinking. Figure 2–7 illustrates the interplay between mutually

high level of vocabulary	high level of metacognition	high development of semantic memory	highly developed personal narrative	independence in learning and problem solving

FIGURE 2–7. *Essential Characteristics (Amplifiers) of Literacy Ability*

amplifying components of language, memory, and thinking (Chapter 5—on reading—links back to this chart).

When I do teacher workshops, I call this diagram "The Secret Stuff!" It's the stuff *most directly connected* to reading ability and academic performance, although it is much less likely that developing these is the explicit *focus* of the academic curriculum. Multiply mismatched CLD students whose schooling is grounded in and organized around systematically developing explicit school-matched ways of using and organizing language and thinking (without being asked to jettison their own communities' preferred ways) are fortunate, indeed! They are developing independence in the skills that *automatically* empower so many dominant-culture students. How that might be accomplished is the focus of Chapter 3.

Notes

1. I've had a few students who attained CALP proficiency in three years, and some more mismatched students have needed more than seven years. The length of time is usually directly connected to the literacy orientation of a child's first or dominant language (see also Collier 1995).

2. I highly recommend authors like Lisa Delpit and Theresa Perry, who write very powerfully about language and dialect from an African American perspective.

3. In an as yet unpublished study, a colleague and I conducted four memory experiments with about forty-five third and fourth graders (with parent permission) in three different towns (two in western Massachusetts and one in southern Vermont) to test out whether semantic memory and academic performance could be correlated. We found evidence of greater semantic memory access in higher-achieving students. We hope to get this study published soon and are hoping someone will do a follow-up study on a larger scale.

4. Through the blessing of this Thinking Skills program, I have found that some students who are unversed with semantic categories also have difficulty recognizing them as separate qualities. For example, they think initially that changing an object's size also changes its shape. This can obviously have a huge impact on a student's school learning, especially as he gets older and school learning gets faster, more complex, more linguistic, and more abstract.

Teaching and Learning in the Classroom

A first-grade ESL-inclusion classroom has just had a lesson on camouflage as a part of its ocean unit. The follow-up activity is to make a construction paper collage of a camouflaged fish or other undersea creature. I go around to check the ELL students' comprehension. I ask, "If I'm a red fish and a shark is coming, what color seaweed should I look for?"

Each student says, "Red!" or whatever color is the appropriate response. They seem to have learned.

However, I notice that a couple of the students have started to cut a different color for their camouflage than they used for their fish. I call them over to a quiet spot and ask them to bring their pictures. I repeat the shark question, and again the students reply appropriately. Then I ask, "So, Vuth, your fish is green. If I'm a shark and want to eat your fish [making a scary face and gesturing a swimming motion toward Vuth], what color seaweed will your fish need?"

Vuth looks down at a pile of construction paper on the floor. "Yellow," he says.

"What did we learn about camouflage today, Vuth? You're making a camouflage picture. So if I'm a shark and I want to eat your green fish . . . you don't want your fish want to get eaten, do you?"

"No!"

"So you'd better hide him! What color seaweed will you use?"

He looks at the pile. "Mmm . . . blue."

"Tell you what, Vuth. I'm going to ask Maria the same question. Let's see what she says, OK?"

But Maria does the same thing as Vuth, looking down at the construction paper! She has a blue fish and says, "Green."

WHAT WAS Vuth's and Maria's confusion? As it turned out, they were unclear about an apparently simple academic awareness in the classroom: that teaching and learning activity in a classroom are connected. When the direction did not come *explicitly*, the students gave priority to making the picture pretty and colorful, in line with what their teachers had so often given them good feedback for in the past. This scenario, which is related to the problem surrounding the instructional use of *so* discussed in Chapter 2, gives rise to several important questions about teaching and learning within classroom activity:

- What are the domains (i.e., areas of instruction or attention) a teacher should be aware of in the teaching-learning process when working with CLD students?

- How can interactions within the teaching-learning process be optimized?

- How can the student's learning needs of the moment be identified and prioritized?

- How can the frameworks of culture and language introduced in Chapters 1 and 2 help us become more effective teachers?

The following principles help address those questions:

1. Successful teaching of CLD students addresses all the domains of the sociocultural framework, bridging mismatches between learner, language, classroom culture, and academic content.

2. Discriminating between *quantity* and *quality* in learning is essential to working successfully with underachieving CLD students.

3. The process of learning has three identifiable stages. We need to know which stage we are in.

4. Student attention is key.

5. Successful teaching of underachieving CLD students means reducing the clutter.

6. Learning needs to be grounded.

7. Academic lessons with CLD students need clear content and language goals.

As with the previous chapters, take a moment to think about your initial reactions to these principles.

Principle 1: Successful teaching of CLD students addresses all the domains of the sociocultural framework, bridging mismatches between learner, language, classroom culture, and academic content.

Just like a prism shows us that white light is actually made of many colors, a sociocultural framework refracts the teaching-learning process into its many component parts. When working with CLD students, we must constantly be aware of the interplay between culture, thinking, background experience, language, and student individuality. Any learning interaction between a teacher and a CLD student may potentially be focused on, shift to, or need to account for any one of these aspects at the intersection of student, teacher, what is being learned, the language medium through which it is being learned, and how it is being learned. One possible way to conceive of this interrelationship is through the diagram in Figure 3–1.

Two things are implied in this diagram. First, we must understand the sociocultural context of school, and second, we must have formed a genuine, respectful relationship with our CLD students. If we perpetuate gross inequality in our classroom and/or do not try to form strong relationships with our students, then whatever else we do is doomed to fail.

But let's say we have. Then we enter this diagram. The center diamond represents a learning moment in a classroom. The middle octagons represent four main components that come together during academic instruction of the teacher teaching, the student learning, and what is being taught/learned. Around the edges are issues of language, cognition, social context, and a student's cultural background and personality, any or all of which may negatively impact or positively amplify learning. Think of this figure as a synthesis of the

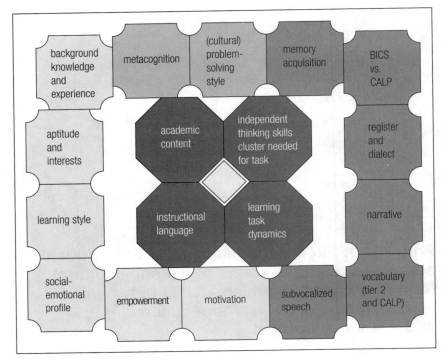

Figure 3–1. *Puzzle Chart Containing the Components of the Teaching-Learning Process*

first two chapters, with the addition of *metacognition* (see below) and issues that you already pay attention to: a student's social-emotional profile, aptitude and interests, and learning style.

Together, these represent the various domains—*that is, areas of the curriculum and issues of language, culture, or teacher-student interaction*—that might need direct teaching, scaffolding, or attention. For school-matched students, we can conceive of the outer cultural and linguistic cells as overlapping lenses that *focus* the power of instruction and learning, while for many CLD students, they are *diffused* through domains of mismatch or confusion. Teaching school-matched students, we don't often have to move to explicitly working within the outer cells other than those on the left-hand side, but when we teach non-literacy-oriented students, we often do.

One very important aspect of the teaching/learning process that is frequently revisited in this chapter, but does not have a separate cell in Figure 3–1 is *attention*. I do not mean just the attention of our students, but our own as well. The need for attention or focus is present throughout nearly *all* the domains in the diagram—not just is the student paying attention, but *how*.

Another important concept not in the diagram that you may recall from the first two chapters, discourse community, also pervades many of the domains by helping us conceptualize what they are.

A colleague has likened the diagram in Figure 3–1 to a chest of drawers. As we teach, we open a number of drawers until we find just what we are looking for. When we teach CLD students, we may need to open and look inside a larger number of drawers to determine our instructional focus with a student or make the lesson comprehensible. The labels on the drawers call out to us when we're teaching, telling us that they may need opening and looking in, as well as what we can expect to see inside them.

Principle 2: Discriminating between *quantity* and *quality* in learning is essential to working successfully with underachieving CLD students.

One distinction that this diagram is helpful in making, especially in a context like in my own school where some CLD students are very mismatched to the shared discourse community norms of most students and teachers, is quality versus quantity in learning. Remember that discourse community norms are both explicit and implicit. Quality learning is often the *implicit* norms of the dominant learning community, while quantity learning is the *explicit* information curriculum (the academic content domain) or the *what* of learning. Quality learning is the *how* and *why* of learning, which lies within *all* the other domains. It is what we do with the content curriculum on the inside. A *quality curriculum* is one that pays attention to all the issues of culture and language described in Chapters 1 and 2, and issues of teaching and learning taken up in this chapter. Quality curriculum is another way to say *hidden curriculum*. Figure 3–1 labels various quality-learning drawers.

I do *not* mean to imply a value judgment, that school-matched (i.e., dominant culture) ways of thinking, feeling, believing, and acting are a better quality than those of different discourse communities, or conversely, that the home-learning apprenticeship of non-school-matched communities is of an inferior quality. But we also cannot avoid the fact that successful school learning is defined largely in terms of *amplified quality-learning skills* that match dominant-culture, literacy-oriented expectations (especially in the dominant-culture classroom). That means some CLD students must learn the information curriculum *and* school-matched ways of learning and using language, and thus have double the work to do. Our job is to recognize that non-literacy-oriented CLD students thus have a double burden, and understand how our teaching must change to help make that load more manageable.

My own thinking about *quality learning* evolved while watching our Cambodian American students over several years. They'd had first language and culture support, ESL-inclusion classrooms increasingly attuned to helping scaffold their (quantity) learning needs, and were in a school that has highly skilled, motivated teachers. In the inclusion classrooms, the teachers tried very hard to form genuine relationships with their students; regulated the language of instruction and learning; made the implicit explicit; actively tried to combat social, cultural, and academic disempowerment; and had lots of active, engaging group projects to stimulate learning. Yet, while the Cambodian students' (and other lower-achieving CLD students') performance and achievement had certainly improved in inclusion classrooms, many continued to underachieve relative to other students—even other populations of ESL students—when left to their own devices or when in noninclusion classrooms. This continued into secondary school. Apparently their *internal, independent ways* of integrating and processing classroom learning experiences had not significantly changed enough to match classroom expectations at our school and in our district, in spite of all the support they received and, more important, the explicit way that it had been enacted for them right before their eyes over the years. Or, in the words of Meir Ben-Hur, Director of Learning Applications at Cognitive and Achievement Solutions (2001): "Why is it so common then, that the cognitive and affective dispositions that are necessary for higher academic achievements are not enhanced through the learning that happens in the context of those academic disciplines?" (2). As I developed a reflective practice around this issue, I came to understand the difference between *quality* and *quantity* in learning.

If a particular group of CLD students forms the center of gravity of a classroom community, then the *quantity* curriculum should be learned through the *students' shared quality-learning norms.* (There are many excellent examples of this, such as the KEEP program in Hawaii; see Tharp and Gallimore [1988] and Au [1980]). If, however, CLD students are a minority within, and very mismatched to, the dominant classroom community, as they are in our school, then for them to attain independence in the school's discourse community norms, quality-learning transformation must be front and center as a teaching-learning goal.

A transformation toward school-matched quality learning is in a student's best long-term interests, because it puts the reins of learning more and more in his control.

I admit that this can seem to cause a real tension in how we teach and what we teach given this era of high-stakes testing and quantity-learning focus. In fact, the quantity-learning focus that many teachers, and certainly many policy makers, think is the key to students doing well on tests—cramming them with information like force feeding geese to make paté—is not only wrong, it is ultimately toxic because it sucks up all the time in the school day, and the life and enjoyment out of it. A balance of quantity and quality learning, with the *emphasis* on quality, is actually *much* more helpful to underachieving students, because what is really in their long-term interests is to become adept in literacy-oriented ways of thinking and using language (while maintaining a strong sense of cultural identity). But even so, I look at it this way: if suddenly it were ordered that July-blooming flowers must open in May, it would not happen even if I pretended it could, or demanded it, no matter how much fertilizer I stuffed in the ground, watered the plants, or prayed. And the reality remains—I *still* have to tend to my July-blooming flowers appropriately. As we become more knowledgeable about ourselves, our classrooms, and our students, we see much more, and more deeply. Teaching becomes a reflective process of *inquiry*. Then it is up to us to work best with what we see and understand to be true.

What Are My Students Really *Learning?*

A good example of discriminating between quantity versus quality occurred recently in one of my ESL reading classes (mixed third and fourth graders). We were working on reading fluency. We had given it a clear three-part definition (it has to flow like a river, we can't trip over words, and our expression must match the story) and practiced in class. In class, the students seemed to understand. So I gave them homework to practice with a couple of their favorite pages from a book that was 98 percent within their decoding range. They would show off their good fluency the next day by reading those pages aloud.

They came in enthusiastically the next day, proudly saying they'd done the homework. Yet when the time came, they did not read very fluently! But I had a feeling that fluency was not the real issue at that moment. In fact, they each rated themselves as not having done a very good job after their out-loud reading that day, so they understood fluency better than they had performed it. I said, "But you said you did a good job practicing it at home."

"We did!"

"So how come you didn't do a good job with it today?"

"I don't know," they said in unison.

"Tell me, how did you study at home?"

Two of the three girls answered, "We practiced the two pages," which with further probing I realized meant that they'd read them *once*; the other girl said, "I read it twice." In other words, they had *not* actually felt that they had done a good job practicing *fluency* at home—in fact, they hadn't monitored that at all! They "did their homework," assigning a random time for it. Or put another way, they were leaving the evaluation of their learning solely up to me.

That was the more important quality issue at that moment, not fluency (i.e., the quantity). I asked them, "How would you know if you'd studied enough at home?" to which they hemmed and hawed and finally just shrugged. So that day in class, we spent nearly the entire hour talking about how we know enough is enough and did no further work on fluency. We put the *quantity curriculum* aside in favor of the *quality curriculum*. The following are some quality-learning statements we have generated and posted on our wall over time, and refer back to as needed:

- Being organized is better than being random.

- Knowing is better than just being lucky.

- Know what you know.

- There are similarities between things that seem different, and differences between things that are similar. Think and look carefully!

- Have a strategy before you start.

- Be sure to follow the rules (that is, the rules of how to perform an academic task appropriately and successfully).

- If you know what mistakes you often make, you can stop yourself from making them.

- Use a model to check back to if you have one.

- Labeling your thinking (using clear, descriptive language) is very important to successful learning.

As you can see, these are some explicit statements about the implied classroom discourse community norms of thinking and learning of successful students, that is, the quality curriculum. Not only do these students and others need these, and other, norms to be named explicitly, but they also need structured practice time to become more aware of them as elements of the learning environment and to become more skillful using them.

It is not fair, but non-literacy-oriented CLD students have to learn *much* more than other students (the quantity *and* quality curricula) to function independently in dominant-culture classrooms. They also need to fill in gaps in background knowledge for the quantity curriculum to be properly understood at times. With all that, we could say that for long-term value, focused work within *any* domain is just as valuable as any other.

Take, for example, a hypothetical science lesson about why Saturn has rings. One could not say that content learning is any more valuable than focusing on any of the possible domains of quality learning or language that a student needs to develop. One could even make the argument that the content knowledge (the quantity)—why Saturn has rings—may be the *least* important thing he could be learning when juxtaposed against domains of more long-term, quality-learning value. When we account for quality-learning domains as well as quantity learning, it makes us think more deeply about what our students may need most in the moment.

Principle 3: The process of learning has three identifiable stages. We need to know which stage we are in.

Think back to a new thing you learned—for example, how to play a musical instrument or how to ride a bike. What was the process through which you first learned it? Was being shown once enough? How did you come to master it (to whatever degree you have)? Based on that information, fill out Table 3–1.

Who taught you?	
When, where, and how were you taught?	
When in the process did the teaching stop?	
Describe your reactions to the teaching, either positive or negative.	

TABLE 3–1. *May be copied for professional use. © 2008 by Ken Pransky from* Beneath the Surface *(Heinemann: Portsmouth, NH).*

Vygotsky (1986) describes a four-stage process of learning, of which the first three are most important for us as teachers of CLD students. You might find that your reflection on your own learning could be encapsulated by this process:

1. *The need for a clear, explicit, external model.* This may be visual or verbal or involve some other sense. However, a clear goal or model must be scaffolded externally by a more competent peer or adult. This stage is like gears 1 and 2 of a five-speed car, which just get the car moving.

2. *The internalization of the model (or concept) by the learner.* This stage is a much longer process. The skill of good teaching comes into play here: one must slowly hand over responsibility for the learning, and ownership of the concept, to the learner, not letting go of everything too fast, yet not holding on too long. This is the stage of structured practice. This stage is like gears 3 and 4, the ones you spend the most time in on your way to cruising speed.

3. *Independence*; the student has constructed her own meaning of the model, the learning goal, or concept. At this stage, the learner may even be resentful of attempts to interfere, which would imply that she still needs help. This is like fifth gear, or cruising speed.

Do you find that this framework roughly resembles the process you went through in the learning that you described in Table 3–1?[1] If not, why do you think that may be?

The second stage of this process is the key one for us: knowing when to offer support and how much, when to withdraw it and to what degree, when to just let students be, and how much and what kind of practice time to structure. One way to characterize stage 2 is *activating student awareness, thinking, and knowledge.*[2] The less we need to do or say to activate that awareness, thinking, and knowledge, the better.

For example, if I am working with a beginning reader who is developing the skill of using a picture and an initial consonant sound to figure out words, and I see he begins to read in a book without also looking at the picture or, conversely, looking at the picture without checking the words, I might ask, "What else do you need to do to be a good reader now?" or say, "Now you also need to . . . ," and let him finish the sentence. If he can't, I might add, "Now you need to *l-* . . . ." If he still can't respond, I might add, "Now you also need to *loo-* . . . ," adding parts of the phrase until he can finish the sentence: "Look at the picture (or word) too." That's quite different than continuing to tell the student, "Look at the picture first," if he forgets or automatically expecting him to know because he did it yesterday. There are many ways to work in this stage with students, from verbalizing to using visual cues to having (older) students keep learning logs they can refer back to. I'm sure you employ many great strategies to do work in stage 2 already; this is just a reminder of how important it is to constantly be attentive to where students are in the learning process.

As much as I can, I try to think of how to make students take on an increasingly larger share of the heavy lifting in stage 2. I've done things like keep a small piece of rope or chain on the table to remind students to make connections, use icons and symbols that stand for larger concepts, which I can point to as needed, and keep a plastic bucket around to remind students that as learners, it is their responsibility and effort to "fill their own bucket" with the sweet water of learning in our school (an image we talk about first). I am still playing around with how to "Zen" the second stage, in other words, conveying meaning as simply as I can.

Understanding and skillfully working within the second stage in quality-learning domains as well as in the academic content domain is one of the keys to successfully teaching underachieving CLD students.

Even so, I confess to shuddering over how often I have modeled something clearly, structured a little practice time—and bingo, moved on to something else! The press of time and *quantity* can squeeze stage 2 processing out. Then *quality* suffers. This is especially true with some of the less obvious instructional domains represented in Figure 3–1.

One way to think about Figure 3–1 is that many of the domains represent what Vygotsky calls *zones of proximal development* (ZPDs), that is, when a person is learning with support that which is slightly beyond her ability to learn independently. Because the learning framework presented in this book emphasizes the intersection of language-based *interactions* and the cultural nature of learning tasks, the ZPD concept is particularly helpful in conceptualizing our teaching interactions with CLD students. This is the essence of working in the internalizing stage.

It is not enough just to understand this concept in relation to the academic content ZPD. We consciously need to ask ourselves, "What is appropriate input (ZPD) now (out of the domains in Figure 3–1)? How do I know? And how do I focus a student's attention there?"

Principle 4: Student attention is key.

Wherever a student's attention and focus are, *that's* where his brainpower is being directed. It seems obvious enough, yet as I've noted, some students seem not to have learned certain things even after years of exposure to them.

> Mullah Nasruddin was seen crawling around in the dirt in the late afternoon. He was wandering near a street light that had just come on. He seemed to be looking for something. Some townspeople went over to help.
>   "What's wrong, Mullah?"

SKILLS AND SCHEMATA

Another lens that helps clarify the learning process is cognitive load theory (Sweller and van Merrienboer 2005, 1998). It describes learning as essentially what we do in working memory toward the creation of skills or patterns of thinking (called *schemata*), which we store in long-term memory. Experts are defined as those who have multiple schemata and skills stored up to apply to new problem-solving situations. It is sufficient practice (i.e., stage 2) that gets new learning into long-term memory as schemata and skills to apply in the future.

A key point is that the space in working memory is quite *limited*. That means that new learning may be compromised by the amount of information and variables—important or extraneous, intrinsic to the task or distraction from the outside—that can clutter up precious but limited working memory space. When faced with new learning, the more we can overlay a preexisting schema or skill from long-term memory onto the new learning context, the more we combine and integrate information into familiar patterns, which in turn frees up (or cleans out) space in working memory for more focused learning to occur. Many of these are quality-learning schemata and skills, as well as language skills. This helps explain why students from the dominant culture are generally successful in dominant-culture classrooms—they have many appropriate preexisting schemata and skills (e.g., amplifiers) of experience, information, patterns of thinking, and language that support and enhance classroom learning. However, the flip side is that non-literacy-oriented students do not have (all) these skills; thus, the schemata and skills of classroom learning tasks, which are built into the tasks in the way they are organized and the expectations of learning they carry, act as distractors. They are confusing or misunderstood elements that take precious working memory space away from learning and solving problems. For example, a student thinks, "How am I supposed to know that??", or "What am I supposed to do now?", or "I don't get this language!", or "Oh, no, I'm the only one who doesn't seem to know what to do!" Maybe the student's mind is taken up with concern that the class is moving so much faster than they are, or they misunderstand some language and don't realize it, or they feel disempowered. There are any number of possible ways that working memory space is diverted from the actual problem solving by being confused, overloaded, nervous, misunderstanding, or spinning out on a line of a non-task-oriented thought. (For more on this, see the discussion about Principle 5 on page 92.)

"I lost my purse! I need it back! I had a lot of money in it!"

"We'll help!" And they got down sifting through the dirt and scraggly grass by the side of the road.

Soon a number of other townspeople came over and helped, all crawling around by the roadside, but no one could find it. Finally, one of the older men said, "Mullah, we've looked and looked. Are you sure you dropped it over here?"

"Oh, no," said Nasruddin. "I dropped it over there." He pointed towards a high-walled alley which could by now barely be seen through the darkening dusk.

"Then by Merciful God, why on earth are we on our hands and knees way over here, you donkey!?" everyone shouted.

The Mullah shook his head at such obvious ignorance. "Excuse me, but don't you know there's no light in the alleyway? That's why I came over here, so I could see better." (Adapted from *The Exploits of the Incredible Mullah Nasruddin* [Shah 1972])

How we direct our own attention is key, too. How often do we end up looking for answers within the structure of our assumptions about teaching, learning, and language and the quantity curriculum? It's surely where we can see best, but not necessarily where our answers lie.

MEDIATED LEARNING EXPERIENCES

One very important concept to understand in any discussion on student focus is the mediated learning experience (Feuerstein et al. 1980; Kozulin 1999, 2001b, 2002; Ben-Hur 2001). It is one of the theoretical bases for the Feuerstein Instrumental Enrichment (FIE) thinking skills program used in more than eighty countries around the world, though hardly known here. It is ultimately a very optimistic way of looking at academically underachieving students: Dr. Reuven Feuerstein, who developed mediated learning theory, says that if a child is not learning, the mediator must always take responsibility for that situation by figuring out a more skillful, more appropriate means of mediation, because *all* children can learn.

The MLE school of thought ascribes certain characteristics to high-quality, culturally appropriate interactions between parent or other adult (teacher) and child that promote *flexibility, depth, and breadth of thinking.*

Mediation operates on two levels. Active mediation in literacy households points the child in the direction of developing literacy skills and schemata, *whatever the cultural and language background.* That informs a teacher's understanding about the need to adapt the learning environment in diverse classrooms to build on students' own cultural and linguistic strengths as they

acculturate to the new language and culture. The deeper level informs our understanding that *some* students come to us poorly mediated to whatever degree for whatever reason, such as high stress, forced immigration, violence, or severe impoverishment (also see Saco-Pollitt, Pollitt, and Greenfield 1985). Their internal landscape needs to change for them to become successful, independent learners at school.

Mediation *molds the learning of the child to a culturally appropriate end by culturally and linguistically familiar means.*

Well-mediated learners from *whatever* culture or class spontaneously and independently compare new experiences with old, analyze them, and more skillfully respond to them. "Do I understand this well? Is it like what I already know or different, and if different, exactly how?" This is what expert learners do with the multiple schemata they have formed. All children take meaning from immediate sensory experience, but creating learning that *transcends the moment* is a learned, culturally grounded behavior. Although different types of

(Continues)

MEDIATED LEARNING EXPERIENCES *(Continued)*

learning skills may be mediated in different social classes (Tzuriel 1996), well-mediated children from *any* culture or class are more considered, perceptive learners who operate more skillfully in new circumstances than poorly mediated children.

Think back to Figure 1–3. If the cultural grounding is not there, children do not develop the full range of expected thinking and problem-solving skills of their parents' culture, and that is reflected in the ways they use language. Kozulin (1998) describes what happens with some immigrant families, because of intense stress, being in survival mode, or not being able to integrate into the new culture or language while at the same time not continuing to transmit the traditional culture. I think we all have seen this in some of the families we have worked with.

> On the sociocultural level, the lack of mediation is often associated with the rejection or breakdown of the system of cultural transmission. The influence of this condition on the child is twofold. The child becomes deprived of those devices of mediated learning that were incorporated into the traditional cultural schemas and rituals of his or her parents. At the same time, parents themselves often abandon or are forced to revoke their prerogative as mediators because the old culture is perceived as irrelevant, and the new culture is not yet mastered. As a result, the child is left to confront the world on a "here-and-now" basis without the help of the transcending devices of the cultural-historical tradition. (75)

MLEs add flesh to the bones of the ZPD concept. The real focus of an MLE is always the learner's *internal landscape* (quality learning). Out of a number of mediational characteristics named in the literature, there are

three essential ones without which an interaction cannot be an MLE:

- *Transcendence:* Explicit connections are made with the help of the guiding adult between the present learning experience, similar past experiences, and future possible experiences; also referred to as bridging.
- *Intentionality and reciprocity:* The specific focus and purpose of the interaction is made clear. In addition, both the mediator and the child are clear that the real intention of the mediation is *not* solving the present problem or mastering the present situation, but rather the development of the child's thinking. It is crucial that the child has the opportunity to actively demonstrate her understanding of the learning focus (i.e., at the point of intentionality).
- *Mediation of meaning: Each* aspect of the learning interaction is made meaningful; or, as I like to think of it, *meaning-full.*

These essential factors of learning, which are naturally a part of mediating parent-child interactions, must be squarely in the consciousness of the moment for both the learner and the teacher at school. For students who would *not* spontaneously engage in their own internal bridging and intentionality and reciprocity, the modeling of these qualities of good learning is crucial. Thinking about learning in the context of these characteristics has made me much more aware of what is going on in front of me, when quality-learning issues may be affecting quantity learning. I constantly ask myself, "What am I *really* teaching? What are my students *really* learning? What do they really need to be focusing on now? How do I know, and what do I do about it?" Now that such reflection has become a habit, I am much more likely to think of asking my *students* those questions, too, or at least probing for their understanding. I feel more sure of myself as an effective teacher since I began using this lens to understand the learning challenges of my academically neediest CLD students.

Students are learning wherever their intentionality *and* reciprocity are. This helps clarify the subtle yet deep distinction between *exposure to* and *instruction in* and explains why students do not learn some things even after years of what seems like explicit exposure to them (the issue that was raised on pages 78–79). Their attention had not explicitly been pinned down there (intentionality), and they had not been required to respond enough, or at all (reciprocity), vis-à-vis those elements of quality learning. Intentionality and reciprocity force the student and teacher to work harmoniously in the second stage of learning. Attention is key!

A mediator enables the child to scaffold a culturally integrated perspective on his experience, which would likely not have been possible without mediation. Yet at the same time, the learner must be an active agent in this process. The dynamic interaction between learner, mediator, and what is being learned—and the change that happens to *all three* in the process of interacting—is a powerful way to look at learning interactions.[3]

Another enlightening aspect of mediated learning theory is its division of learning into three distinct phases: *input*, *processing*, and *output*. They guide our thinking about a student's learning in the moment: Is she having difficulty because she has not taken in data in a considered way, or taken in too little or inappropriate data? Or is she having difficulty processing the appropriate data she has taken in? Or is she having trouble communicating what she's learned? These added layers of our thinking deepen the meaning of the ZPD.

The input phase is crucial, because if students have not been skillful there, it does not matter how carefully they process it and communicate their thinking. With patch-

> *Poorly mediated students frequently flit across the surface of learning, being attracted to the most obvious input: the biggest, loudest, brightest, shiniest . . .*

work or threadbare input, it's hard to sew up our learning, which often needs details and care. It's like just basting a pair of pants together—they might look OK at first, but they'll unravel quickly!

For more on the background and theory of mediated learning and other important learning theory from Feuerstein, as well as projects his organization has undertaken, I highly recommend you visit www.icelp.org/asp/main.asp.

To clarify, I do *not* mean that

- all CLD students are not mediated or poorly mediated
- all socioeconomically struggling students are not mediated or poorly mediated
- all immigrant students are not mediated or poorly mediated
- one's first thinking about a struggling CLD student should be that she is in need of mediation

I *do* mean that

- for very mismatched students for whom scaffolding in a variety of domains does *not* enable them to change their *independent* ways of thinking and learning to become of more school-matched quality, an awareness of mediated learning theory can help us understand their learning needs better and teach them more effectively
- the mediated learning model is a helpful frame for thinking about *any* learning interaction, with *all* students

SPECIAL EDUCATION

When we think a CLD student may have special needs, the nature of the referral process should change by definition. There are so many ways to get a false read with CLD students because the many possible different ways of thinking, feeling, believing, and acting may masquerade as special needs to a teacher unfamiliar with the sociocultural framework, and because the testing process itself may perpetuate a false read. But while the larger problem is that we must guard against the overrepresentation of CLD students on special education caseloads, some children from CLD communities do have special needs, and they should not be denied services based on philosophical bias. So where does that leave us?

Beware of any source that tells you there is a solid, clear answer on how to make decisions during the referral process for CLD students. Similar to the case this book makes that how we *think* is ultimately the most important thing when we teach CLD students, and not just what we do, it is also the key point in the referral process (also see Echevarria, Vogt, and Short 2008, for a similar perspective on referring CLD students). The following are several perspectives to consider:

- *It's often political:* The referral of children of color by white, dominant-culture staff is by nature a political process: privileged, dominant-culture teachers making value judgments about a CLD student's culture, intelligence, and ability. There is no escaping this fact, and we have to come to grips with what it may mean during any referral of a child of color.
- *There are cultural differences:* The very term *special needs* or *special education* translates into the equivalent of *mental retardation* in many languages and cultures. This must be understood if we are to have any chance of bringing parents on board and helping them understand what it means here.
- *Parents' perspective is key:* We must get the parents' perspective on their child as a learner and user of language in their own discourse community first. Developing some sort of interview that gets at this is a very valuable step. If parents have questions about their child's learning or language development within their own cultural and linguistic context, that is like a green light to the referral process. If, however, from the parents' perspective, the only place where a child seems to have language or learning problems is at school, to me that is at least a yellow, or even a red, light.
- *Compared with whom?* A student's academic progress should be viewed relative to the academic progress of other members of their discourse community (if possible), not against the "average" (dominant-culture) student. If we are unfamiliar with the cultural learning patterns and language practices of certain students, we need to ask for help and the perspective of other teachers who are familiar with that community, or that family, and not just jump to our own conclusions in isolation from that cultural information. (Of course, this text says we should be doing this anyway as teachers, not just if we think a referral is in order!)
- *Time:* We have to be careful not to let the artificial notions of the time we expect it will take for things to academically fall into place for the average child to overcolor our decision making as we think about and measure non-literacy-oriented CLD student progress, either as a reason for referral or during the referral process.

- *Bias in the process:* Once a non-literacy-oriented CLD student is referred, the skids are often greased to the determination of a special need (especially with students who are poorly mediated). The student is likely going to perform under the norm on some if not all testing whether he has a special need or not, so what will the testing process prove (see next bullet)? That is why it is so important to be considered and careful at the start of the referral process.

- *Bias in test materials:* There is cultural or linguistic bias in many test materials! Districts need to research the least biased testing possibilities, consider what language is the student's academically dominant one, and take any results with a grain of salt. Districts that have bilingual school psychologists are somewhat covered, at least for any students who speak the school psychologist's language, but the impact of dialect (in whatever language) on test performance is not well understood. So it is not the results but their interpretation that matters. This means that we need to find a way to incorporate a cultural informant or expert in the student's language to help interpret test results. However, direct translation of test items is not the answer, especially on language testing, as translations may skew what is being tested for, which also may not translate directly between languages.

- *The gray area:* In the bad old days (which I've heard are still around in some places), just the fact of not speaking English well was "proof" of a special need. Hopefully, that is not the case at your school! But even then, it is often very hard to distinguish between academic struggle due to a special need or

due to a student's being undereducated or in need of more explicit mediation. It is a gray area where the easy out is to refer, but that is not often the empathetic or knowledgeable course of action to take.

- *The sociocultural framework:* The first, most important step we can take to get a better handle on CLD student referrals is to develop a reflective mindset that transforms our teaching practice in more empathetic and knowledgeable ways. Then we more easily discriminate between quality and quantity in learning, make language a focus of inquiry and instruction, help deconstruct and demystify our classroom discourse community's ways of thinking, feeling, believing, and acting, focus on helping students developing literacy-oriented amplifiers, reduce distractors in learning, become much more sensitive to the issues that are *really* affecting a student's academic performance, and help students develop more independence in learning successfully. We are then better able to offer an informed perspective about CLD student referrals both in terms of what a student's progress has been like in such a learning-enhanced classroom space as well having a clearer perception of just what issues are at play, either masquerading as or genuinely being a special need. Referrals of CLD students that come out of academic performance in "typical" classrooms should be viewed as suspect until proven otherwise (barring parent agreement or some medically established condition), especially if CLD student referrals are by teachers who have referred many CLD students in the past.

If we see that students are not learning effectively even when we have clarified and adapted the learning environment according to issues of culture and language raised in Chapters 1 and 2, or they are not developing the capacity to achieve at higher levels *independently* over time, then our attention may need to shift to the student's cognition. It's almost like systematically working our way through the drawers in Figure 3–1. We start with ourselves and move toward the student through the layers of language, academic focus, and learning interaction, and then even inside the student if necessary. This is a general list—there are, of course, many details within each of the following:

Sympathy

✓ Have I tried to build a good relationship with my student?

✓ Have I understood her personal interests and learning style?

✓ Have I taken steps to incorporate the cultures of all my students in my classroom?

Empathy

✓ Have I tried to learn about the student as a thinker and user of language from the perspective of his own discourse community?

✓ Am I continuing to incorporate a social justice perspective in my work?

✓ Have I scaffolded the academic content?

✓ Have I accounted for my use of instructional language?

✓ Have I clarified the content and language goals of the lesson?

✓ Have I accounted for difficult language in text?

✓ Have I accounted for cultural mismatch in learning tasks?

✓ Have I been explicit about our classroom discourse community's implicit learning (quality-learning) norms?

✓ Have I monitored social and academic disempowerment closely?

Knowledge

✓ Have I been helping the student acquire school-matched quality-learning skills and schemata?

✓ Have I been helping the student acquire school-matched language skills?

✓ Have I been helping the student develop a stronger tier 2 and tier 3 vocabulary?

✓ Have I been helping the student acquire a school-matched narrative?

✓ Must I also account for the student's cognition?

Metacognition: A (Skeleton) Key to School-Matched Quality

Students need to be able to pay attention to themselves as learners before, during, and after the fact of learning. Metacognition was addressed in Chapter 1 as a key component of literacy orientation. Developing self-direction by children is a result of the mediation of a western, middle class/affluent parental style (Nieto 2000; Morgan, Alwin, and Griffin 1979)—although, of course, this does not mean that no child from more socioeconomically struggling households (or other cultures) develops this skill. But the important point is that being more self-directive and independent requires the parallel development of metacognitive skills.

Although not all cultures similarly develop independence in children, literacy culture seems to be a leavening agent for other cultural norms. For example, my Chinese, Korean, and Japanese students, though often not speaking much if any English to start and from cultures that traditionally value more conformity and respect for following adult direction, usually have little trouble adapting quickly to our school norms given a culturally supportive classroom environment, and typically become successful students in the new cultural paradigm. It's a combination of maintaining a strong primary cultural and linguistic identity, being well-mediated, and having literacy-oriented skills that scaffold the acquisition of any new or unfamiliar school-matched skills.

Many school learning tasks, especially analytical, exploratory, and other "top-down" tasks, rely a great deal on metacognitive competence. Metacognitively aware students tend to be active, independent learners by definition. Students without well-developed metacognitive skills *must* learn to become more self-aware as learners.

I'm sure you incorporate metacognitive reflection in your teaching in some way. For instance, you may ask students to explain their thinking in math or keep a learning journal. For underachieving learners, however, reflection should *not* just be done in relation to the content learned (quantity), but should be more about the *process or details of their learning* (quality). For example: "*X* was hard because . . ." or "I do *X* better now because . . ." or "Next time I see something like *X*, I will . . ." We often ask students to reflect on *what* they have learned more than *how* they learned it, what they needed help thinking through and why, and how they might organize for future similar learning. We don't want our students to continue to sweepingly say things like, "*It's* hard," when all of "it" may not be, or immediately need our help just because something *looks* new. What enables students to get out of those ruts is, in part, the ability to reflect on their own learning and experience.

However, when teaching CLD students, how we work with metacognitive awareness is not so straightforward. Aside from the host of possible sociocultural problems if metacognitive discussions are done primarily as all-class or large-group activities (see the section on cultural patterns in Chapter 1), some CLD students may not have the cognitive schemata and linguistic skills to reflect on their learning unaided. It is not a universal, natural skill that all children possess; it is not developed to the same degree in young children in all communities. Furthermore, communicating one's metacognitive awareness is usually practiced in standard dialect, formal register English, which not all students own. Literacy-oriented students with school-matched organizational speech (see Chapter 2) tend to have highly developed metacognitive skills, which creates a self-contained, mutually amplifying loop of learning.

In spite of the strong pull of the quantity curriculum, we need to help students develop these crucial quality-learning skills!

Principle 5: Successful teaching of underachieving CLD students means reducing the clutter.

When we focus on the nitty-gritty of applying our thinking about stage 2, the ZPD, mediated learning, and quality learning, how does it all work? I return to Sweller's cognitive load theory as a very helpful model that clarifies the challenges many CLD students face in their learning. Figure 3–2 conceptualizes how the memory system operates relative to new learning experiences.

A student receives sensory input in a visual and/or auditory (or other) form. It stays very briefly in short-term memory, which acts like a holding tank before sending it along to working memory. Of course, the input phase is an extremely important part of the learning. Without clear, focused attention here, learning will not go further. But if the student's attention has been appropriately focused, as has our lesson goal, data gets sent along to working memory.

If you recall, working memory space is limited. So a lot of competing information must be sifted through and discarded or combined, otherwise precious working memory space gets cluttered up quickly. To that end, the student needs to draw on applicable schemata and skills he already has stored in long-term memory to clean out working memory space by organizing data into patterns. This enables more working memory capacity to focus on the problem at hand.

For example, if I were to print a recipe here for making Chinese dim sum, who would be more likely to visualize the final product, let alone do a better job

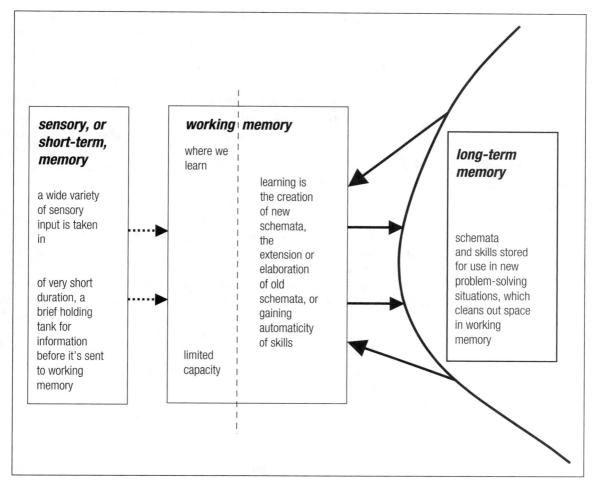

FIGURE 3–2. *Context of New Learning*[4]

making it the first time around: Cook A, who is very familiar with Chinese cooking, or Cook B, whose repertoire is Italian food? Obviously, Cook A will have a much better understanding of the ingredients, how the flavors will combine, maybe even parts of the process, like using a bamboo steamer. In other words, Cook A has schemata and skills that will inform the new experience. Cook B may need to read the recipe more than once, may not have a feel for how the steps or flavors will go together. Some of the terms may be unfamiliar, and his first time may be full of mistakes, even though he is quite competent within the parameters of his own cooking expertise. Of course, both cooks are similar in that they both already have schemata for reading recipes and understanding cooking basics. Therefore, the print, its layout on the page, the vocabulary of cooking, and so on will not be distractors as they would be for someone whose cooking expertise does not extend beyond boiling hotdogs. And the learning of both cooks will happen more readily if their attention is not distracted by a meowing cat or a loud TV at the input phase, and their processing stage is not complicated by thinking about a financial problem, or a needy child, or burning cooking oil.

Think about the domains in Figure 3–1 as being either schemata or skills.

Learning at school is no different. Learning takes place within linguistic and cultural contexts governed by certain implicit and explicit rules, expectations, and assumptions, and the acceptable performance of that learning requires certain skills and understanding.

Further, each schema or skill either exists in long-term memory and can be applied in the classroom to maximize working memory space (in addition to enhancing the learning experience) or is an element of the learning experience that *compromises* working memory space or *distracts* the learning from the intended goal. Figure 3–3 illustrates the *huge challenge* of learning for many CLD students in dominant-culture classrooms.

Cognitive load theory helps illustrate how quality-learning issues either maximize working memory space for quantity learning or clutter it up. The working memory space of many non-literacy-oriented CLD students is affected by contextual, linguistic, and cultural factors that are not part of their long-term memory expertise. By obviating some things (i.e., regulating our instructional vocabulary, providing comprehensible input, and creating language and learning goals), scaffolding some things, helping students draw on past schemata for others, and focusing their (and our own) attention at the right places, we can maximize working memory for focused learning to occur. The more expertise in multiple domains they get (i.e., quality), the less they will need our help in the future, because they will have more skills and schemata to draw on. This explains why quality-learning development is so important.

The less we pay attention to what students need in the present moment in any domain, the more distractors there may be.

Amplifiers

As with mediated learning, I feel very fortunate to have come across Michael Cole's concept of amplification. In Chapter 2, it was introduced regarding semantic memory organization: how the predisposition to organize information in memory semantically, the organization of the school curriculum, and the way it is taught mutually resonate to the advantage of literacy-oriented students. Our focus of attention must always be partly on what amplifiers students need to develop as they are learning the quantity curriculum.

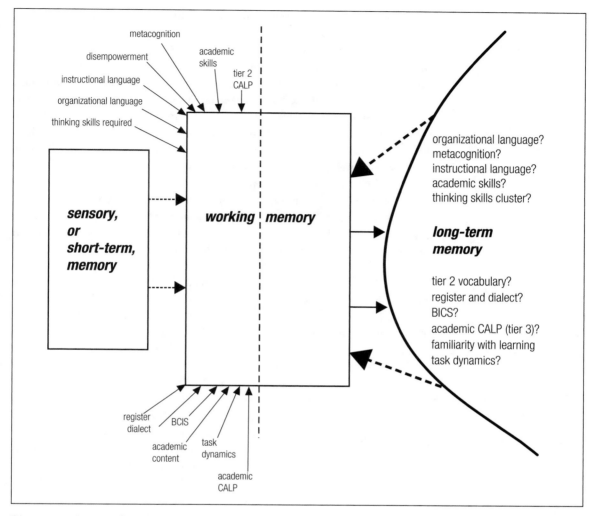

FIGURE 3–3. *Context of New Learning*

Amplifiers are a type of quality background knowledge. *Quality amplifiers* are the foundational elements of literacy orientation from which all other learning-related issues of language and thinking (except specific special needs) spring. The following examples clarify how amplifiers work beyond the issue of semantic organization.

The first example is quantity oriented; the information curriculum has amplifiers, too. Knowing addition is an essential amplifier for learning multiplication. Conversely, I can add numbers together faster when I

The various domains and the cognitive and language skills and schemata in Figures 3–1 and 3–3 can be thought of as amplifiers.

know how to multiply. The quantity curriculum is partly constructed by layering amplifiers year by year.

The second example is related to language. When I learned Farsi in Iran, I automatically learned the Arabic alphabet (how Farsi is written) and many vocabulary words with Arabic roots. When I took an Arabic class one summer, I quickly learned to read and could make good guesses about a lot of vocabulary. My Farsi knowledge amplified my Arabic learning, and conversely, learning more about the Arabic root system amplified my Farsi vocabulary. Tapping into a Latino student's Spanish ability is a great way to activate an amplifier for learning many tier 2 and 3 CALP words in English.

Now, a quality-learning amplifier: Let's say I am faced with a complex openbook social studies question on a test. I generate subvocalized internal speech that goes "Remember, look back at notes, also at essay model teacher passed out last month, also at book. Gotta know exactly what question is asking; this'll all help me do well." My organizational speech will help me launch into the task in the first place as well as amplify my performance, and getting a good grade will reinforce the value of my organizational speech. However, if my organizational speech is just "This looks hard" or "Uh-oh!" not only will I *not* be organized to do a good job on the question, but some of the very things I need to do to do a good job will lie outside the immediate access of my consciousness.

The various elements of thinking, language, and culture all act as amplifiers, or they become distractors if a student does not have the appropriate, school-matched elements.

They say the more we read, the more vocabulary we learn. Yet if my store of tier 2 vocabulary is weak, I will not comprehend enough of the text solidly enough to learn unfamiliar words from it. A larger store of vocabulary amplifies new vocabulary learning, which in turn adds to one's store of words, but without a solid vocabulary amplifier, the "truism" about learning vocabulary from reading does not hold true. The rich get richer at school because of the amplifiers they have.

That is why ultimately, finding time for the goal of helping non-literacyoriented students to develop quality-learning amplifiers should at least be as important as their learning the academic curriculum. It would be a great project for a study group of teachers to try to generate a list of amplifiers across different domains.

Principle 6: Learning needs to be grounded.

One of the most important things to understand about teaching is that learning must be grounded in what students know. Of course, any teacher would say that this is true and is what she, in fact, does. However, in the context of this sociocultural framework, and when we work with students whose cultural, linguistic, and experiential backgrounds differ from our own, grounding takes on a broader meaning than we might otherwise have considered. There might need to be grounding in any of the following:

- content learning on which the new lesson is being built
- background knowledge
- background experience
- vocabulary
- task dynamics
- academic script (organizing language)
- other language issues

Most likely, it will need to be in some combination of these.

"You mean, there's really a town *under the water down there?"*

A third-grade classroom is busily at work learning about the history of the Quabbin Reservoir, a landmark of local importance in western Massachusetts. It was made in the early twentieth century by damming up the Swift River. In the process of creating it, several towns in the valley had to be evacuated. The unit focus is on the evacuation of the towns in that historical time.

The class is a textbook constructivist classroom with a phenomenal teacher. They read a book by a local author about the making of the Quabbin, they have maps and filmstrips, they keep a journal, they make matchstick towns in diatomaceous earth valleys and flood them. A Cambodian girl, Darline, eagerly participates in all the activities. The teacher is very attentive to her learning and adapts materials as best she can. It seems like a perfect situation for her.

Then as a culminating activity, the class takes a field trip to the Quabbin. They picnic and explore the area. Darline has a wonderful day. They troop back up to the bus parked at a scenic overlook. Just as Darline is getting on the bus, she turns pensively back to the scene and stares. The teacher asks, "Darline, is anything the matter?"

"You mean, there's really a *town* under the water down there!?" Darline asks, in apparent disbelief.

So for the entire unit, in spite of her apparent engagement in the class and through all the experiential learning activities, Darline had missed the main point! How was that possible?

As the teacher and I thought about it, we realized that Darline had few experiences that we would think of as typical of a child growing up around here. She had never previously been to the Quabbin, unlike many of her classmates. Apparently, during the unit, it seemed so outlandish to her that a town could be under the water that she assumed it must be something else. The learning that there *used to be* a town there, with much but not all of it moved away, was missed because it was not *grounded* in anything but abstraction, in spite of the unit activities. But when she finally saw the reality of the situation—there was, indeed, a huge lake there, and yet wasn't there supposed to be a town there, too?—she reverted back to her thinking about a "real town" under the water, and her learning of the unit vanished. Was there really a town under the water down there?

Darline is a very smart girl, and she had certainly constructed meaning . . . but on an abstract base of clouds.[5]

"We have chickens in Cape Verde!"

Another example occurred recently in a first-grade ELL-inclusion classroom. The kids were excited about an embryology unit and impatiently awaiting the teacher to bring in the eggs. Just one student, a Cape Verdean boy, was not really caught up in the excitement. Every morning he asked, with kind of a quizzical tone, "When are ya gonna make the eggs?" The teacher thought maybe it was just a language issue—"*make* the eggs"—yet the boy also seemed not too interested in the picture books she'd put out that showed how chicks developed, which he'd looked through in sort of a perfunctory, bored way. She would patiently explain how she would not be making eggs, but the boy kept asking the same question each morning, and not showing much interest in the unit.

Then one day as he was staring at the empty incubator, he suddenly exclaimed, "We have chickens in *Cape Verde*! I get it, the chicks come out of the *eggs*!" Beaming, he immediately grabbed one of the books and looked intently at the pictures. "Oh, I get it! This is inside the egg!" He spent a long time carefully examining the pictures. Of course, the teacher had been talking about this very thing for several days, but it wasn't until the student got grounded in his Cape Verdean experience that he could make sense of it.

Many of us use K-W-L charts (what I *know*, what I *want* to know, what I've *learned*) to set up lessons or books, which is certainly a way to get at background knowledge. But again, while a K-W-L chart can be a great tool, we have to consider that, like grouping, the activity itself does not guarantee anything. For instance, if it's a whole-group lesson in a dominant-culture classroom, who typically dominates the discussion, and therefore whose experiences and prior knowledge are most likely go up on the chart, representing what "the class" knows and what questions "the class" has? And will a CLD student volunteer information that she isn't sure about or she thinks will sound funny or confusing, especially if face is culturally important to her or she feels disempowered? What if the CLD students don't know the information or experiences that others in the class have generated as known? Some—even many—important background pieces may still be missing for some CLD students if we assume that the K-W-L activity by definition gets at background knowledge and build our lessons from there.

Building (and accessing) background is essential when working with CLD students (Echevarria, Short, and Vogt 2008). We just need to be considered about how we go about it.

Principle 7: Academic lessons with CLD students need clear language and content goals.

If one is working with a class with an MLE perspective in mind, then articulating clear language and content goals in a lesson to focus student attention is a natural step. The SIOP (sheltered instruction observation protocol) framework stresses the inclusion of both language and content goals into lessons (Echevarria, Short, and Vogt 2008). Many teachers have content goals, of course, even if they do not articulate them clearly up front or bookend a lesson with them.

But the idea of a language goal can seem confusing: how are language and content goals different? Because a primary issue of learning for CLD students is developing school-matched language awareness and use, language must be at the forefront of the mind of every teacher of CLD students. In the broadest sense, a language goal can address any domain of language (see Figure 3–1). However, for starters, the simplest way to think of language goals is to see them in contrast to content goals. The following exercise might help clarify the idea of language goals.

Exercise

Say a first-grade class is going to engage in an activity to learn about islands. The students will be making clay islands on paper plates. The teacher wants them to firm up their understanding of what makes an island an island: that it is land surrounded by water. At the same time, language weaves through the entire activity. There is not only academic vocabulary but also language that bounds the activity, both in the doing and in the sharing afterward. A student may be unable to participate meaningfully or completely in the activity because he lacks the necessary language, or does not really understand what to do with what he learns.

Sort the following five goals under the *content* and *language* categories:

interacting within one's group (asking for things, being polite, etc.)

knowing the key words and concepts

following directions

describing one's island to the group

defining an island

Content	Language

I would put "knowing the key words and concepts" as the only content goal and everything else as language goals. A student could know the target concepts yet still not be able to communicate them clearly. She could participate meaningfully in the entire lesson *independently* only if she could understand the directions, interact appropriately with group mates, explain what an island was (using the key concepts), and describe her personal island creation. Any one of those could be an excellent language goal for the lesson. Depending on the students and their needs, whichever goal or goals are chosen, then the others may need to be scaffolded. But *reciprocity and intentionality* must be a part of the interaction around the chosen language goal(s), and the goals must be made *meaningful*.

It might be useful to further divide the frame for thinking about language goals into *conceptual* (defining an island) and *procedural* (following directions, describing one's own island, interacting within the group). I might use the "There is/are . . ." structure as my language goal for describing the island if it's targeted to ESL students. Or I might use the words "First," "Second," and so on as a procedural language scaffold and goal. I might decide to provide group-interaction language for students who need

Language goals are extremely important for CLD students. They set up a clear language expectation before the lesson begins. However, setting multiple language goals just creates cognitive overload in students and works against their learning.

it. Whichever goal I choose, I must highlight and clarify the appropriate language structures or vocabulary before the lesson, make sure they are used during the lesson, and be sure to continue to highlight those language components *after* the lesson. Another important area of language to mine for objectives is instructional language (see Chapter 2).

It is equally important to be clear about both language and content goals with students. One trap about content goals (what we want students *to learn*) is that we can sometimes confuse them with activities (what we want students *to do*).

> *Activities, themselves, are not content goals, no matter how wonderful they are.*

A metaphor I like to use for thinking about goals is that I'm going somewhere, say from Boston to New York. That destination is the lesson goal. The car you go in is the activity. You can get to New York in any number of different kinds of cars, some rides being more enjoyable than others. However, even if you get in the most comfortable, most enjoyable ride, if you don't know where you're supposed to be going, though the ride may be fun, you probably won't end up in the right place.

Clear content goals help frame activities so their purpose is clear. If you cannot encapsulate the content goal for yourself in a clear sentence that can be communicated to your students, such as "Today we are learning . . ." or "By the end of the lesson, you will be able to . . . ," or make a question that must be answered at the end of the class, then it is likely that the goal of the lesson will be lost, at least on students with fewer school-matched skills and schemata. Even if they can participate successfully at that time in the activity, they will not be able to identify what they can carry over to future learning, and will not be able to reflect metacognitively on it (e.g., The ride was fun—but where *were* we headed, anyway?!).

Exercise

Label the following as either *activity* or *content* goals:

using cubes to create arrays of 100 _____

finding factors of 100 _____

skip counting on a 100s chart _____

making conjectures about factors of 100 _____

Although all of these are listed as "unit goals" in the fourth-grade teacher's manual *Arrays and Shares*, part of the Investigations series (Economopoulos,

Tierney, and Russell 1998), I would label only "finding factors of 100" and "making conjectures about factors of 100" as content goals. Using manipulatives and skip counting are activities, not goals. Furthermore, from the perspective of making clear content goals, we should not just use the words a particular text or curriculum guide gives us. For example, what does "finding factors" really mean? To students with BICS understanding, *finding* means "There it is." But that implies you know what you are looking for to begin with. Here, *finding* has a CALP meaning in the classroom: "discovering," which is much more metacognitively loaded and active. You have to come to your *own* conclusion about what is being looked for. And aside from the question of whether CLD students would even know what *conjecture* means, is a content goal of "making good guesses" about factors of one hundred really what the teacher hopes the student will learn? And even if that were an acceptable goal, would all students know *how* to decide if their guesses were good or not?

In our school, teachers are being asked to post content goals for math in their classrooms. In discussions about setting these goals, some teachers have commented on how hard it is to distill some of the complex and abstract concepts in Investigations math into simple learning statements. If it is hard for teachers, imagine how hard it is for students to know what they are learning!

In sum, making and communicating (appropriate to one's students) clear content and language goals are a must for effective teachers of CLD students. It must be a conscious process for teacher and students alike, helping clarify the intentionality(-ies) of a lesson, focus student reciprocity (attention and response) at those points (though, it must be stressed, only one at a time), and create a more coherent lesson package.

Skills Practice Focus or No Skills Practice Focus, That Is the Question

If learning and language are organized culturally, then the validity of any learning or language norms is situational, relative to the cultural context (Lave and Wegner 1991). So in diverse classrooms, there is likely to be some clash of learning norms by definition. One issue related to this is skills versus concepts and understanding. Before summarizing this chapter, I would like to return for a moment to the seemingly obvious and innocuous addition of "academic skills" to Figure 3–1.

Lisa Delpit addresses this issue in *Other People's Children* (1995). She makes a powerful case that for CLD students, skills are equally important to future social and economic success as concept understanding. In contrast, contemporary progressive pedagogy has typically devalued explicit skills practice in favor of concept understanding and creativity with multiple solutions to problems, making the case that students will learn skills over time (Bailey and Pransky 2005). This basic case was made in whole language about phonemic awareness, in process writing about language skills (like spelling), and generally is the backdrop of constructivist philosophy (i.e., the Piagetian constructivism of Brooks and Brooks [1999], not what is known as social constructivism [Vygotsky and others]) and other contemporary pedagogies.

In fact, it often does seem that dominant-culture students learn academic skills such as phonics or number fluency without much explicit practice.

A QUICK WORD ABOUT SCAFFOLDING

It is an article of faith in education today that there is objective value in scaffolding complex academic tasks so that underachieving students can participate and "learn" like other students. While I had been a big adherent of that way of thinking, and I know the value of helping less academically proficient students successfully participate in complex academic tasks, I now question exactly where I stand philosophically. For instance, what has more value: the independent ability to *not* need a teacher's efforts to make the curriculum more accessible or the efforts a teacher might make in that regard in the short-term context of a quantity lesson? If a task has been heavily scaffolded for a student, at the end of that lesson, what does the student walk away with? Maybe more information, maybe the satisfaction of accomplishing what others have accomplished . . . yet not necessarily any less of a future need for that degree of support. A study on the differences between "high support" and "low support" learning situations (Fischer and Knight 1990) found that there is often still a big gap that remains between what learners can do in a "high support" learning experience, and what they can do on their own afterward; and the text has already examined the phenomenon that students without school-matched quality-learning skills and schemata do not learn them just because they participate in lessons where they have been used. At the very least, our field needs to take a step back and rethink the whole concept of scaffolding in the context of traditionally underachieving populations of CLD students.

I am *not* advocating a simple, deadening, deficit-oriented, isolated skills-only approach to working with non-literacy-oriented CLD students, going back to the bad old days of unchallenging lessons and boring material that does not spark interest or a desire to learn! Students need to be challenged cognitively and need to feel motivated to learn. I mean finding a balance between "high support" participation (for quantity learning and building empowerment) at times, and at other times, explicitly focusing students' attention on amplifiers and other quality-learning skills and schemata of language and thinking that will be of future, lasting value, and requiring them to use those new skills in challenging ways. This will contribute to their no longer needing our support over time.

However, many dominant-culture children learn literacy-oriented academic skills in the home with parents, either explicitly or through learning games that employ them or activities that focus on them. If we do not give sufficient skills practice time for students who need it, we advantage already advantaged students while disempowering others. In *A Mind at a Time*, one of the leading educational experts in the country, Dr. Mel Levine (2002), says that fluency with skills—for example, sounds in reading and writing, number relationships and facts in math—is *essential* to learning. Cognitive load theory buttresses this assertion by defining *expertise* in a given domain as not only possessing multiple schemata but also having automaticity with the appropriate skills, and that lacking appropriate fluency skills is a significant distractor in problem solving.

One other aspect of skills of all kinds is that they are very much tied to context (Fischer, in Wozniak and Fischer 1993; Rogoff and Lave 1999). One has to be a meaningful participant in a given sociocultural context to both acquire and appropriately use the skills required. In a classroom, the acquisition of academic skills is tied to feelings of inclusion and empowerment, how much a student is enabled to participate, and whether the meaningfulness of classroom activity is clear and grounded.

Summary

A number of years ago as I was starting to evolve on my own path from sympathy to empathy and knowledge, I was breaking out of the typical theoretical bounds of my field, casting about for ideas that would help me be a more effective teacher with my underachieving CLD students. In retrospect, I realize I was in the process of constructing the framework presented in this text. At that time, I was holding just some of its strands.

One day when I was working with a Cambodian girl in a fifth-grade ELL-inclusion classroom, she suddenly surprised me by looking up and saying in a serious voice, "When you teach me, Ken, I *understand*!" I by no means offer this anecdote to pat myself on the back, or to claim sole knowledge of how to reach underachieving CLD students, but the way she emphasized the word "understand" really struck me: she somehow felt *different* about her learning, it went *deeper*, and she *knew* it. And I understand far more now about being an effective teacher than I knew then.

By expanding our notion of the possible domains in which we can focus our learning interactions, we are able to work with students more inclusively, in ways that develop quality learning, addressing the various issues of culture and language that were described in Chapters 1 and 2. The less we consciously think about, the more we may unintentionally disempower CLD students.

Three models support the development of quality-learning schemata and skills. One is Vygotsky's three-stage theory, because it helps us stay continuously focused on where the child is in the learning process within a given domain. If we don't nurture the learning stage of internalization—that is, focused practiced with increasingly reduced scaffolding—we do not give students the chance to take ownership of new ways to interact with information and use language and to develop independence. This is true for developing both problem-solving schemata and automaticity with skills, in fact, in all the different domains of the framework. Vygotsky's ZPD concept deepens the meaning of working within the second stage.

The second model is mediated learning. MLEs help us reconceptualize learning interactions so that four important qualities are present: mediation in interpreting experience that connects to the past and relates to possible similar future experiences (transcendence), a clear focus of learning and expectation for direct student response and participation at the point of learning focus (intentionality and reciprocity), an infusion of meaning in all aspects of the learning interaction (mediation of meaning), and the opportunity for students to reflect on their thinking (metacognition). The effect of this way of working is most dramatic within the context of a formal thinking skills program, but explicit attention to these qualities enhances any learning experience, for teacher and students alike. It builds a deeper, transformative learning and strengthens students' cognitive abilities.

The third model is cognitive load theory, which helps us see (1) the need for a clear, sharp focus in both ourselves and our students; (2) the need to minimize distractors in learning (which may be any element of Figure 3–1); and (3) how learning is developing schemata and skills in working memory, which through practice are transferred to long-term memory to be applied in future learning situations. Cognitive load theory also helps us clearly see how amplification works. Vygotsky's learning stages, mediated learning, and cognitive load theory combine to create a very powerful three-pronged model of learning and instruction.

It is important to create clear, specific content and language goals. All students benefit from clear content learning statements, but it is especially advantageous for many CLD students. Language goals help clarify content goals and enable CLD students to participate more accurately and meaningfully in learning activities.

We need to learn the full range of possible instructional domains for working with CLD students, covering language, classroom culture, academic curriculum, and student. We need to focus clearly, both for ourselves and our students, on exactly what learning goals we have, be sure our students are engaged at that point, and give students sufficient structured practice to further the process of moving that learning into long-term memory as a new schema or skill. Scaffolding may well need to occur in other domains to be sure working memory is not overwhelmed with confusing or distracting information or input, but we must be aware that those scaffolded elements have not, themselves, been learned. Over time, students' learning must be focused in all the possible learning domains so that they can develop academic independence and empowerment.

Overall, I have been getting good results with struggling CLD students both on our internal assessments and on state-mandated testing by operating within this sociocultural framework. It works!

Notes

1. The present-practice-use frame for vocabulary development introduced in Chapter 2 is very evocative of these learning stages.

2. This can take different culturally appropriate forms. Rogoff (in Wozniak and Fischer 1993) uses terms such as *apprenticeship* and *appropriation* to describe various levels of the internalization process.

3. I often wonder whether the increased stress on families, the lack of quality time families spend together, the increasing use of TV and video games as "parents," and so forth help account for the rise in attention deficit disorder (ADD) diagnoses in young children—is it a lack of mediation, even in the most affluent of families?

4. I have started drawing a simplified version of this diagram for some of my older students to try to help them see how memory works, how I will try to help them use their memory system more efficiently to learn, and what they must do, themselves, to optimize their working memory.

5. This is why I try to take relevant field trips at the *beginning* of important content units.

Literacy

THE STATISTICS are daunting! According to the most recent national NAEP (National Assessment of Educational Progress) test results (nces.ed.gov/nationsreportcard), students of color continue to significantly underperform relative to white students in reading. ELLs score the lowest of all subgroups, which is only to be expected, considering they are taking the test in their second language before becoming fully English proficient. But the larger issue is that there is a huge achievement gap between races, ethnicities, and socioeconomic status in reading.

While there is a complex web of social, cultural, and historical factors that have created the phenomenon of chronically underperforming schools that is beyond the scope of this book, we do need to think more deeply about the reasons for underperformance in reading. While there are a number of excellent resources for teaching reading, and some sound reading programs in many elementary schools, why are those resources and programs still no guarantee of more similar levels of white student and CLD student achievement?

To me, it is clear: unless quality as well as quantity learning are accounted for in teaching reading, we will never get the results we want and CLD students deserve.

With this goal of achievement in mind, the remaining chapters of the book focus on the *application* of the principles and framework for understanding and working with CLD students in reading and math that I presented in the first three chapters.

In this chapter and the next, I

- first, establish a shared meaning of *reading* in its fullest sense;

- second, highlight issues relating to CLD student learning in the context of the various aspects of the reading process; and

- third, focus more specifically on instructional issues and responses that take into account quality learning.

Then in Chapter 6, we will apply the framework to the teaching and learning of math.

Reading: What Is It, Anyway?

What *is* reading? We say "reading" all the time, yet I wonder—could we all define *reading* clearly? And would our definitions match? Do our students know exactly what we mean by "reading"? Shouldn't they? Whatever our beliefs about reading and how we think our students match those beliefs, they inform the assumptions that underlie our lesson planning and moment-to-moment decision making. Our students have assumptions, too. Sometimes the challenge lies in the mismatch of our and our students' assumptions about what we and they are doing, how we and they are doing it, and why we and they are doing it. So take a minute and think of your own definition of reading, or what you consider the process of reading. You might find it helpful to jot it down, as we will come back to it later.

*   *   *   *   *   *   *

It's almost magic. You see the following squiggles on a page: *c a t s*. In an instant, you associate it with a type of furry pet! And if you see these squiggles: *c h z a s t e r y*? You will probably wonder if it's even a real word. Maybe it's another language? More amazing still, anyone who shares your language and can read will come to similar conclusions about both sets of squiggles! How does this wonderful thing happen?

We have to start grounded in this inseparable connection between reading and language when we teach CLD students.

I'm sure you know some of this already. Take the squiggles *c a t s*. The brain cognizes the squiggles, recognizes them as letters, and then assigns them appropriate sounds. It chunks them into a word (*cat*) plus a morpheme (-*s*; i.e., there's more than one) and matches the result up with your storehouse of words (lexicon), which in turn is integrated semantically and grammatically into whatever string of other squiggle sets it appears with on the page. Developmentally sound and supportive beginning reading programs are designed to support how the brain magically transfers squiggles into sound and how we can infer, predict, and strategize based on our *overall language ability.*

For me, the interesting question becomes: Many of us are paid to teach reading, at least in part, but within the process of teaching reading from kindergarten through sixth grade, what are we actually *teaching*? What are merely pre-existing skills and schemata that we are *accessing* or *activating*? That's the fundamental question, because not all students will have those skills and schemata to access or activate. If we are less the teacher and more just an activator, it's right at that point that underachieving students are disadvantaged.

For most literacy-oriented students, learning to read seems almost effortless. Maybe they sometimes need a nudge or two here and there, but their overall language skills take over, and it all just happens. We can make it more or less enjoyable, more or less meaningful, but that's the extent of it. Grade-level standards of reading represent levels of text complexity and vocabulary, but not really more skills associated with the *process* of reading. Maybe we stretch the students' understanding of characterization, style, and other elements, which may even be more about the writing of the book than the reading of it, and we may focus longer on reading nonfiction text for academic purposes. But it seems like the more one reads, the better one gets, and the more one's language and maturity grow, the more complex text lies within one's ability. The *psycholinguistic* model of reading accounts for a lot.

However, it does not answer the question I posed earlier: What do we actually *teach*? And why don't non-literacy-oriented students become just as proficient readers as literacy-oriented students with the same reading instruction?

There are two reasons that bind the two questions together. The first reason is that non-literacy-oriented students lack some or many of the cultural, cognitive, and linguistic *amplifiers* of literacy-oriented communities. Those are the very things we activate but usually don't teach. The second is that the process of reading at school is primarily a *sociocultural* process, not a psycholinguistic one! At the point of *giving meaning to language*[1] and *enacting* reading, we immediately become enmeshed in linguistic and cultural norms, regardless of the neurological and psycholinguistic capacities that children from all communities share. When we overlook the cultural roots of reading and how it is also a sociolinguistic and sociocultural process, we disadvantage CLD students.

> *Reading is really a set of cultural practices based in certain ways of using language and thinking.*

Lev Vygotsky, the Russian psychologist and originator of sociocultural learning theory, tells us that our psychological tools (i.e., thinking, which is predicated on language, which is predicated on culture) and the culture's tools (i.e., using signs to convey a culturally shared meaning of language) interact in a particular way. If you show the squiggles *c a t* to a literate Arabic speaker who does not know English, he will not be able to make sense of it. Even the sound-symbol system is a profoundly cultural tool. And the more familiar you are with cats in real life, the more those decoded squiggles will mean to you. The process of reading cannot be conceived of apart from the particular cultural and linguistic context it is set within.

First Things First

For many CLD students, a prerequisite for developing sufficient independent reading skills at grade level is full empowerment and membership in the classroom community.

In Chapter 3, I noted that being firmly grounded in context is a prerequisite for developing the skills needed for a given activity. If students are not firmly grounded and empowered in our classrooms, it is not likely that they will develop the full range of skills they need to be independently proficient readers. Empowerment is always first!

Literacy Culture and Classroom Literacy

Before examining the reading process in depth, here's a little quiz: Which of the following is most closely correlated to success in reading at school?

a. the type of classroom reading instruction

b. the number of books in the home

c. being read to in the home

How many of you picked c? That is the urban-myth answer I think most of us would guess. But in the very interesting book *Freakanomics*, Levitt and Dubner (2005) cite a very wide-ranging study conducted in the 1960s by the U.S. Department of Education whose statistics show that, contrary to popular belief, reading in the home does *not* directly correlate to academic performance outside of the context of there being many books in home; therefore, the answer is b, whether or not reading the books actually happens or whether reading happens in homes with few books! How could that be?

The number of books is a sign of parent education and socioeconomic status, two very strong predictors of academic achievement in children. There is something in the home apprenticeship of those children in language and learning that helps position them for school success. In other words, it's what literacy-oriented students bring with

It's a mirage that we teach *much of anything about reading to literacy-oriented students!*

them to school from their homes that enables most to become automatic good (enough) readers early on.

Figure 4–1 illustrates the main literacy language amplifier schemata and skills (introduced in Chapter 2) that enable literacy-oriented students to attain benchmark levels of reading ability so easily.

There are many types of literacy. Some literacies are functional (e.g., shopping lists); some emphasize rote memorization (e.g., religious text). By "literacy-oriented," I mean *interpretive literacy*. The personal interpretation of text requires a particular cluster of thinking skills, high metacognition, and a particular type of language and memory use and organization. (Along with high metacognition, one has appropriate *organizational speech* for literacy activities, but this seems to be a secondary amplifier.)

Formal, scientific thinking is grounded in the type of thinking that gives rise to interpretive literacy. It is the preferred way of thinking and using language in school. Interpretive literacy transforms cognition.

DIFFERENT LITERACIES

Sylvia Scribner and Michael Cole (1981) conducted some landmark literacy research with the Vai people of Liberia. The Vai have developed their own unique script. However, Scribner and Cole found that "Vai-literate" Vai did not perform any better on literacy-oriented cognitive measures than nonliterate Vai. On the other hand, Vai who had been schooled (in English or Arabic) did. Vai literacy has a specific and limited function in Vai society and is not interpretive. So it's only when society and culture organize *around* literacy that the ways children are acculturated are affected and their ways of thinking are transformed.

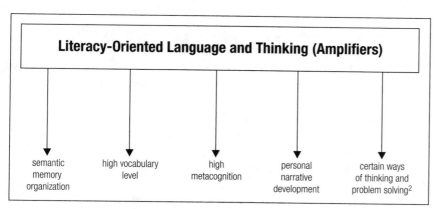

FIGURE 4–1. *Literacy-Oriented Language and Thinking*

So, we enact reading instruction that is in the long-term best interests of our struggling CLD readers by systematically targeting the development of the linguistic, cognitive, and cultural amplifiers of literacy-oriented communities. Schools should systematically organize around it across grades because, as the saying goes, "It takes a village . . ."

Is Reading the Same Everywhere?

A few years ago, I had an interesting pullout group that needed to be hastily formed midyear with the arrival of two new fifth-grade ELL students. One was a Saudi Arabian girl and the other a Cambodian American girl who had attended an inner-city school in New York.

"Fatimah" was a classic ESL student. She had L_1 literacy skills and had experienced no disruption to her schooling. She came to us testing as an intermediate ESL student. "Sothary" was Khmer dominant upon entry into school in New York but without school-matched CALP skills in Khmer. All her academic work and CALP building (such as it was) had been in English, her second language, which was probably her dominant language by the time she came to us. When I first assessed the two girls, I found they both read English at a third-grade level but for different reasons: Fatimah because it was her second language, and Sothary because that was her level of comprehension in her dominant CALP language.

After we got started, I noticed that the types of questions we typically ask at our school about reading—inferential questions, questions about characterization, and so on—seemed difficult for both of them, even as Fatimah's English skills grew. I found this intriguing because I expected Fatimah's reading progress to quickly surpass Sothary's based on their language profiles. So to understand them better, I interviewed them about their experiences as readers in their previous schools.

I learned that Fatimah's reading experience was markedly different from reading at our school. There was a lot of reading aloud, the emphasis was on accuracy, and as I understood it, interpretation of text was almost solely left up to the teacher (at least at Fatimah's grade level). There was also a lot of recitation. Sometimes she had book reports to do. Overall, Fatimah described a situation mainly in the teacher's clear control of both content and process. She said her teachers considered her a good reader and she was proud of that fact.

Sothary reported something quite different. She'd attended a pretty rough school in Brooklyn, with large, often disruptive classes. I realized that reading there was a form of crowd control. If you did your work quietly, you were evaluated as a good reader. The students had books that they read and journaled about with "I liked/I didn't like" types of responses. Sothary said the teacher almost never looked at what the students wrote in their journals or conferred with them. In contrast to Fatimah's school experience, reading for Sothary was mostly in *her* control, as long as she was not disruptive. Sothary saw herself as a good reader based on her previous teacher feedback, and indeed her school transcript reflected that fact. Nonetheless, she was reading almost two years below grade level, at least according to how we measure it at my school (we use the Qualitative Reading Inventory, or QRI, for grades 3–6).

So I had two students who had self-images of being good readers and who had been evaluated as good readers within the contexts they came from. Well, if pressed, I doubt her previous teacher would admit to Sothary really being a good reader. But Fatimah's case really gave me pause: If the way we teach and measure reading is "right," and it is different to some degree in Saudi Arabia, are Saudis "wrong" about how they teach reading? After all, Saudi children grow up to be literate citizens of their country, possessing all the literacy skills they need to get jobs as scientists, bankers, teachers, authors, and other professionals. So how could I think of her as lacking some of the requisite reading skills for her age? I realized that although the cultural and linguistic differences (both ESL and a different cultural narrative) were significant in the short term, they were also superficial in the sense that Fatimah was a literacy-oriented student. Although her culture, language, and schooling experiences were very different from ours, she was culturally grounded and well mediated and had strong CALP in L_1. I just needed to figure out how to bridge the gap of cultural expectations and empower Fatimah as a reader in this new discourse community.

I decided to cast my instruction as "reading here" versus "reading there." In other words, Fatimah was lacking nothing, but rather *here* (my school) was the problem. So it was my job to clarify this on behalf of my school. After I explicitly worked with and clarified the sociocultural mismatches of reading here versus reading there with Fatimah and Sothary for a while, Fatimah's progress quickly began to outstrip Sothary's, as I had initially expected. Sothary, though apparently so much a part of American culture and a proficient English speaker, was not as culturally grounded or well mediated, and certainly not from a literacy-oriented home. The whole experience of reading for her was much more laborious.

Children apply their underlying language proficiency (Chapter 1) to the task of reading and writing. For children with first language literacy, the process of learning to read in another language is fairly easy once any differing letter or sound system is accounted for. As long as support or clarification is given in areas of particular linguistic (the vocabulary and grammar of text) and sociocultural (book context and knowledge base, doing reading, and cultural narrative) mismatch between a child's L_1 and L_2, L_1-literate ELLs can attain grade-level proficiency without much difficulty, given sufficient time, like Fatimah.

But for children who are not literate in L$_1$, or who do not have school-matched CALP in L$_1$ (be it English or another language), it is a much more complex process, like it was for Sothary. These are the students who perform most poorly and whom we need to think about the most. For them, each of those aforementioned areas needs to be explicitly *taught* and practiced, not just supported or activated. It leads me to ask, again: What skills and schemata in language and thinking do literacy-oriented students have that non-literacy-oriented students have not developed? The answer to that question should then be our teaching focus.

The Importance of Multicultural Literature

If we do not find ways to bring our students' cultures, languages, and experiences into the classroom, we are not even manifesting the sympathy we need to be successful teachers of CLD students. Text is no exception. Luckily, there are ample resources available for teachers who wish to use good multicultural literature in their classroom (such as an National Education Association resource, www.nea.org/readacross/resources/50multiculturalbooks.html, for a simple list of good material), as well as resources that describe the rationale for it for those who need convincing (such as Freeman and Freeman [2004] for a short article on the subject), so I will not make the case for it here. But it is important to touch on how it addresses a key issue affecting reading performance, *background knowledge*. Background knowledge directly relates to two other principles described earlier in the text: the principles of actively combating disempowerment and that all students need to be grounded for optimal learning to occur. A personal connection to text also increases motivation.

When children are more familiar with both the implicit and the explicit context of a book, they naturally comprehend text better. CLD students are then better able to answer inferential questions and other questions that probe characterization or plot more deeply when they can draw on their own experience to inform text meaning. After all, that is the same advantage that most mainstream children typically enjoy as readers!

The motivation of students to read books centered in who they are often enhances the attention they pay to reading skills, too.

Further, when teachers use books centered in their CLD students' identities, they are saying, "I value who you are and I am making sure that everyone else learns more about you, too." Feeling a valued member of the classroom community enhances the acquisition of skills.

With the growing number of books written by a multicultural authorship and about diverse cultures and experiences, we must make the effort to bring our students' cultures and life experiences into the classroom by using multicultural literature.

The Reading Process

Figure 4–2 shows how I understand the full process of reading as a sociocultural process. These steps may overlap at times, but they are all aspects of classroom reading, and each gives rise to issues that impact CLD student performance.

Of course, students often read at school in a reading group, in which case step 7 can be seen as framing the whole process, as can the fact that everyone

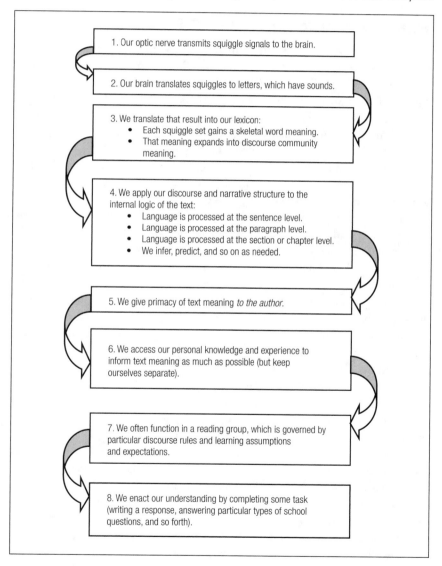

FIGURE 4–2. *Steps of Classroom Reading. How many of these steps did you include in your own definition of reading?*

brings his own background knowledge and experience (step 6) to start the process of reading. However, even looked at in that way, these two aspects of reading are still essential to the process of reading comprehension in their respective places in the chart. They may strongly influence the student's processing of text as well as the way he demonstrates what he knows and how he is assessed as a reader.

Reading Instruction and CLD Students

CLD students certainly benefit from the same sound beginning reading instruction in steps 1–4, such as in guided reading programs. However, we must give *comprehension and vocabulary development* a central place in our instruction, so that a student's reading development is moving simultaneously across a broad front, with language development, narrative development, vocabulary development, fluency, and decoding skills all being attended to as the need arises. We also need to actively help CLD students connect their perhaps very different background knowledge and experience to text; conversely, whenever possible, we should ground the experience of reading in culturally relevant text. And we also must think of language in a different way.

For example, students may misunderstand important *metalinguistic* terms (abstract linguistic terms that organize language concepts), such as *sound, letter, word,* and *sentence.* We may not work enough, or explicitly enough, on the distinctions. I have known CLD students who were still confused by the terms even into second or third grade, regardless of how often they had heard those words used in context in kindergarten and first grade. If asked to count words in a sentence, they would count letters in a word; when asked to focus on sounds, they named letters. The term *sentence* is another metalinguistic term that is often not well understood by students.

A student intern of mine once bumped head-on into this metalinguistic issue with the seemingly innocuous word *question.* He was trying to get a very wiggly, distractible first grader refocused on a lesson, but he first asked her what behaviors would get her stickers (a behavior system the classroom teacher had instituted for this student). She didn't really respond, so he asked her again. This time she sat up straight, though again didn't respond verbally. He asked her to *repeat his question* ("What do you need to do to get stickers?").

She *answered* his question: "I need to listen."

He said, "But are you listening? I asked you what my question was. What question did I just ask you?"

She said, a little more hesitantly, with a rising inflection, "I need to listen?"

He got frustrated and said, "But you're not listening, Salome! Listen to my question. What do you need to do to get stickers? Now, what words did I just say?"

This time, she repeated them verbatim! In other words, when the intern asked her to relate to questions on a metalinguistic level ("What was my question?"), she simply did what she had always been asked to do with questions in the past: she answered it. It was only when he switched his language to the concrete ("What words did I just say?") that Salome understood what he meant.

The metalinguistic use of words like *word, sound, letter, sentence,* and *question* is quite common in reading instruction, and students must be clear about what we mean by them or they'll lose out on the full impact of our instruction. When teaching about less tangible things such as metalinguistic awareness, the need to sharply focus attention—ensuring that intentionality and reciprocity are present—is paramount.

Another ESL-related issue that arises here is prediction of unfamiliar word meaning from context and syntax. A student's new language might not be developed to the point that text syntax is familiar, and there may obviously be a mismatch of background knowledge. We should be alert to this if we teach reading to ESL students.

Of course, in teaching reading in general, we should be constantly mindful of the following:

- Vygotsky's three stages, to give sufficient focused practice time while giving the reins of learning more and more over to the learner across multiple skills and schemata

- mediated learning principles, for focusing attention, making the learning interactions meaning-full, and helping bridge present learning to past and future experience

- cognitive load theory, to be sure that students' working memories are not overtaxed and that they are developing literacy language schemata and skills

Prereading Skills, Phonemic Awareness, and Non-Literacy-Oriented CLD Students

Another issue that has a strong impact on the acquisition of reading skills at steps 1–3 and beyond is prereading skills. Kindergarten programs have many activities that practice these skills. However, just participating in formal, academic activities where those skills are used is *not* the same thing as learning them if a child does not already have them.

The following prereading schemata and skills are some of the more essential ones for successful reading. In addition

For children to learn prereading skills, intentionality and reciprocity must be focused through structured interaction at the point of their thinking and decision making, within the context of something they already know well.

to skills typically thought of as prereading skills, I have added several from me-diated learning theory and my experience with it (see Chapter 3):

- sequencing (and explaining one's sequencing decisions)
- comparing and contrasting
- categorizing
- paying careful attention to (visual) sense input
- visualizing the completion of incomplete data
- holding two things in the mind
- holding one thing constant in the mind while something else changes
- restraining impulsivity
- being able to strategize
- rhyming[3]

Until these are in place, children will struggle to read at grade level. Further, if children are loaded up with mechanical reading skills *before* those prereading skills are in place, it can give a false picture of what the child will be capable of doing unassisted in the long term, even if they get early reading sup-port (such as Reading Recovery). It is essential that we give systematic preread-ing skills development sufficient *explicit instruction* and *time*. I do not mean to replace working with meaningful text, but also to set aside time to develop these skills *outside* the context of text.

Recently I was working with a first-grade struggling reader from Cape Verde, "Luis." I asked him to put together a twenty-four-piece Sesame Street puzzle. I explained that he was going to be making the picture on the box with the puzzle pieces. Although Luis had seen students making puzzles before and wanted to do it himself, he did not bring much, if any, puzzle-making experi-ence to the task. However, what I wanted to see was not if he could put it to-gether, but how he would approach the task as a problem solver. Would the haphazard way he approached reading be echoed in his puzzle making?

Luis sat on the rug with a big smile on his face, opened the box, and *imme-diately* picked out the *top two pieces* and tried to put them together. When they didn't fit, he dropped them back in the box and *randomly* grabbed two more pieces near the top of the pile. He did this two or three more times before just looking up mournfully at me. He never once looked at the picture on the box (though I had told him that was the picture his puzzle would make) or sat back at any point to mull over what was in front of him; he did not even look carefully at the shapes or colors of the pieces he had picked up.

Together we spent time figuring out good strategies for puzzle making—putting the edge pieces together first, checking back at the picture on the box, and looking at both the shape and the color of the pieces. Little by little, with scaffolding, he was able to name what to think about to be a good puzzle maker (practicing organizational speech) and put together a novel puzzle with a bit more skill and deliberation the following day (though a lot more practice was needed for him to become a skilled puzzle maker). Gaining more skill made him proud, and eager to do more puzzles, an activity he enjoyed. From this springboard, we segued into productive reading work based on his experience with frustration over the fruit of random or egocentric decision making at school (e.g., picking up pieces to fit together just because they were his favorite color or because they happened to be closest to him in the box), his satisfaction with having better strategies to accomplish his goal, tangible experiences we could refer back to as needed, and more practiced, school-matched organizational and planning speech, which I could bridge to the task of reading.

Academically struggling students often have to learn that at school, their thinking must be oriented first to what the outside context *asks of them. Put another way, students cannot just impose their will and intent on the outside context and be successful academically. Academically savvy students know this instinctively.*

Again: to experience the advantage of developing school-matched ways of thinking and develop the stronger metacognitive awareness that this demands, struggling students may well need to first work *outside* the quantity curriculum. (The concept of transcendence implies that we will then help students explicitly connect that learning back to the quantity curriculum.)

Reading instruction for young children should always be relevant, meaningful, and enjoyable.

This sharpened focus and openness helps develop reading skill.

I usually begin to see a drop-off in performance around second grade, and certainly in third and fourth grade in at-risk CLD readers relative to our grade-level norms no matter how relevant, meaningful, and enjoyable their early reading programs had been (and the early reading program at my school is excellent), if quality-learning amplifiers such as prereading skills are not explicitly developed. The question always comes back to what amplifiers enable unassisted grade-level reading performance as children get older.

Developing versus Applying Prereading Skills

Applying phonemic skills to text at beginning stages of reading—such as guessing a word from a picture and first consonant sound—requires the ability to hold two things constant in the mind at the same time. For students who experience difficulty strategizing with text, just practicing more *in the context of text* (quantity) does not necessarily affect the underlying *cognitive* issue, which is the thinking skill itself (quality).

I often do a letter box activity after I've first introduced a sound, such as *b*. I have a shoe box in which I put little objects that start with *b*, like a belt, a bear, and a balloon. I give a few clues about an object, and the students have to guess what it is—of course, the primary consideration is that the object must start with *b*, a fact I keep reminding them of. However, in the excitement of the game and the impulsivity of the moment, many of my struggling early readers cannot maintain the *b* sound in their head. If my clues start "Remember, your word has to start *b* . . . *b*. . . . So, what do I have [*looking in the box*]. . . . Hmm, OK, ready? It's a fruit . . . ," more struggling readers will often immediately shout whatever fruit they happen to like best. I recall "Luana," a Cape Verdean first grader, blurting out "Apple!" After she was refocused on the goal of the game and the *b* sound she needed to keep in her mind, I said, "OK, it's a fruit and it's yellow . . ." She called out, "Mango!" Only after she was refocused a third time did she realize that it had to be a banana.

Luana also did not yet understand that the fruit *she* liked best (mango), or the most common English fruit word in *her* experience (apple), was irrelevant in that context. She actually knew the *b* letter has a *b-* sound, yet she was not able to keep that steady in her mind in the face of the other, more attention-grabbing elements of the activity. Until students have the ability to hold two things consistently in their mind at this more concrete level of cognition, and/or rely on the outside context to inform their thinking, and/or restrain their impulsivity, they will be unlikely to consistently perform even basic strategizing independently in the much subtler and more abstract realm of text.

Learning Sounds and Letters

As we move into the reading process, decoding skills obviously become important. It is essential for students to acquire an automatic recall of basic consonant sounds, or working memory gets overloaded quickly and reading breaks down. I recommend a particular order for teaching phonemic awareness to CLD students. The best sound-symbol correspondences to start with, especially for ESL students, are frequently appearing, strong consonant sounds where the name of the letter *starts* with the sound, and the sound is consistent: *b*, *d*, *p*, and *t* are my starter letters, but not *s*, *f*, *m*, and *n* (the name of the letter starts with ĕ); *v*, *z*, and *j* (they are not high-frequency letters); or *c* and *g* (they have two sounds). Also, in order to avoid confusion, I use this order—*b*, *t*, *p*, *d*—so that practice with sounds made at the same spot in the mouth (*b* and *p*, and *d* and *t*) are more separated in time to avoid possible confusion. After those four, when the concept of sounds for letters has been established, I introduce *s* because it is such a crucial letter in English (aside from being a strong sound and a high-frequency letter, it's also used in plurals, the third-person singular present-tense verb ending, possessives, and contractions). After that, it depends how long I have to work with students on individual letters in the second stage before they more readily internalize the concept of sound-symbol connections and can learn the rest independently, but I choose frequently appearing letters that have stronger sounds (*f*, *m*, *c* [*k*], etc.) in no particular order.

Two sometimes difficult English letters for ESL students are *n* and *r*. We sometimes pronounce the *medial n* as a nasal sound that gets overwhelmed by the consonant next to it (i.e, pencil, finger), and the English *r* strongly colors neighboring vowel sounds (in addition to being confused with *l* in some languages). Another example of phonemic confusion is that young students may hear an initial *tr-* combination as *jr-* or *chr-* in speech (e.g., *tree*) and have difficulty both encoding and decoding it in text. Different dialect speakers may merge sounds like *th* into *f*, while ESL students with first languages that have no *th* may turn it into an *f*, *t*, or *d* sound. Misperceived words in an ESL student's oral language repertoire can easily affect text comprehension, if students are looking for something that's not there, or if what they read does not match what they expect. (Spelling is dealt with separately in the next section.)

First language interference or dialect difference often dictates what types of letter-sound errors CLD students make.

When students are practicing consonant sounds, it's important to call their attention to the fact that consonant sounds are not produced with a completely open mouth. Something is almost always touching or moving—tongue, teeth, lips, and so forth. If a student says that the *b* sound is "baa," the accentuated, open-mouth vowel sound tacked onto the end will complicate her ability to sound words skillfully in writing and cause confusion. The *b* sound is just "b-."

Vowels

Every language has its own particular array of vowel sounds; some have more, some less. In English, there are at least sixteen vowel sounds, with a variety of spellings. In contrast, a language like Spanish has just five, each with a single spelling. The English vowel system can seem overwhelming—and bizarre—to second language learners!

When students have developed a stronger awareness of consonant sounds beyond just an initial position, they can better understand how the vowel sound(s) bridge the more obvious consonant sounds. But when I do get to vowel sounds, I have found a particular order for working with

Vowel sounds should not be a focus until a student already has strong phonemic skills in recognizing consonant sounds at least at the beginnings and ends of words. English short vowel sounds can be particularly problematic for ESL students.

Getting clarity about where in the mouth we produce these sounds, and how facial muscles move differently as we make them, is helpful for students who have difficulty discriminating between sounds based on their language background— but don't expect instant changes in pronunciation or the ability to discriminate subtle vowel sound differences that are not in a student's L$_1$.[5]

them helpful: short *a* (as in *at*) and short *o* (as in *on*), then short *u* (as in *up*). These tend to be the easiest to discriminate and produce for many second language learners. After that, I have a contrastive period with what are typically the hardest vowel sounds, the short *i* (as in *in*) and *e* (as in *bed*).[4] After that, students seem ready to start tackling long vowel sound spellings (which are more complex, though long vowels are easiest to pronounce and recognize), but sometimes short vowels may still need revisiting.

Word families, or word chunks (e.g., one-syllable words that end in a particular vowel-consonant cluster, such as *-at*), are a good way to integrate vowel work for ELLs.

Academically Struggling CLD Students and Phonemic Awareness

Even though the prevailing thinking about second language learners is that phonemic practice should occur with meaningful words, I have found that for students who struggle phonemically (especially with vowels), nonsense words can also be very helpful. I do this with mediated learning in mind. I realized that during spelling practice, some students were searching their minds for words they knew, but not really paying attention to the vowel *rule* I wanted them to be learning.

For example, if it was a lesson in the short *o* sound, and the word was *hop*, many of my non-literacy-oriented students would still instinctively read it as *hope* upon first seeing it. Rather than focusing on the phonemic goal, they searched for a word they knew that looked like the text; most knew *hope* more readily than *hop*. In other words, they are orienting the text to themselves, instead of themselves to the text. Or even if a discrete lesson in the short *o* sound was successful, they might come across a short *o* word in a book and read it as a long *o*, or even replace it with another short vowel sound, to make a word they knew better—what they knew about phonemic awareness (which needs outside-context orientation) still could not be heard over any familiar-seeming words they happened to know (egocentricity). Of course, I do not want students to overrely on phonemic awareness and decoding, either; I want them to achieve a balance of skills and schemata, always used in the service of text comprehension.

Nonsense words help focus students' intentionality and reciprocity at the point of the vowel rule; if the students do not have the word in their head to search for, it's a waste of time to try! This helps students maximize their working memory for the spelling rule, itself, by not taking up space with a search for words that look like the target word.

One final thing I've found very helpful for second-grade and older students is giving them a list of words with a simple rule following some in-class practice and then testing their understanding of the rule *with totally different words, including nonsense words,* the next day. In other words, they have to focus on studying the rule at home. It is quite a shock at first, because they want to memorize the list. But that is very different than learning the rule! I tell the students that they need to look back at the rule and say it out loud between each word on the list. I want to train them to think, "There's an *e* by itself; it probably says *eh*," when they come across an unfamiliar word containing a single *e* in text. It's my intentionality to help at-risk readers build appropriate subvocalized speech through this process. (I deal with exceptions to a rule when we come across them, but I try not to initially clutter up the rule with them, as working memory gets overtaxed.)

> *It's not only the phonemic skill but also its application that needs to be practiced and mastered by at-risk readers.*

While phonemic skills are essential to reading, they are the least of what reading really is. Programs that emphasize phonics skills over making meaning and strategizing should be looked at with great skepticism. Aside from deflecting attention from meaning making, which is the essence of reading, our sound-symbol system is just too complex. The chart in Figure 4–3 looks at just

Spelling	Sound	Examples
a	*a*	fat, pack
	ah	father, bark
	u	a, afraid
	aw	all, chalk
	ay	nation, razor
	eh	catch (can be pronounced /kĕtch/)
a . . . e	*ay*	place, rake
	a	scrabble, battle
ai	*ay*	rain, afraid
	eh	again
ay	*ay*	ray, tray
ae	*ay*	sundae
aw	*aw*	draw, crawl
au	*aw*	caught, taut
	a	laugh

FIGURE 4–3. *Sound Chart for A*

one vowel, *a*, in the context of the typical vowel pronunciations in my part of the country (and I'm sure I've missed some exception or other).

Further Along the Reading Process

Back to the reading process. Steps 3 and 4 are multilayered, and *sentence-level processing is key*. Higher-order psycholinguistic skills converge with sociolinguistic processes at step 4. In diverse classrooms, the sociolinguistic elements of language—such as discourse community meaning, dialect difference, vocabulary level and narrative structure, and student interaction in a sociocultural context—often interfere with, or even overwhelm, the ability of a CLD student to extract appropriate meaning from text or demonstrate any meaning he has made. When steps 3 and 4 are problematic, predicting words from context accurately is greatly complicated because of a mismatch to the grammar and vocabulary of the text.

Without proficiency in step 4 skills at the level of the text students are being asked to read, step 5—understanding the author's meaning—is not possible. And step 5 is key!

The first four steps lead to step 5, and in turn, it is the jumping-off point for the rest of the process. In some teacher training workshops I conduct, I use an activity in which I ask the participants to sort the steps of the reading process (from Figure 4–2). Many folks have trouble with this idea initially: What do I mean by "giving primacy of text meaning to the author"? And why isn't a student's own interpretation of the text more important? Some have questioned why a separate "author's meaning" step is there at all.

My experience has been that weaker readers often read *themselves* into the text, and this is again related to the fact that some students do not orient themselves as much to the outside learning context as they try to orient the outside to themselves. Of course, students have to rely on background knowledge, and in that sense need to orient the text to themselves, too, but *first* students need to try to orient themselves to text that is often about subjects and from points of view very different from their own experience. Since it is very likely *not* the case that non-literacy-oriented CLD students share background knowledge, or a cultural context, or a literacy language with the author, how likely is it that they can really get what the author is saying without at least a lot of thought, if not effort? Think of all the language issues that were raised in Chapter 2—any or all of them may affect text comprehension. Not orienting to the author first causes wrong or implausible answers to inference questions, other critical thinking questions, and even factual questions about text.

Looking at reading as a sociocultural process clarifies what otherwise may be blurry or even invisible to us about the process of reading. For CLD students who lack reading amplifiers, reading should be more effortful by definition.

By "effortful," I mean deliberately paying attention to the author's language and how it might not match the student's own first guess at meaning. Effortful implies intentionality and reciprocity. That is why I have "accessing our personal knowledge" *after* the step of understanding the author's meaning. Of course, one's personal knowledge of language and of the world pervades the entire process, but here I mean one's *interpretation* of the text. With so many idioms, words with multiple meanings, and unfamiliar cultural contexts and experiences in text, unless the student really works hard to establish meaning based on the author's intent, it is too easy to misread text. I tell my weaker CLD readers that if they read text quickly, it's a sure sign that they're skipping the deliberate step of trying to understand the author's meaning—and thus, they're not really *reading* at all![6]

Another issue that arises between steps 3 and 6 is that proficient readers ask themselves questions as they read, to check their comprehension, to predict, and to compare the text with their own background, knowledge, and experience. Many reading programs for struggling readers emphasize asking questions, making it a part of the explicit quantity-reading curriculum. However, the real issue is that younger students who are not from an interpretive literacy culture are less practiced with metacognition (Chapter 3). That's the quality flip side to that coin. While active practice asking questions about text is helpful and even essential, the underlying issue is not usually solved merely by deliberately scaffolding the act of questioning. We also need to help students develop more metacognitive skill in general. Otherwise, they remain too dependent on the context of a particular program or teacher and are not developing independence in the skills they need.

Particularly as students get older, they must know how to separate fact from opinion, and appropriately convey their opinions, which brings modal verbs (*might, could, ought to*, etc.), other expressions (*be sure, be positive about*), and adverbs (*probably, maybe, almost*) into play as teaching points for CLD students. Students also have to recognize and answer various questions from text and perform their understanding in appropriate ways, be they written or oral. This takes place in steps 6–8. Even understanding text, a CLD student may fall short in these steps and be assessed as a poor reader when that is not really the case. For example, without a strong tier 2 vocabulary, a CLD student's ability to participate in discussions about characterization will be weak.

So in sum, when we say "reading" to our students, I believe that *whole process* is what we should clearly mean and they should clearly understand, in whatever developmentally appropriate way matches the students. By third grade, they should be able to converse about all eight steps, which helps them develop a stronger metacognitive awareness of their own reading. Consciously knowing all the steps affects the thinking of students who had conceived of reading as just steps 1–3 and helps them be more aware of their reading development. Figure 4–4 is a fuller description of the eight-step reading process.

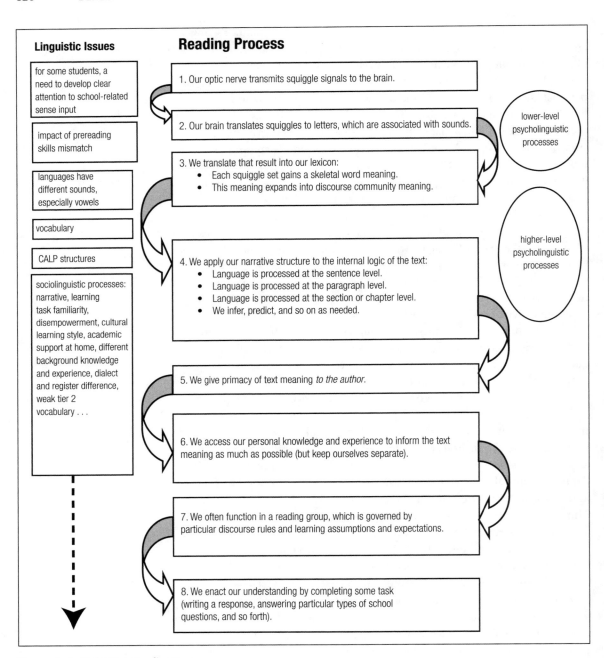

FIGURE 4–4. *Eight-Step Reading Process*

When we move into steps 3 (transitional step from psycholinguistic to sociolinguistic) through 8, students require the following amplifiers to be assessed as proficient independent readers at their grade level:

- school-matched language skills (Chapter 2)

- a school-matched cognitive orientation (Chapter 1)

- a school-matched memory organization and metacognitive awareness (Chapter 2)

- school-matched thinking skills (Chapter 1)

In addition, I should reiterate that the following issues may affect the reading performance of CLD students, as they negatively affect all learning:

- feelings of disempowerment

- lack of motivation

Finally, the chart in Figure 4–5 matches CLD-related issues in reading more specifically with the various steps in the reading process (not an exhaustive list).

Figure 4–5 is a general framework for thinking of reading issues and CLD students, as well as a guide to places where teachers may want to focus a student's intentionality and reciprocity during instruction. But although it is pretty comprehensive and a good guide, the truth is still that in addition to the issues in the chart, some of the core quality-learning issues—like thinking skills development, language transformation, and vocabulary development—take systematic practice over years to develop independence in, which reinforces the ability of a student to read independently at grade level (remember, attention to the development of quality-learning schemata and skills should not only be happening in the context of text).

We need to move up the football field three yards at a time and hand off the ball to next year's teacher. And of course, she or he needs to continue from there, not go back and start a whole new line of attack! We don't get to the goal line by throwing long-bomb quick fixes (because there are none). The more teachers collaborate between specialties and across grades to help students develop quality-learning amplifiers, the better it is for students.

Steps in the Reading Process	Possible CLD Student–Related Issues
prereading	lack of appropriate prereading skills: holding two things constant; organizing; focusing attention; comparing; spontaneously connecting to past experience; restraint of impulsivity; categorizing; systematic thinking; undeveloped metacognitive awareness
squiggle signals go to the brain	lack of visual discrimination lack of sustained, clear focus
squiggles translated to sounds and words	different alphabet different directionality lack of underlying literacy orientation undeveloped auditory sequencing skills different L_1 sounds (especially vowels) undeveloped metacognitive awareness lack of practice in systematically strategizing
words integrated into our lexicon: • *skeletal meaning* • *discourse community meaning*	discourse community mismatch lack of English vocab (especially CALP) limited English syntax knowledge different background knowledge or experience misunderstanding of the importance of "small words" (see "Just Small Words?" in Chapter 5)
discourse level and narrative meaning: • *words form sentences* • *sentences group into paragraphs* • *paragraphs form together* *we employ higher-level psycholinguistic processes*	limited English syntax knowledge different verb-tense system dialect and register mismatch narrative structure mismatch (cultural) lack of transition word vocabulary lack of understanding of function of paragraphs

FIGURE 4–5. *CLD-Related Reading Issues*

	narrative stage underdevelopment
	lack of sufficient practice inferring, predicting, etc. (especially in academic context)
	underdeveloped metacognitive awareness
primacy given to author's meaning	student reads self into text
	mismatch of background experience or knowledge
	lack of success in steps 1–4
we apply our own experiences and opinions	lack of understanding of modal verbs and adverbs expressing degrees of certainty
we function in a reading group	mismatch of background experience or knowledge
	lack of understanding of group norms or expectations
	lack of appropriate social language forms
	disempowerment
	lack of familiarity with academic questions (e.g., How do you know . . . ? Why do you think . . . ?)
we enact our understanding	errors in language production (written or oral)
	fear of making errors in public

FIGURE 4–5. *(Continued)*

Notes

1. It might be said that psycholinguistics and sociolinguistics (the meaning of language in its sociocultural context) overlap.

2. In Chapter 2, "certain ways of thinking and problem solving" was phrased as "independence" in problem solving.

3. Rhyming is an essential skill for good reading ability in English. All students do not come to school with the ability to rhyme, and it is not innate! Some students need to be explicitly taught rhyming. By this I mean their intentionality

and reciprocity need to be brought to bear on what the rhymes are, and they need sufficient practice time with rhyme. If they do not have rhyming skills upon entry into kindergarten, they do not necessarily pick up independent rhyming skills just through participation in common kindergarten activities that use rhyme, like chants and songs.

4. It is very hard for students whose first languages do not have all of our short vowel sounds (like Arabic or Spanish) to consistently produce the sounds orally. In conjunction with that, they will mispronounce or misunderstand words during reading. Minimal-pair games are good for this—activities where students have to produce or discriminate between words that vary only by the short vowel sound (e.g., *pick* and *peck*). But it takes a while for students to get these sounds down.

5. For young students, I use the image of "spaghetti sounds" (sounds for which we do not cut off the airflow right away, such as the short *a* and short *o*) and "rice sounds" (when we do cut short the airflow, like the short *i*, *e*, and *u*). Spaghetti noodles signify longer sounds, and rice grains, shorter.

6. I periodically have students read books of their choosing or books I assign at their independent reading level for homework, which I only briefly check up on. If reading is always effortful, enjoyment is lost. Cumulative effortful reading in the classroom slowly but eventually changes independent reading habits.

The Secret Stuff

What *Most* Ensures Successful Performance
in Reading

THERE ARE a wide variety of specific is-
sues that can affect the reading performance of CLD students, but the amplifiers
that *most* contribute to long-term independent grade-level success in reading are

- narrative

- vocabulary

- empowerment

I have banged on the empowerment drum many times
in this book already, so I will not go into it in detail here
again. But without empowerment in the classroom community, a student's motivation is seriously impacted, and
he'll be unlikely to develop the independent skills he needs
for academic success regardless of reading program or
methodology.

*Active attempts to empower students
within the classroom culture are a
prerequisite for successful reading.*

Narrative Revisited

As you read in Chapter 2, there are two issues with narrative: (1) different cultures have different narrative forms,[1] and (2) there are developmental stages (culture and language appropriate) of narrative organization. When working with CLD students, we must acknowledge and account for cultural differences in narrative; otherwise, the assessment of a student's reading and especially writing may suffer. We confuse *difference* with *error*. However, if a student is literacy orientated, we can bridge the gap fairly easily if we contrast the differences between a student's particular cultural narrative form and that of English and graphically make English narrative structure clear. Being behind in the developmental stage of personal narrative (one possible result of a nonliteracy orientation), though, has a longer-term impact on academic performance and is a harder gap to bridge.

Remember Fatimah from the last chapter? She sure could weave a mean oral narrative! Although the Arabic narrative form is not identical to English (issue 1), she transferred her substantial, well-developed L_1 narrative skills into L_2. When she lacked the appropriate vocabulary, she asked for the *best* English word so she could better describe her narrative. Ironically, even though English was clearly her second language, Fatimah could construct a much better English narrative in all respects than Sothary (also from the last chapter), who was English dominant! Not only did Sothary not have a culturally appropriate Khmer narrative, her developmental narrative stage in English was way behind (issue 2).

The following are two oral versions of *Cinderella* produced by hypothetical fifth graders that reflect narrative development differences. The first is a version that students like Sothary might produce; the second one is closer to what a student like Fatimah would create.

Once there was this girl, you know that girl who was all dirty and stuff and had a bad life? And, like, a grandmother or something helped her and stuff? And she married this prince. Her name was Cinderella. Well, that girl, she had to live with this bad woman, who wasn't really her mother, but it was like her mother. And that mean lady had two mean daughters and they were really, really, really mean to Cinderella. And then Cinderella went to this kind of dance and stuff and the prince fell in love with her! And she lost a shoe and then the prince found it and then he looked for who the shoe belonged to and he found Cinderella and then they got married and they lived happily ever after.

Once upon a time, a nice man and his wife had a pretty little baby girl. They were all very happy together, but sadly, the mother got sick and died. After a while, the father married again. But the lady he married was horrible. She had two grown-up daughters who were just as horrible as she was. Right away, the new wife began to act very mean to Cinderella. She made her do all the hard work of the house: scrubbing the floor, cleaning the dishes, cooking the food, and looking after her two terrible step-sisters, who treated her in cruel ways. Cinderella felt she would never be happy again.

Then one day, someone came from the palace. . . .

I don't think I need to go on in version 2. If I asked you which version illustrated a better reader based on the *oral* retelling, I'm sure you would say the second. Aside from simple, repetitive language structures, a minimal vocabulary range, and a paucity of story elements (e.g., a sketchy beginning), the "Sothary version" basically just lists events and does not center the story in the character's internal landscape of feelings and thinking.[2] This student will have a lot of difficulty independently producing writing and deeply comprehending narrative and expository text because of the simple way she structures her thinking, as exemplified by that oral retelling. The key instructional goal for her should be to help her develop a more complex, richer personal narrative that contains all the elements appropriate to the developmental stage for her age. Oral language comes first!

Narrative encompasses not only the macrostructures of language and thinking but microstructures like connecting words.

One significant way in which narrative helps comprehension is filling in the pieces when authors do not write links between sentences.

An author is just as likely to write, "It was raining. The children stayed inside for recess," as he is to write, "It was raining *so* the children stayed inside for recess." It is mainly by superimposing one's own narrative atop the author's that the *so* link becomes clear. However, if a child is at an . . . *and then* . . . *and then* . . . narrative stage, that is likely what he will use as the implicit link between sentences, and thus comprehension will be subtly, if adversely, affected: *It was raining and then the children stayed in for recess.* Or the student may simply ignore the need to link every sentence in text either explicitly or implicitly altogether, and then sentences tend to float in isolation. Either way, the ability of a student to be successful at giving primacy of meaning to the author (step 5 of the reading process) is negatively affected.

We'll revisit this narrative-related issue again later. If a child is not able to independently produce personal narrative at the appropriate stage when younger, she is unlikely to be a successful independent reader in dominant-culture classrooms when text explodes in complexity at around the third- or fourth-grade level—even if she had performed adequately in early-intervention reading programs. The focus

The development of school-matched oral language skills precedes the development of full text comprehension.

of early-elementary reading programs should include developing narrative skills as a major component of what some students practice and learn, and it should be worked on with older readers who remain narratively behind.

A Case Study in Reading with Fifth Graders

The following is a summary of a series of reading classes in an ELL pullout class for two fifth-grade CLD students. (This group was mentioned in Chapter 2 in the discussion of vocabulary.) It illustrates the many different ways that CLD students' comprehension of the text can be blocked, and acts as a segue between narrative, which was addressed earlier, and vocabulary, which is revisited later in this chapter.

If you recall, I was working with these two students in a book from the Soar to Success series, a book kit for below-grade-level readers that focuses on the comprehension process. We were using the fourth-grade kit. Figure 5–1

FIGURE 5–1. *Back Cover of* Fire! in Yellowstone *(Ekey 1999)*

shows the back cover of *Fire! in Yellowstone*, a book about the terrible forest fires that blew out of control in Yellowstone National Park in 1988.

Before reading, we talked about some key tier 3 words on the back cover—*controversy*, *philosophy*, and *ecology*—and the theme of the book: the controversy surrounding the philosophy to let natural fires burn rather than put them out right away. To activate their background knowledge, we spoke about what they knew about fires based on their fourth-grade experience with a fire safety unit (sponsored by the local fire department). Both students said that they would side with the philosophy that says it's best to put out fires right away. In fact, they were surprised that anyone could possibly think differently about it after their fire safety unit.

I reminded them that the purpose of reading is *first and foremost* to understand the *author's* meaning (step 5). In this case, that meant they could not be sure that they knew what side of the controversy the author was taking, even if the issue seemed clear to *them*. In fact, the author might not be taking a stand at all! It would be one of their main jobs as readers of this book to figure it out, and I would check with them about what they thought afterward. This helped set the purpose for reading and helped avoid a meaning mix-up at step 5.

> *It is very important to articulate a clear purpose for reading to CLD students (like setting a language or content goal in a content lesson) and return to the purpose at the evaluation of a student's reading or during postreading work.*

Also before starting the book, we visited the library to see pictures of Yellowstone and locate it on a map, to help supply a *concrete* base of information on which they could scaffold a sufficient understanding of the (abstract) text. They had never traveled there or seen pictures of what it looks like. When they were at least more grounded visually, we were ready to start the book.

We used a method of reading where one student read aloud while the other was responsible for paraphrasing, or else they both read a section silently and took turns paraphrasing. This continually focused their attention on understanding the author's meaning. Sometimes I have students come up with what they think are good "school questions" for the passage, but I always follow up with questions that either connect to earlier information in the book, ask for inferences, or probe their understanding of the book's CALP language, the underlying structure of the text, and sentence- or paragraph-level meaning. I also periodically model aloud how I think about the text.

When it came to vocabulary, the students were responsible for identifying words they didn't really know. Without students being able to identify that they don't know a word, much of a text can be misunderstood. So it is important to name and deal with this issue directly. CLD students need to recognize the difference between three basic types of words:

1. words they definitely know

2. words they definitely do not know

3. words they've just heard before

It's that group of vaguely familiar words that students really don't know but may have heard before that can interfere most with comprehension.

Words they have never heard before or cannot decode are easy for them to identify, as are familiar, everyday words that they can decode (although they still need to be aware that sometimes even these words can be used idiomatically or have other meanings, and be aware of the huge difference between decoding and understanding).

I tell my students that words they have heard before but really don't *know* are "death words," because they often kill comprehension. Students have heard lots of words, even multiple times, and still have at best a vague understanding of their meaning. How can one understand the author's meaning if one *really* knows only about 75 to 80 percent of the text language? This will happen at some point because we can't keep underachieving CLD students reading at very low levels year in and year out, which is where a strict vocabulary approach to book selection would keep them. These two students knew I would ask them about every word they might not know, and if there were too many they had been lazy about identifying, they'd get extra homework. So they tended to be quite vigilant!

Following is a page-by-page synopsis of some parts of our discussions over the first few pages of the book (my questions appear in italics; their responses and discussion follow each question; I have numbered the lines for easy reference in the follow-up activity), which altogether took about five classes (forty-five minutes per class). The corresponding pages are shown in Figures 5–2 through 5–4.

Prereading

1 The students identified trouble words from back of book (which I read aloud as they read

2 silently and paraphrased for them): *vivid, bleak, swept through* (in addition to

3 *controversy, philosophy,* and *ecology*).

4   We discussed the fire controversy and found Yellowstone on a map.

Page 5, Paragraph 1 (see Figure 5–2)

5 They read fine, but the paraphrasing was shaky. There were no words they identified

6 as problematic, so I knew I had to probe their understanding carefully.

7   *"What was different that year?"*

8   "Spring came early." (a direct quote from the text)

9   *"What might that mean?"*

10   It turns out they didn't know what made it spring. They were confused because

11 the start of spring was just a date for them—how could that date come early? So we

12 had to digress to talk about spring being in relation to the earth's tilt in its rotation

In 1988, spring came early in Yellowstone National Park. Snow that usually stays until June melted away under bright, sunny skies. Little rain fell.

The elk, moose, and grizzly bears grazed on an abundant supply of grass and other plants. Old Faithful geyser gushed as tourists snapped photographs. Yellowstone did not appear to be in a drought, but the forest was dry.

Far left: Elk graze, undisturbed by the antics of the geysers. Even during the fire, most animals were calm despite the raging fires and the activities of the firefighters and soldiers.

Upper left: A bear and cub near Mystic Falls. Most animals escaped the dangerous fires.

5

FIGURE 5–2. *Page 5 of* Fire! in Yellowstone *(Ekey 1999)*

13 around the sun. We reworded the first sentence in the text to "The warmer weather

14 of April and May came earlier that year, maybe in February or March."

15   *"So, is that all the paragraph tells us?"*

16   "The snow melted."

17   *"Doesn't it melt every year?"*

18   "Yes . . ."

19   *"So why do you think the author bothered to put it into this story?"*

20   They had no idea why the author would bother to do that. Of course snow melts

21 when it's warm! So we talked about how melting snow keeps ground wet, so trees

22 have enough to drink. So if the snow melted early, then the ground would get dry

23 before it usually does.

24   *"Anything else in this paragraph that connects to the theme of the book?"* (They

25 knew what *theme* means.)

26   "Little rain fell."

27   *"What does that mean?"*

28   "The rain was small."

29   *"What do you mean, 'small rain'?"*

30   "It was little." I realized they did not know what *little* meant when used in that

31 CALP sense. They thought each "piece" of rain must have been tiny! They had not

32 identified *little* as being a word they didn't know, so we put it up on our word wall.

33 We talked about why they had passed over this word. They realized that what they

34 had thought of first—small pieces of rain—didn't make a lot of sense, so they

35 should have been more vigilant.

Page 5, Paragraph 2

36 First we spoke about vocabulary: *grazed, abundant, geyser, gushed, drought.* Then

37 they read and paraphrased.

38   *"So, why was the forest so dry?"*

39   "It was in a drought."

40   *"Why?"*

41   "Spring came early. . . ?" (answered with a questioning inflection, as if unsure)

42   *"What did we say that meant?"*

43   They answered that question, then the question *"So, why was the forest so dry?"*

44 with the implications of the early spring for the upcoming fire. They also now added

45 that the snow had melted earlier than normal and mentioned the lack of rain.

46   Words in captions: *antics, undisturbed, calm, despite, raging, activities.*

Page 7, Paragraph 1 (see Figure 5–3)

47 They asked about *bolt.*

48   After reading, they could paraphrase with their own words, except the last

49 sentence, which they spoke verbatim.

50   *"What does that last sentence mean?"*

51   "There was smoke."

52   *"Is there always smoke with fire?"*

53   "Yes . . ."

54   *"So, it's kind of like the snow melting on the other page. Would the author put it*

55 *in if it weren't important to understand the problem?"*

56   "No . . ."

In June, a bolt of lightning struck a tree and started a small forest fire. Soon, lightning struck in other areas and started more fires in Yellowstone and on nearby forest lands. Each fire sent up a small column of smoke.

At first, park rangers allowed the fires to burn. Rangers had learned that fire has always been a vital part of the forest ecology, or the relationship between living things and their surroundings. Fire clears away old trees to make room for new plants and trees. Fires are as important to the growth of the forest as sunshine and rain.

Far left: Fire creeps up the dry trunks of trees near Grant Village in Yellowstone.

Left: Fishing in the Firehole River. At first, people went about doing their normal activities.

7

FIGURE 5–3. *Page 7 of* Fire! in Yellowstone *(Ekey 1999)*

57   *"So why did the author put this in about the smoke, do you think?"*

58   They didn't have a guess. We discussed putting in description to make a scene

59 come alive versus just writing facts that might not seem so interesting by themselves.

60 The smoke here is just a device to draw the reader in but has no extra information to

61 give about the circumstances surrounding the fires that year.

Page 7, Paragraph 2

62 They asked about *vital, growth, relationship* (i.e., it is obviously not a family

63 relationship here, and that's the only sense in which they understood the word).

64 They read and paraphrased. I asked just one question, because they stated their

65 paraphrase confidently.

66 *"What had rangers learned about fire?"*

67 They answered with the pertinent information in the paragraph and could

68 elaborate on it.

69 Words in caption: *normal.*

Page 9, Paragraph 1

70 They asked about *drive game, centuries.*

71 They could paraphrase accurately and suggested reasonable ways that Native Amercians

72 might have used fire to drive game for hunting.

This was not the first time Yellowstone had seen fires. Every year lightning starts fires. In fact, centuries ago, Native Americans used to light fires to drive game to hunters and to improve wildlife habitats.

Most of the fires that start go out by themselves. Those that burn usually burn only a few acres. But 1988 was a different year. The heat of the summer and lack of rain left the forest very dry.

The fires in and near Yellowstone grew bigger. A careless woodcutter started another fire.

The North Fork fire south of the town called West Yellowstone. This damaging fire was accidentally started by a woodcutter in Idaho's Targhee National Forest, only 200 yards from Yellowstone.

9

FIGURE 5–4. *Page 9 of* Fire! in Yellowstone *(Ekey 1999)*

Page 9, Paragraphs 2 and 3

73 They asked about *acres, lack.*

74   Interestingly, they had difficulty paraphrasing. One on them said, "*A few* fires go
75 out quickly."

76   "*What does* most *mean?*"

77   "Some."

78   "*Like if I had twenty cookies and I gave you most of them, how many cookies*
79 *would I give you, do you think?*"

80   "Like, seventeen?" We had a discussion about *most, some,* and *few* and how
81 knowing their meanings clearly is important at school. After the discussion, they
82 rephrased it to "almost every" fire.

83   "*Why does the author tell you 1988 was a different kind of year?*"

84   "The summer was hot."

85   "*Isn't the summer hot every year?*"

86   "Yes . . ." (spoken pensively)

87   "*So what was the problem that year?*"

88   "The summer was really hot. . . ?" Again, an answer asked. At this point, we
89 reviewed how books connect information from page to page, and how good readers
90 make a point of thinking about what's happened before in a book to help them
91 understand what they are reading now. In fact, it's the reader's responsibility to
92 connect it on her own. We went back over all the information about early spring,
93 the early snow melt, the lack of rain, and so on, and talked about how all this was
94 being brought back *implicitly* on every page by the author. Every page is not isolated,
95 but connected, and the words on one page add to what was before it. In other words,
96 the author did not have to restate that earlier information as a summation of the entire

97 list of factors that came together to create that bad fire year because it was expected

98 that a good reader *would do it on her own*. Then she could restate what she'd

99 learned on the previous page about why that year was "bad" and apply it to the

100 information on this page.

Exercise

The lines of the previous summarized discussion are numbered. In the chart in Figure 5–5, I list the line number(s) with some blank lines next to them.

Discussion Focus or Lines of Dialogue	Domain(s)
Preview of vocabulary	
Talk about fire	
Locating Yellowstone, etc.	
Reading back of book	
Highlighting vocab, putting it on the word wall, etc.	
Reading aloud and paraphrasing	
My questions (in general)	
Lines 5–14	
Lines 15–23	
Lines 24–35	
Lines 36–46	
Lines 47–61	
Lines 73–82	
Lines 83–100	

FIGURE 5–5. *Discussion Chart*

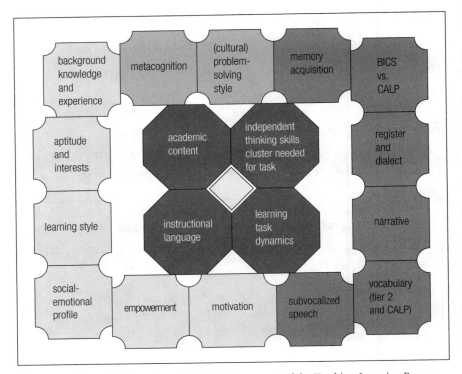

FIGURE 5–6. *Puzzle Chart Containing the Components of the Teaching-Learning Process*

Write the domains you think were being worked with in each part of the lesson in the space provided. The diagram from Figure 3–1 is reproduced in Figure 5–6 for your convenience. My thinking about the domains I had been working with are shown in a filled-out chart at the end of the chapter (Figure 5–10 on page 163) for your comparison.

More on Tier 2 Vocabulary, Idioms, and CALP Words

Without sufficient vocabulary, too much of a text is confusing, misleading, or incomprehensible. The following are two versions of a short oral lecture about the settling of the Iranian plateau that I use in teacher training workshops to illustrate BICS versus CALP language. The first version illustrates how such a text might be heard and understood by a hypothetical intermediate ELL or

English-dominant CLD student. To understand that student's experience, imagine that you are a student who is not fully proficient in literacy-oriented English. Maybe you are an ESL student, or maybe you are a dominant/monolingual English speaker with less developed CALP. I made three types of vocabulary-related changes to the lecture in version 1 to simulate the type of misunderstandings and miscomprehensions that often arise:

- Sophisticated, probably unknown CALP words were changed to Farsi (the language of Iran)[3] words; in other words, the CALP words will be unintelligible.

- Idioms were written out with the literal meaning of each word separately (i.e., the way an unknown idiom would be processed).

- Words that might be misheard or misinterpreted because they are CALP versions of BICS words or are likely unfamiliar CALP words were written as they might be processed (i.e., they are close in sound to familiar BICS words).

Version 1

Today we're going to look in a new place the qadim history of Iran. Iran is one of the oldest tamaddon in the world. It is believed that the eggshell cement of the Iranian flat O by kuchegaaraan might have been as early as seven thousand years ago! As kuchegaaraan followed their listened to of animals as they gray colors bar tebq-eh the seasons, they swept the floor across the wide stairs of central Asia into what is today Iran, maqiming the flat O. All amma most gift day Iranians are not kuchegaaraan, that's how it all began.

The first kuchegaaraan were Aryan qoms. Did you know that the plant roots of the gift day Iranian language and English are the same? For example, *faamil* is *family*, *maadar* is *mother*, va gheireh. A few people's real eyes that western tamadon is a family member so closely to Iran.

The Iranian flat O is Maine khoshk. There are large sand and salt deserts flunked by mountain ranges and divided by a thin piece of haaselkhiz land. As groups of kuchegaaraan maqimed in the flat O, they became sad entry. They started some of the world's first science experiments with keshaavarzi. What a a'aaneh to tamaddon! Don't you agree?

Think about how your understanding was affected: you *almost* were understanding, then some zinger or other would intervene. How did you feel? If you felt frustrated, that is how many of our students feel, too.

Now, read the actual text and compare the two. How much did you get?

Version 2

Today we're going to explore the ancient history of Iran. Iran is one of the oldest civilizations in the world. It is believed that the actual settlement of the Iranian plateau by nomads might have been as early as seven thousand years ago! As nomads followed their herds of animals as they grazed according to the seasons, they swept across the wide steppes of central Asia into what is today Iran, settling the plateau. Although most present-day Iranians are not nomads, that's how it all began.

The first nomads were Aryan tribes. Did you know that the roots of the present-day Iranian language and English are the same? For example, *faamil* is *family*, *maadar* is *mother*, et cetera. Few people realize that western civilization is related so closely to Iran.

The Iranian plateau is mainly arid. There are large sand and salt deserts flanked by mountain ranges and divided by a thin strip of cultivatable land. As groups of nomads settled in the plateau, they became sedentary. They started some of the world's first experiments with agriculture. What a contribution to civilization, don't you agree?

> *Vocabulary obstacles are one of the main reasons I emphasize understanding the author's meaning as such a crucial step for underachieving CLD readers!*

Although I've used this exercise in the context of oral language, the same issues arise in reading for CLD students. These various types of vocabulary obstacles occur on the printed page as students independently process a mix of familiar and unfamiliar language.

Underachieving CLD learners may see things at school as *isolated, in-and-of-themselves moments*, either when trying to follow instructional language or in text. This may be because they are bottom-up learners awaiting explicit adult direction that does not come or because they are poorly mediated. They may not make the independent, spontaneous connections of more proficient learners. They may well process words individually without reintegrating them at the phrase and sentence levels, so if they happen to know a meaning for a word, they are satisfied. They will simply read on without integrating everything back into the author's intent to see if that is the way the word was used by the author. Yet a word could be part of an idiomatic expression, a phrasal verb, or a word with multiple meanings. The student may never ask the crucial question "Does this make sense?" at the sentence and paragraph levels because he is satisfied with "This makes sense to me" at the *single-word level*. In other words, he'll stop partway through step 3, and therefore won't really be reading.

In looking back at the two students reading the book on the Yellowstone fires, the only word they could not ultimately *decode* was *geyser*. So, what interfered with their text comprehension was a combination of tier 2 words, idioms, and narrative-related issues. Altogether, combining the words they picked out of the text that they felt they might not know (both unknown words and vaguely known words they were unclear about), and the word *little*, which I added to that list during the reading, they did not know roughly 7 percent of the text (including the captions). That's not a debilitating quantity—indeed, the percentage was often much higher for them in grade-level chapter books—but if we examine the 7 percent, we see that it included many of the *essential CALP words* that allow the reader to enact the crucial step 5 of the reading process: understanding the author's meaning.

> *How we name a need shapes our response to it. That's why it is so important to interpret what we experience with our students from a deeper, more informed perspective.*

So were the two students weak readers? Did they need remedial reading support or double dosing? Or did they really need vocabulary development and narrative practice?

Historically, the tendency in education is to evaluate CLD student need in juxtaposition to school discourse community norms and evaluate areas of mismatch as deficits. Besides being disrespectful of CLD students' families, languages, and cultural backgrounds and experiences, that way of looking at students limits *us* as well. In this case, it would cause us to say, "These students are still poor readers," or "They don't comprehend text very well yet." It undervalues and underassesses what students can actually do once we account for a broader range of specific mismatch issues. In this case, once narrative and vocabulary issues were accounted for, they did a good job paraphrasing and answering questions. That would indicate that the students *really* needed more practice with developing personal narrative, vocabulary development, and more practice with metacognitive skills in recognizing when their comprehension was breaking down (because of vocabulary and narrative mismatches). But is that necessarily what they'd get if they were identified as needing more "reading services," remedial reading instruction, or even more comprehension practice?

In the first-grade ESL-inclusion classroom I work in, the classroom teacher and I have talked about "peachy words" with students. We highlight student attention on words that seem "juicy" and "yummy" as a way of building vocabulary during our read-aloud time. The students just about all agree that peaches are delicious and can relate to the juicy image. Sometimes we highlight peachy words before a reading, and sometimes we ask them to make some motion of their own to show they've heard a peachy word during story time—they might mime pulling a peach off a tree, or licking their lips, for example.[4] We stop the story and ask what word they thought was a peachy word, and we talk about what it means. After the story is over, we cut a piece of orange or pink construction paper into a peach shape, write the word on it along with a simple meaning, then hang it on our construction paper tree that we have "growing" on a wall. When possible, we cluster the peaches into groups of words with similar meanings or categories. We try to recycle those words in our conversations and instruction, and the words are there for students to use in their writing. The stronger students in class really run with this idea and often come in asking excitedly, "Is *x* a peachy word?" about a word they heard at home or in a movie or saw in a book. They are modeling making connections between school and outside school for the other students, and we take time to talk this up. This year, we are doing a WOW (Wonder of Words) word wall instead of a peach tree, with words on bright pink construction paper that we've deliberately highlighted during class for that purpose. During writing time, many students go over to that wall to look for good words for their writing. However one does it, highlighting the words and having kids use them is the key.

One trick about this is regulating the language in picture books so that certain vocabulary sticks out. I rarely read picture books verbatim. If I regulate the language for my ELLs, then not only can I hold them more accountable for listening and group participation because more or most of the story is comprehensible, but I can also highlight useful tier 2 words (typically verbs or adjectives) that lend themselves to the peachy image. Picture books are often filled with very literate, complex language. Thinking of the present-practice-use frame established in Chapter 2, we know that just exposing vocabulary-weak students to this text does nothing for their vocabulary development (nor will they understand the story).

In addition to establishing a culture of appreciating language in general and vocabulary in particular with our peach tree, we tell lots of riddles and puns, which help CLD students see that words can have multiple meanings. We notice an increased interest in words even among non-literacy-oriented CLD students in the ways we foreground vocabulary, in both their oral as well as their written vocabularies. Students often become interested in what their teachers seem excited about.

I also want to reemphasize that text is a great place from which to cull tier 2 words, useful idioms, and phrasal verbs. Flipping the usual way of thinking about it, I think of reading as a means to helping CLD students increase their vocabulary and overall language development, rather than the other way around. That is always my baseline purpose for working with students in text.

Just Small Words?

Read the following paragraph, which I showed at a teacher training workshop. I asked the participants what the most important word in the paragraph was. What do you think?

Where Yu Li lived, they had few of the things that people in town had. There was no electricity. No telephones. Few roads. Most goods were carried on barges on the canals. The farmers would take their produce and load it onto the barges to take it to town markets, where it could be sold. But the barges carried more than corn, honey, wheat and vegetables. They carried news. Through the bargemen, people in the countryside would learn of what was happening in far-off places. (Schlein 1999, 29)

Actually, *but* is the key word in this paragraph. Just going by the quantity of words, the description of river trade seems to be the important idea. However, the main idea is that in this Chinese town news traveled by river and *but* signals the transition between ideas. CLD students need help seeing the importance of these "small words" in highlighting meaning. They are related to the more recognizable group of transition words (*however, moreover, when, therefore, after,* etc.) but their importance is easily overlooked. It's almost like longer words gain more importance at school to many students!

CALP words like *yet, even, still, only, besides,* and *just*—short, seemingly innocuous words—signal an important change in the author's intent that is delivered almost in an *offhand* way. CLD students must learn to recognize them: I teach my students to say, "Uh-oh!" when they come across them during classroom reading. Of course, they need to transfer that awareness to their internal processing when reading silently on their own.

Other Barriers to Comprehension

Of course, although the most important overall, vocabulary and narrative are not the only issues that affect text comprehension. The following issues are also important to keep in mind.

CALP Language Structures

Following pronoun referents through paragraphs is another difficult area for CLD students, particularly if they refer to more than one person or idea. Just about all students know *that* when it refers to one thing (e.g., *That is my pencil.*). But when *it* or *that* stands for a whole sentence or concept(s), CLD students often do not understand the referent. For example: *The Appalachians formed a huge physical barrier for the American colonists, and Native Americans still lived there in strength. That is why it took so long for the colonists to begin to expand westward.* Many of my CLD students would not understand that the word *that* in the second sentence refers to the *entire* previous sentence, which in fact are *two separate reasons* that prevented westward expansion. So an answer to the question "Why did it take so long for the colonists to begin to expand westward?" would need to include *both* reasons to be 100 percent correct.

Sentence structure can also be a barrier to full text comprehension, especially in nonfiction. Compound sentences, complex sentences, gerund (-ing) phrases, flipped sentence structures (e.g., *I couldn't find the store without the map* versus *Without the map, I couldn't find the store*), and sentences connected with semicolons all make comprehension challenging. Asking students to periodically paraphrase aloud what they read helps us see which types of language are tripping them up. Asking sentence-level questions that probe the relationship in meaning between the various parts of compound or complex sentences, or the meaning underlying the linkage of two sentences (or sections of text), also directly addresses how students are processing text language.

This is step 4 of the reading process. We might not think to ask such questions of literacy-oriented native English speakers, presuming that those elements of language are not a barrier to their comprehension. However, until a CLD student demonstrates the independent ability to process and use text language at grade level, those types of questions are essential.

Underline the sentence below that you think would probably be the easiest to understand for a CLD student:

I didn't go because I thought that mean kid would be there. He scares me.

Because I thought that mean kid would be there, I didn't go. He scares me.

Thinking that mean kid would be there, I chose not to go, as he scares me.

As that mean kid scares me, I chose not to go, thinking he would be there.

It should be pretty obvious that the first sentence would be much easier for a CLD student to process than the others. The longer and more complex the sentence, and the more sophisticated the construction, the harder it is for underachieving CLD students (and of course, ESL students) to understand. Following are a few effective instructional responses to complex text:

- Rewrite it using simpler sentences.

- Help the students process the meaning.

- Have a stronger reader read the text onto a tape for the less proficient reader to use when he reads it.

- If the text is really hard, read the passage onto a tape for the student and editorialize on the meaning as you go.

Print and Text Organization

Two other barriers to comprehension are the print itself and the text organization. These are issues influencing the input phase of reading, step 1. Do your non-literacy-oriented CLD students consciously process font changes—italics, boldface, underlining, size—and try to understand why the author used them? These features may seem so obvious on a page, but not all students really process them. If a student is not being careful and very discriminating about what he sees, he is already a candidate for poor comprehension—and the reading process has barely even started! Recognizing and interpreting differences in font type and size is an especially important skill to help comprehend nonfiction text.

Remember that poorly mediated students (see Chapter 3) often lack skill in the input phase of learning activity.

The following anecdote illustrates how students do not necessarily process what may be quite clear to us. I was doing the first page of the "Organization of Dots" unit of the Feuerstein Instrumental Enrichment program (see Chapter 3) with two students. In this task, students have to find geometric shapes of increasing complexity within various dot clouds. The first page had the simplest shapes and the least complex dot matrices. There were big and small black dots and big and small blue dots, so four distinct kinds of dots. It is important to note these characteristics because they are easy cues for finding the shapes on that first page. Figure 5–7 is a partial reproduction.

I wanted to see what they took in on their own, so I asked them to tell me what they saw in the frames after we established that the first frame on the page had the model shapes students would need to find on the rest of the page.

They said, "Dots."

I said, "Look again. Can you tell me more about what you see?"

Staring hard, they replied, "There's just dots!"

"Do you notice anything about the dots?"

They put their heads close to the paper and frowned as they looked. They finally said, "Are you trying to trick us again, Ken? They're just dots!"

Yet when I asked specifically about color and size, they of course could tell me the two colors and two sizes. They just had not accorded these details relevance as they processed the visual input. In the same way, students see font differences and punctuation, but may not always process them as they should. (And just imagine how hard it is for such students to attend to the subtleties of language or concepts.) The *quantity* side of this coin is obviously that "When you see *x* (e.g., italics) in this text, it means . . ." The *quality* side of this coin is, "When good learners see differences, they try to make sense of them and understand why." Both sides of the coin are equally important.

Successful readers actively try to make sense of the various visual cues in text.

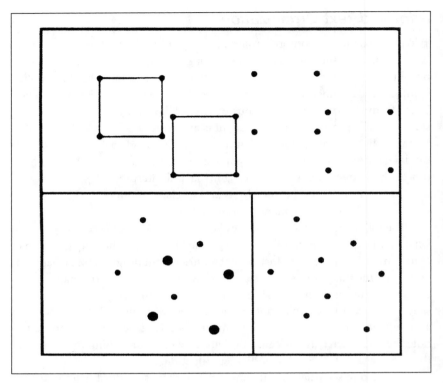

FIGURE 5–7. *Organization of Dots*

Many underachieving readers must improve their attention to the input phase of reading. This also connects to developing appropriate organizational speech and metacognitive awareness. (More on the biggest step 1 issue of all for underachieving readers—registering those tiny dots called periods—follows on page 156.)

Paragraphs

Do weaker readers really understand what paragraphs are in spite of all the times they hear the word and even the practice time spent on them? I try to define paragraph usage as two concrete things:

- First, it's a physical shape of words on a page.
- Second, it shows the reader when *something changes*—time, place, speaker, plot event, topic, and so on.

Paragraphs are an important comprehension processing point. In nonfiction, paragraph organization is particularly helpful to comprehension because it often divides up text into the supporting details of a main idea. In my experience, less proficient readers fly across paragraph breaks like they weren't even there. If paragraphing is not recognized, comprehension suffers.

Being more effortful in this way slows down reading (the rate of speed, not student progress). But that's OK! I often mix effortful reading practice in my class for the students who need it with more enjoyable reading at home that they just have to summarize or talk about briefly the next day. The further CLD students are from reading at grade level, the more they should deliberately practice stopping and processing.

> *Some students must make it an automatic habit to pause at paragraph breaks to process the text they have just read. If they have not understood it, they must automatically be in the habit of rereading it until they do understand or can ask a specific clarifying question of the teacher about it. We also need to be sure to mediate meaning about* why *this is necessary.*

Sentence Links

The narrative-related issue of sentence links is worth revisiting. I have always found it fascinating how the implicit linkage of proximate sentences—in text, or in instructional language, or by the markers of an instructional sequence—is overlooked or misinterpreted by many CLD students. I often stop in a reading and ask students what connecting word they could put between two sentences or what information has been dropped. Their answers often surprise me.

For example: *The man tried the handle. He shook it. He had to look for another way in.* (*Then* might be inserted between the first two sentences, and *because the door wouldn't open* was dropped before the end sentence.) If I asked my underachieving CLD students, "Why did the man look for another way in?" I would likely get some plausible answer from *outside the text* that they would generate from their own experience or imagination (e.g., he didn't want to make noise by opening the door in case it squeaked). CLD students who are not proficient readers bring in their own experience or ideas to the text as a *substitute* for step 5 (understanding the author's meaning) instead of a supplement to it. That is why I now emphasize the entire process of reading with my older students (third grade and up), with a focus on step 5. I go so far as to tell my CLD students that the main purpose of reading is to understand the author's meaning.

In fact, simply asking your students, "What is reading?" can yield very revealing insights into what assumptions students have about reading that may negatively affect the way they read. When I've asked this of my students, the weakest readers have tended to define reading just in terms of "reading the words." I have to directly address their assumptions about what reading is before I can expect them to progress, making their concept of "reading" more meaning-full.

Fluency

Fluency is a very important element of success in reading. Until a student can read text fluently, the processing of the language will be choppy and slow and will interfere with comprehension. Fluency is reached when longer sentences are chunked and read as meaning chunks (and the reader's inflection matches text meaning):

> In other words, a student should be able to read this sentence like this. But if the student has trouble processing phrases or appropriate chunks together, she will experience difficulty understanding the text.

Therefore, fluency practice must be an essential component of any struggling CLD student's reading program until he reaches an appropriate level of fluency. I have found these fluency issues to be the most common and essential for students to overcome:

- leaving sentences read choppily (i.e., not rereading poorly read sentences)
- lack of awareness of what words go together as phrases
- lack of awareness of common prefixes and suffixes (which slows fluency down)
- inattention to punctuation (e.g., so words that are not meant to be chunked together are read together)
- inattention to paragraph breaks (ditto)

Students should be clear that *fluency* basically means two things (however that is conveyed to students; see Chapter 3, "What are my students *really* learning?," page 79):

1. being sure you understand how the words go together to make meaning
2. being sure you can read it like you'd talk it

Students must get in the habit of independently choosing to reread choppily read sentences more smoothly. Rehearsing text aloud until it smoothes out is excellent practice. A student can choose his favorite section of a book and rehearse it until fluent as if he were an actor, then read it to a person of his choice (teacher, other adult, student, administrator). Or you can tape the student reading an easier book for younger students to use.[5] There are many ways to make this practice fun. But there must be an out-loud component to fluency practice for struggling CLD students, both so the student can hear himself read and we can hear what his reading sounds like. However, I do not advise teachers to automatically have students read aloud in front of the whole class, especially if a student is a reflective learner.

Reading fluency is predicated on understanding which words need to go together. As CLD students reach fourth or fifth grade, they should start getting practice in identifying prepositional phrases, predicates versus subjects, and different types of clauses. This is not so they learn the special grammatical terms for each, but as a means to recognize *how words connect together in standard dialect English.*

Of course, fluency does not ensure text meaning by itself! Many of us have worked with excellent word callers who do not understand much if anything of what they "read" so beautifully. Fluency is merely one important skill of several that comprehension is built on, all of which must be in place for independent reading ability at grade level. But it certainly can't be ignored.

Songs can help CLD students see how we chunk words, as phrases are frequently sung together. This is true of many nursery rhymes (think of how we sing "The Eensy Weensy Spider") as well as various songs. (Though this will surely date me, one of my favorite songs for this purpose is "Cry, Baby, Cry," from the Beatles' *White Album.* Each verse is sung distinctly by noun, verb, and/or prepositional phrases.) Children love to sing anyway, but focusing their intentionality and reciprocity on word chunking turns it into a useful fluency exercise.

Timothy Rasinski also has good ideas for building fluency in his book *The Fluent Reader* (2003). One of his suggestions is to have students learn to recognize common phrases that contain the three hundred most frequently used words that early-elementary students will come across in reading (which he divides into three one hundred–word lists according to frequency of use.) For example, *you and I, the people,* and *up in the air* are in the first list.

Fluency is too important to remain an abstract or mysterious concept to CLD students. Its purpose should be clear to both our students and ourselves: it connects how one reads to understanding what one reads and gives the reader a concrete way to know if she is doing it right.

Reading aloud is also valuable for CLD students to do because comprehension is often enhanced when they take in text through both their eyes and their ears.

Punctuation

Those little dots and squiggles we call punctuation are hugely important to giving meaning to text, which aids in fluency. To understand basic punctuation better, CLD students need to realize how it corresponds to oral language. Because metalinguistic terms are often poorly understood by underachieving students, telling a student that a period means it's the end of a complete thought or complete sentence may well have this meaning: "A period means it's the end of a *bhtdrvmolihhytgz.*"

I've heard teachers tell students periods mean they need to take a breath. Then when I ask those students what they think the teacher meant, they just take an exaggerated breath! There is no understanding that the pause is actually related to *making meaning.*

I tell students that periods in writing are the places we briefly stop *when speaking aloud.* On paper we need to show it with a period because the reader needs to know when the writer would stop if she were talking. Other ending punctuation marks are periods with additional signs to show "a stop plus something," either a question or a strong emotion. So periods are related to *speaking.* To illustrate this, I speak to students aloud with no pauses, or pauses in the wrong places, which helps them see what this feels like. Their awareness that they need *me* to pause so *they* can process my language helps me link to the fact that in the same way, the author puts periods in so the reader can process the language. In addition, just like they have a hard time understanding when I speak without pausing, their reading comprehension suffers accordingly when they do not pause to think over what they have just read and skip over punctuation. CLD students must understand that skillful attention to periods helps their comprehension, whereas inattention to periods hinders it.

If students do not read basic punctuation (and paragraphing) well, it is a good bet that they have not been paying close enough attention to text meaning.

Depending on language background, some ESL students tend to use commas in some places where we put periods in writing. I sometimes put up signs that say, "No Comma Zone!" or ask kids to ceremonially take the commas out of their pockets and throw them in the basket. I address commas only after I see that my students have really become grounded in the use of ending punctuation. A related issue that arises, especially (though not only) with ESL students, is when students begin to put periods at the end of dependent phrases: *I came home late. Because we got lost.* I accept this until I get to more sophisticated sentence-combination work when I pair up period and comma usage with the types of sentences being written. Students cannot learn everything at once, and I want to maximize working memory space, so I try to eliminate confusion by streamlining instruction and sharpening student focus on one thing at a time.

Students must be able to follow dialogue in novels, which means they need to understand quotation marks well. There are different ways to write quotations and to break them apart. Students must become fluent in quickly processing quotation marks in all three ways they can be written:

"Quotation marks are important," said Ken.

Ken said, "Quotation marks are important."

"Quotation marks," said Ken, "are important."

How we use quotations can even change language meaning:

Ken said, "José, stop it!"

"Ken," said José, "stop it!"

In addition, students must understand that quotations can be written without the *he said* phrase in dialogue, when it is the paragraph change that signals a change of speaker.

Responses to Reading

One issue that appears later in the reading process is responding to text:

- There may be school questions about reading.

- There are various types of response activities.

- Students may not understand where their focus should be.

CLD students should know that when they read at school, there is a certain expectation about what they will be getting out of text (which connects to setting a clear purpose beforehand), and teacher questions target those things. Reading for pleasure, we can pay attention to whatever we like; we may be quite happy with the *who, what, where, when*, and the basic *how and why* of a book. Yet we rarely confine ourselves to those basic questions of students; if we do limit ourselves to those kinds of questions, especially with underachieving readers, we should stop!

Underachieving readers must be asked the same kinds of probing questions as are asked of stronger readers. If the various elements of language (e.g., vocabulary and sentence structure), background knowledge, visual cues, punctuation, and so on are being monitored and scaffolded as necessary, students must be asked to dig deeper into text. We need to keep narrative in mind, too, to enable students to do that more independently.

As children get older, school questions about text are often about implied meaning, predictions, character study,[6] and point of view. School questions about reading often bear little or no resemblance to questions that non-literacy-oriented CLD students are asked in their life outside school! Students must develop independence in aligning their reading comprehension with school questions. I'm sure you already *set a clear purpose* for reading before students read and/or have students read the questions they will need to answer *before* reading the text, which often helps them be more ready to engage in postreading activities.

One question in particular that can be confusing is the very common school question *Why do you think. . . ?* It is tricky because it actually has two meanings. One meaning (convergent) asks for the author's idea and proof from the text as to how or why you think so, the same as a *How do you know. . . ?* question. The other meaning of *Why do you think. . . ?* (divergent) simply asks straightforwardly for one's opinion or conclusion. CLD students often mistakenly give just this latter meaning to the question.

It is important that CLD students realize the dual possibilities inherent in this common school question, but even so, they need to understand that their answer to *either* of those two meanings *must be grounded in the text.* When these questions are asked about a character's decisions, students must be able to put themselves in the character's shoes to answer well, yet this may be quite difficult if the students are unclear about or unfamiliar with the story line, character types, or place (e.g., when a child from the inner city who has never left it reads about a camping trip or a child reads historical fiction without familiarity with the history). The ability to put oneself in another's position is a function of age, narrative development, and mediation.

Text Analysis

When working with CLD students, it is important to be able to scan text they will be reading to identify possible trouble spots in any of the areas discussed in this chapter. With practice, we can learn to pick out academic vocabulary or concept words to preview and note possibly unfamiliar idiomatic phrases, tier 2 vocabulary, places where sentence links have been dropped, places where meaning is strongly implied but not explicit, and so forth. It gets easier the more you do it, and really helps you both anticipate and pinpoint comprehension breakdowns more skillfully.

Reading Strategies for Better Standardized Test Scores

When CLD students are—very unfairly!—made to take standardized tests with native English speakers, they need a set of strategies that will enable them to perform above their actual comprehension level. After all, fair is fair! I tell my students that those strategies are tricks. Not only do CLD students need to be taught these tricks, but they need to be put in situations that simulate the test day periodically so that when that day comes, the strategies will be well internalized.

One year, one of my fifth-grade (English-dominant) Cambodian American CLD students took the Gates-McGinnity standardized reading test with his class. He told me he thought he did well. He scored a 4.1 (fourth grade, first month) in vocabulary, which I'd roughly expected, but just a 3.6 (third grade, sixth month) in comprehension. Not too good!

Non-literacy-oriented CLD students need to be able to score higher in comprehension than their vocabulary level. Otherwise, they will always be working below grade level, as their vocabularies will often remain below the dominant-culture norm.

Though the student in question was not reading at grade level, his score was well below what I thought he could and should have gotten. Of course, because the Gates is not normed for ELL students, in some respects I could care less how he did on such a test (not state mandated or going on his report card, etc.). However, I wanted to prove a point to this student, so I asked his teacher to let him retake the comprehension portion of the test after we had reconstructed the tricks we had worked on to pass the very challenging state-mandated fourth-grade MCAS (Massachusetts Comprehensive Assessment System) the previous year, which he obviously did not apply to this new situation. With some prodding, the student remembered the tricks but admitted doing none of them on this test. The strategies in Figure 5–8 are the ones we use; you might already teach students these or similar strategies.

The last step is the most important for those two most common types of test questions. There is something about the physical act of underlining at this point that focuses students' attention on the author's words. Also, I discourage the use of highlighters on tests because I think it is a *distractor*: the color attracts attention and occupies a student's precious working memory space, and I often see students using a highlighter to highlight much more than they need to. Those big areas of electric green, yellow, and tangerine sure are pretty!

Amazingly, after my student retook the test using these strategies *and emphasizing the last underlining step*, his comprehension score shot up to 7.4 (seventh grade, fourth month)! That's nearly *four grades* higher than his initial score! Of the twenty-nine comprehension questions he retook, he got twenty-eight of them right. More amazing still, his 7.4 score included his mistakes among the eleven questions (distributed over three reading passages) he did *not* redo! Of course, he was not really reading at that level (Gates scores tend to measure high); on the other hand, he was not reading as low as his initial score would indicate, either. When I asked him what had changed between the two

1. Read the questions first.

2. Scan for print differences (italics, bold, etc.) and think about why they are there.

3. Read.

4. Use a pencil to underline important information, based on the questions or text.

5. Stop at paragraph breaks to recap meaning.

6. Answer questions; decide which question type:

    a. a *reader response* question requiring a straight personal opinion, or

    b. a *factual* question (grounded in the text), or

    c. a *reader response* question requiring the use of factual information, or

    d. a question about language or linguistic knowledge

7. *If factual* (b or c), *go back to text and underline the answer* in pencil

FIGURE 5–8. *Reading Strategies for Better Standardized Test Scores*

tests, he said, "My thinking." I was very happy! That was exactly the conclusion I'd hoped he would draw.

These strategies have yielded good overall scores on the standardized tests my non-literacy-oriented CLD students must take.[7] It takes consistency, clarity, and practice; teachers must avoid making it drudgery and should integrate test-taking strategies and teach/integrate short answer and open response questions within the regular academic curriculum when possible throughout the year. You might ask, "What is our field coming to?" to have to worry so much about this stuff. I agree 100 percent! But what our students have to deal with, they have to deal with. There is a way to enhance test scores while not sacrificing quality learning!

Summary

When we teach CLD students, we must be very clear in our minds in what domain, and which schemata or skills we want ourselves and our students to focus on. What is typically thought of as reading instruction may not target the real obstacles to a CLD student's grade-level performance, because all of steps 1–8 have not traditionally been conceived of as constituting reading instruction, or at least not as systematically or explicitly supported for as long a time.

It is also crucial to remember the cognitive load model of learning presented in Chapter 3. One can conceive of all the issues raised in Chapters 4 and 5 that impact CLD students' progress in reading as being skills or schemata that proficient readers have stored in long-term memory and bring to bear on working memory as needed. There are skills and schemata of language, culture, and thinking and those that are reading specific (e.g., decoding). Conversely, students without expertise in those skills and schemata become distracted or confused, compounding the difficulties of skillfully processing text in limited working memory space, wherever they happen to be within the reading process. This model helps us deconstruct the reading process in its broadest sense, hone in on those areas of greatest need for our CLD students, and sharply focus our instruction accordingly. Then we must ensure intentionality and reciprocity (see Chapter 3), transcendence, and mediation of meaning in our learning interactions with students and give students sufficient structured practice time (stage 2 of Vygotsky's three-stage continuum). And remember, empowerment is the backdrop to all of this!

Personal narrative and vocabulary are the two issues that for older at-risk CLD readers most significantly affect text comprehension, yet reading programs typically do not focus specifically on them. Developing a school-matched personal narrative and expanding one's vocabulary base must be an *integral* part of many CLD students' reading programs. The earlier this starts, the better.

One good rule of thumb is that the development of reading by CLD students is directly related to their oral language development. The former usually leads the latter. That can help inform the specific activities we may wish to design to further the comprehension of a particular text. However, whatever we do to help enhance the learning experience for a CLD student must arise from our knowledge of the student and the reading process.

The following areas were identified as needing either scaffolding or direct instruction to enhance the reading comprehension of CLD students. In parentheses are the steps in the process discussed earlier where these issues may affect comprehension (reproduced in Figure 5–9 for your convenience):

- tier 2 CALP vocabulary (steps 3–5)

- general CALP (steps 3–5)

- idiomatic usage (steps 3–5)

- pronoun referents (step 4)

- sentence complexity (steps 3 and 4)

- paragraph-level processing (steps 4 and 5)

- narrative structure (steps 3–5)

- background knowledge (steps 3–6)

- reading group dynamics and task expectations (steps 7 and 8)
- visual cues and organizational cues (steps 1 and 3–5)
- improved fluency development (steps 4 and 5)
- personal narrative structure (steps 3–5)
- test-taking skills (step 8)
- types of questions used in reading groups (step 7)
- different sounds in different languages, particularly vowels (step 2)
- prereading skills (steps 1–3)

EIGHT STEPS IN THE READING PROCESS

1. Our optic nerve transmits squiggle signals.

2. Our brain translates squiggles to letters, which are associated with sounds.

3. We translate that result into our lexicon:
   - Each squiggle set gains a skeletal word meaning.
   - That in turn is transformed into discourse community meaning.
   - Language is processed at the sentence level.

4. We apply our narrative structure to the internal logic of the text:
   - Language is processed at the sentence level.
   - Language is processed at the paragraph level.
   - Language is processed at the section or chapter level.

5. We attempt to give primacy of text meaning *to the author*.

6. We access our personal experiences to inform text meaning.

7. We often function in a reading group, which has its own discourse rules and learning assumptions built into it.

8. We enact our understanding by completing some task (answering particular types of school questions, writing a response, etc.).

FIGURE 5–9.

Note how may of these issues are involved in steps 3–5 of the reading process for CLD students.

As students explicitly work with these various areas of the reading process, they should be *creating new scripts for their organizational speech* (see Chapter 2).

Discussion Focus or Lines of Dialogue	Domain(s)
Preview of vocabulary	CALP, academic goal, vocabulary
Talk about fire	background knowledge
Locating Yellowstone, etc.	background knowledge
Reading back of book	CALP, academic goal, background knowledge
Highlighting vocab, putting it on the word wall, etc.	vocab
Reading aloud and paraphrasing	academic skills, dialect, thinking skills
My questions (in general)	academic skills, dialect, thinking skills
Lines 5–14	dialect, background knowledge, CALP
Lines 15–23	CALP, thinking skills, dialect, academic goal
Lines 24–35	CALP, thinking skills
Lines 36–46	CALP, thinking skills, dialect, academic goal
Lines 47–61	academic goal
Lines 73–82	CALP
Lines 83–100	CALP, academic goal, dialect, thinking skills

FIGURE 5–10. *My Filled-in Chart for* Fire! in Yellowstone *Discussion (see page 143)*

For example, for metacognitive reflection after a lesson on taking visual cues from an initial look at text, a student may be asked what he's going to do to enhance his performance the next time he reads nonfiction, and he might say, "Next time I read nonfiction, I'm going to be sure to pay attention to font sizes and changes and figure out why the author put them there" (i.e., stage 1 or 2 of Vygotsky's three stages of learning). And then when he next reads nonfiction text, he should be asked if he remembers what he said he'd planned on being sure to do (i.e., stage 2). Those reminders must become increasingly student owned until it is a part of their independent functioning (i.e., stage 3). As students experience more success as readers by working with the various issues raised in this chapter, their organizational speech will certainly contain those new awarenesses—after all, students know what is helpful to them and what is not!

When reading is looked at with a sharper focus, when sufficient modeling and practice time are given where needed, and when new reading skills and schemata are internalized and become a part of their organizational speech, even academically at-risk CLD students are capable of greatly enhanced independent performance in reading.

Notes

1. For example, English is topic centered while another narrative style is topic associative. There are a variety of different cultural narrative styles, and it is good to learn more about them.

2. A major leap occurs when a child's narrative vaults into the landscape of feeling (centered in the character's internal feelings and problem solving) from the landscape of action (centered in outside events) This should happen in early-elementary grades. The child is beginning to account for *other* in a more focused and perceptive way, and this awareness comes out in her spontaneous personal narrative. I see parallels between a lack of mediation, which keeps one egocentric for longer periods of time (see Chapter 3), and staying in the landscape of action long after one should have evolved out of it (like Sothary), because one is still relating events mainly from one's own perspective.

3. It is almost coincidental that I am using Farsi words in this way about an Iranian subject. I wanted to use words that most readers would not know, and I didn't want to make up nonsense words in English, so I transliterated real Farsi words for this purpose.

4. Having young students perform physical actions of some kind or other when listening to stories—about words, or when a new character enters the story, or when the problem in the plot comes up—ensures better comprehension through the active participation it requires of them.

5. The school catalog Crystal Springs sells ten-minute blank cassette tapes.

6. Students must have a good store of tier 2 vocabulary relating to personal attributes to do this well.

7. This same student also jumped from a low Needs Improvement (NI) score on the MCAS in fifth grade to Proficient (P) in sixth grade.

Math

A wonderful third-grade teacher was making a digital portfolio about two students working in the school's exploratory math curriculum. He filmed them explaining their work after a unit on multiplication concepts using a hundreds chart and what they thought about it. One of them was a Cambodian girl. In her clip, she showed a hundreds chart and proudly demonstrated that six jumps of seven landed on forty-two.

Then the teacher asked her, "So Sopharany, what's six times seven?"

The student answered very seriously, "Oh . . . about a hundred."

FOR CLD students in dominant-culture classrooms, there are many parallels between learning literacy and learning math. Math is, itself, a type of literacy with its own unique language, and it is being taught in increasingly complex and cognitively demanding ways.

The Problem

Though modest gains have recently been made, as with reading, most CLD students (with the exception of certain populations of Asian American students) do much more poorly in math than students from the dominant culture (although this is not to say that every dominant-culture student is good at math).

These are the most recent statistics (for grade 4) as reported on the NAEP website (also see Chapter 4):

- average Asian student score = 253

- average white student score = 248

- average African American student score = 222

- average Hispanic student score = 227

- average score of students on reduced lunch = 236

- average score of students on free lunch = 225

- average ESL student score = 217

Another important and very influential comparison of math achievement can be found in the Third International Mathematics and Science Study (TIMSS). At the fourth-grade level, the United States ranked eighth out of the fifty nations participating in 2003. By the time our students are eighth graders, though, we slipped to forty-second place. So it appears that in elementary school our math achievement is not that bad compared with those other nations, though we would like it to be higher.

But the TIMSS report does not disaggregate scores demographically. That's a problem for analyzing our scores because our achievement is so disparate. It leads us to think in the wrong way. The countries that outrank the United States on the grade 4 TIMSS list have generally middle-class, relatively homogeneous student populations.[1] I'd gamble the farm that if we looked *only* at the scores of our most empowered, dominant-culture students, we would score very high on the TIMSS list! In other words, our math instruction overall is already quite good for the same demographic groups that do so well in other countries. But to improve math instruction for the benefit of those who do *not* do as well, we cannot end up with a one-size-fits-all solution, which most often fits only the ones who don't need refitting! The basic questions have to be *why* disparate achievement exists and *whom* it exists for.

> *Only by understanding our own CLD students and ourselves, their language and ours, and our own curriculum better can we understand what instruction to deliver and how.*

For example, the overall conclusion of TIMSS and many books on improving math education is that we should look to countries that do better in math to learn better ways to deliver instruction and improve the curriculum. To me, this feels similar to the spate of those "Japanese business models are best" books that proliferated during the Japanese economic boom but quickly disappeared when the Japanese economy went bust. On the inside flap of one recent book on improving math instruction, *The Teaching Gap* (Stigler and Hiebert 1999), one can read the following: "Teaching, [the authors] argue, is cultural." The authors point out features of German and Japanese math instruction that differ from ours and could be good instructional models for us. They have it half right: teaching is, indeed, cultural—but only because *learning* is cultural. I'm sure Japanese and German teachers do engage in very effective, valuable teaching practices, but our cultural context is not theirs. Their answers may not be ours.

It is also an article of faith that teachers in the United States must develop professionally and improve their instructional practices for students to achieve at higher levels. While this is obviously true, the devil is in the details. The rest of this chapter delves into what the details are, identifying some of the devils lurking inside them.

Math Is Culture, Too

In earlier chapters, I made the point that students come to school better or less well prepared to learn in school based on their home apprenticeship in learning and language, and that this is often the dividing line between differing levels of academic achievement. Math is no different.

For example, the Oksapmin people of Papua New Guinea base their counting on body parts (Miura and Okamoto 1999), so they are limited in counting up to sixty-eight at most. With our base ten system, we can conceptualize huge numbers and could count up to infinity if we had the time. The ability to construct math concepts is a cognitive ability all humans share, but math tools are culturally bound (as is the language used to express them). Not all our students come to school with the same set, or sense, of mathematical tools.

Math is a cultural tool. While mathematical reasoning ability does not vary between cultures, the cultural tools of mathematics—numbers and number systems—do (as do mathematical tasks and applications).

Math curricula in our schools are predicated on the mathematical tools and sensibilities of dominant-culture, literacy-oriented communities.

In the last ten years or so, the movement toward improving math instruction in this country has been strongly influenced by the writings of Li Ping Ma (1999). Ma posits a model of quality math instruction based on what she feels are the reasons Chinese students do well in math: Chinese math instructors learn deeply about math themselves, and their math instruction emphasizes collaborative problem solving and a deep understanding of math concepts. While Ma's work does offer some very valuable insights into math instruction, recent research (Wang and Lin 2005) debunks the view that it is *instruction* that most strongly contributes to Chinese student performance.

It turns out that Chinese American students outperform other students in the United States in math *without* the benefit of the particular instructional practices that occur in Chinese classrooms (it also turns out that in math tasks that require more creative thinking, students here generally outperform students in China). Again, it boils down to language and culture. The Chinese language names numbers in a way that seems to enhance the awareness of the base ten number system in young children, giving them an early leg up in conceptual understanding (this would also help explain why Japanese students, for example, also do very well in math, especially at younger ages; see also Miura and Okamoto 1999). In addition, the way Chinese families organize around school seems to have a very strong influence on the math prowess of Chinese and Chinese American children. In other words, Chinese students are generally strong math learners regardless of instructional methodology, mainly for cultural and linguistic reasons.

> *To best teach our own CLD students, we need to realize that there is no objectively best math instruction that transcends cultural context and learner.*

Back to Cognitive Load, Language, Memory, and Thinking

A very interesting study (Swanson and Beebe-Frankenberger 2004) describes the issues that impact students who are at risk for math failure in terms very evocative of cognitive load theory and other issues about language and learning raised earlier in this book. Children at risk for math failure performed below other students on "aggregate measures relating to problem solving, calculation, reading, phonological processing, random generation/updating of short term memory, working memory and semantic processing/vocabulary" (486).

Out of these, *working memory* was considered the key component, playing a critical role in integrating information during problem solving. We can use the framework of this book to analyze the curriculum, the language, the cultural context, issues of memory, and our students' learning preferences, and how they act either as space-cleaning skills and schemata to draw on from long-term memory or as distractions that overburden working memory (see Chapter 3). Math is an interplay of numbers, number concepts, and language, set within particular problem-solving tasks, learned by particular students in a particular sociocultural context.

A recent book, *Executive Function Education* (Meltzer 2008), extends this idea. *Executive function* is an umbrella term for the complex processes the brain employs for flexible, goal-directed, planned behavior. It is a function of memory and cognitive skill, including metacognition, sort

> *Good math instruction is any instruction that helps make particular students more competent with any math, language, and problem-solving schemata and skills in which they do not presently have grade-level independence. At the same time, it makes explicit and scaffolds any other language, cognitive, and problem-solving schemata and skills that a student may need to be successful.*

of the mission control center for complex cognitive work. In a subject like math as it is taught in many schools—with math concepts, math language, and problem-solving schemata all so important—a student's executive functioning must be strong to be independently successful; otherwise, too much will lie outside the realm of his control. I see literacy culture as helping young children develop stronger executive functioning capacity because of the very nature of literacy culture acculturation, which goes hand in hand with independent learning ability and metacognitive development. Conversely, a subject that requires strong executive functioning ability in the way we teach it and in our expectations of how it will be processed will be extra challenging for students who have not developed the full range of appropriate schemata or developed sufficient executive functioning ability. (Of course, this is *not* to say that underachieving CLD students have the special need called *executive function disorder*.)

The suggestions *Executive Function Education* gives for math instruction echo this text's emphasis on seeing classroom learning and instruction as the intersection of cognition and memory systems, buttressed by attention (to which this book has also added language and culture in equal measure). The suggestions also dovetail nicely with this book's emphasis on the need for us to be explicit and intentional about making quality-learning issues an explicit, scaffolded part of the learning environment and of student learning.

Finally, one quick anecdote to tie up this introduction: Cambodian refugee families first started moving to our area in the mid- to late 1980s. Although the children had spent a year or more in refugee camps and their schooling had been chaotic and disrupted, the *one* area of the curriculum most of them could feel competent in was math. In those days, the emphasis was on calculation. Over the years, math instruction in many classrooms at our school has evolved into a set of constructivist-influenced and language-laden practices based primarily in developing conceptual knowledge. Overall, the math performance of our Cambodian American students has dropped until it has now become perhaps the most difficult area of the curriculum for most of them. Reflecting on this not long ago, the wonderful Cambodian paraprofessional at our school said pensively, "It's funny. Cambodian kids used to be so good at math." They still are good at math, just not math taught in the particular way we teach it now.

What Math?

Either Concepts or Skills, or Both Concepts and Skills?

To achieve at higher levels in our education system, students must become skillful problem solvers and be able to manipulate concepts. Without thinking skills and language schemata, and solid concept knowledge, this is not possible. No successful, long-term academic achievement can just be rote in this day and age in our culture. The deeper the learning, the more expert schemata and skills students are developing. CLD students have historically been shortchanged by math instruction that is limited, rote, and unchallenging. This can never be the answer.

But the only answer isn't a swing all the way across the pendulum! Partly in reaction to the bad old days of poor, rote, uninteresting math instruction, and partly out of a new philosophical bias, working mainly with the languageless component of math—number operations—is sometimes derided by progressive educators as number crunching. As a result, explicit practice with number facts, for example, has been elbowed out of the way in some classrooms, as happened with phonics when whole language first exploded on the educational scene in the mid- to late 1980s. Generally speaking, because of the subjective, lesser value assigned to those boring skills, pedagogies that privilege the status of concept understanding (whatever the subject) tend to devalue time spent on skills practice in the classroom (Delpit 1995; Bailey and Pransky 2005).

The rationale is that students will develop number fluency skills through meaningful math activity. Therefore, why spend precious in-class instructional time on them? And indeed, while there are always exceptions, it often does seem that dominant-culture students do not need as much practice to gain reasonable facility with numbers—just as they did not need as much practice with developing phonemic awareness when whole language first came out. But what about the ones who do need more practice? And why? These questions are addressed in this chapter.

Fluency

We get whiplash from our field's tendency to swing abruptly back and forth across pedagogies and philosophies of teaching. Yet the simple reality is that without basic number sense and number fluency, really understanding math concepts is not possible.

The cognitive load model helps us see that there are actually three distinct aspects of math fluency. The first is *mechanical fluency* with numbers—for example, facts recall.[2] While the simple, quick recall of math facts (which can be accomplished through memorization as well as arising out

We create the reality of math by the way we conceptualize and teach it, which is based in culture and philosophical preference. There is no objectively correct or best way to do it that transcends context and learner.

We have to shake our heads free of "the best this" and "the best that." Whatever we choose to do will match some students more than others. As more sensitized teachers of CLD students, we need to recognize that this is the crux of the matter.

Stressing (abstract) conceptual understanding before CLD students are grounded in fluency with the concrete (numbers) and without their developing CALP language skills is detrimental to their achievement.

of math activity) does not confer meaning, it is a mechanism by which working memory space is not cluttered by an extended or random search for answers or numerical connections during a focus on concept building or problem solving. Another advantage of developing automaticity with mechanical fluency is that it can be a crucial component of concept development if done right (see section entitled "Mechanical Fluency Practice as a Bridge to Conceptual Fluency," on page 175).

The second type of fluency is *procedural fluency*. This refers to the steps one must follow to solve a math operation beyond the simple recall of facts. Students must develop procedural fluency in one method or another in mathematical operations, or again, precious memory space is taken up either with working out procedures or with the confusion that arises from a lack of procedural fluency. For example, since organizational skills overlap procedural fluency, some young students may recount manipulatives they have already counted because they didn't move them far enough away. Another example is doing two-digit multiplication and division algorithms, when many students get lost in the complex procedures involved.

The third type of fluency is *conceptual fluency*, which is the application of number sense, number relationships, or number interaction to a given mathematical context or situation.

Developing conceptual fluency should be our overarching goal with all students, but it is directly connected to the other two types of fluency, and may be sabotaged by a lack of fluency in either of them.

I look at it like a closet. There are hangers (number fluency), the act of hanging and organizing the clothes (procedural fluency), and the clothes (conceptual fluency). The closet is obviously there for the clothes—who would want just a neat row of hangers? But without hangers, a sense of organization, and coordination enough to use the hangers, all you get is a messy piles of clothes heaped on the floor, making it hard to find anything, and even if you do find what you're looking for, it's all wrinkled.

As teachers of math, we need to constantly be monitoring—and understanding—which type of fluency a student's attention might actually be on regardless of the activity's, or our own, intent. Think back to the anecdote with Sopharany that kicked off this chapter. While the supposedly meaningful math activity of using the hundreds chart had been enjoyable and engaging, it did not really help her deepen her understanding of multiplication concepts or facts—in fact, it appears as though she just developed the procedural fluency needed to jump around the hundreds chart! That is not to say that such activities cannot be meaningful for CLD students. But as always when working with CLD students, it's not the *what* that is important, but rather the *how* and *why*.

What assumptions do we make about the best way to go about things and what our students are learning as they go?

In Sopharany's case, her focus (intentionality and reciprocity) was not matching the teacher's, nor was there a clear, explicit connection (transcendence) for her from that learning experience to past and future math work. She was also not matched to the cultural learning expectations around metacognition and how to think about and manipulate her learning inherent in that exploratory math activity. She lacked some of the amplifiers needed to engage successfully in that learning task. But, was "math" her difficulty?

The more working memory space is taken up with either or both of the first two types of fluency, the less space is available for the third.

Last year, I worked briefly with a math-weak sixth-grade CLD student I'll call "Juan." He had not developed the first type of fluency through exploratory math activities focusing on multiplication concept building in either third, fourth, or fifth grade, and it was really slowing him down. My goal was to get Juan to understand that he needed to apply his own effort now to learning math facts, as much effort as it took—even if it was not fun. I knew his father was a mechanic, so I began with the following conversation:

KEN: I bet a lot of people bring in their cars for your dad to fix.

JUAN: Yeah, a lot.

KEN: I've never seen your dad work, but I bet I know something about him.

JUAN: What's that?

KEN: I bet he doesn't waste time when he's fixing cars.

JUAN: How do you know that?

KEN: 'Cause time costs money. If he wasted time, it would cost me more if I brought him my car to fix. People don't want to spend extra money for nothing. If he were too slow, people would stop bringing him their cars. But tell me something.

JUAN: What?

KEN: Have you ever watched him?

JUAN: Yeah.

KEN: Pretend my car has a problem and he just figured out what it was. What does he do now to start fixing it?

JUAN: Aah . . . he has to get his tools.

Ken: Oh. And does he know which tools he needs and where he keeps them? Or does he have to look all around for them?

Juan: He knows right where they are.

Ken: And when he gets what he needs, does he sit there trying to remember how to use each tool? Or does he know them really well, too?

Juan: He knows that really well, too.

Ken: So he gets the right tools, he gets them quickly, and he knows just how to use them?

Juan: Uh-huh.

Ken: Then he can spend all his time using the tools to fix the car?

Juan: Yeah.

Ken: I bet you're proud of your dad being such a great mechanic.

Juan: Yeah!

Having established that his dad knew right away where his tools were and how to use them, I was able to scaffold a discussion of the value of knowing math facts. Just like his dad need to be efficient when it actually came to fixing cars after he was able to troubleshoot their problems in order to run a successful business, if Juan knew he needed to multiply or think about how numbers were interacting in a multiplicative relationship, he had to be automatic with his tools, too—that is, number facts—so he could spend more time on the important thing, the thinking involved in problem solving. Partly through the understanding that Juan took away from this conversation, and partly with some gentle persuasion from me by taking lunch recesses away to practice facts when he wasn't learning them efficiently—I should say, *effortfully*—enough, his classroom math performance began to improve. And as I worked with him on this, it turned out that he needed some help in the procedural fluency of successfully memorizing facts (the way he needed to do it), which is one of the things that had gotten in the way of his being successful with it earlier. This also gave us a wonderful opportunity to work on organizational skills and to talk about how effort makes us smart.

The view that says all children develop fluency skills through meaningful math activity not only overlooks the three-pronged nature of math fluency, but it overlooks why, as I noted earlier, many dominant-culture children *do* seem to develop number skills that way. Of course, it is possible that students with high levels of metacognitive ability may, indeed, develop adequate number fluency through math activity focusing on concept building. But the more likely reason is that their home acculturation has often included number fluency practice in one form or another. In other words, as with literacy amplifiers, many dominant-culture children bring the basics of number fluency to school.

For instance, have you, like my wife and I, practiced multiplication facts with your own third- and fourth-grade-age children to help time pass on long stretches of boring highway on a family trip or at home to be sure they were well prepared for school? Integrated numbers into home interactions (e.g., "Look at those pretty flowers in the vase! I wonder how many there are? Let's count them. . . .")? Played number games and sang nursery rhymes and other songs based in counting? Baked cookies and other things with your children, who were active helpers in measuring and counting out ingredients? Had academically oriented children's computer programs? Had them watch educational children's TV? Developing number fluency is a cultural practice like any other learning.

If we do not give sufficient time in the classroom for that practice for students who have not experienced it in the home, or who are not highly metacognitive students, we privilege the already empowered at the expense of underachieving students.

Mechanical Fluency Practice as a Bridge to Conceptual Fluency

There must be an explicit connection made between skills practice and real meaning, and the various permutations of a given number set must also be a part of fluency practice.

Mediated learning theory helps us see that even number fluency practice must be *infused with meaning* and have *transcendence*. Just learning a set of simple algorithms by rote is not enough, and it may even be counterproductive.

For example, if students are learning that $3 \times 4 = 12$, they should be *explicitly* learning over time that it means all of the following:

- 3 groups of 4 things or people equals 12 things or people total

- 3 things or people in a (per) group and 4 groups make 12 things or people total

- 3 added 4 times equals 12 (things or people) total

- 3 things that cost $4 each total $12

- 3 jumps of 4 on a hundreds chart lands on 12

- going 3 (miles per hour) for 4 (hours) equals 12 (miles)

- a rectangle 3 (inches) by 4 (inches) has an area of 12 square (inches)

Learning number facts with its accompanying concept language scaffolds the eventual application of facts to word problems. Infusing mechanical fluency practice with meaning like this is an essential component of mediation (see Chapter 3). Students should also *simultaneously* be learning that the places of the 3 and 4 do not matter, in that $3 \times 4 = 12 = 4 \times 3$. I have my students learn fact families as triangular relationships, in that if they have two of the numbers, they automatically know what the third will be. In the context of multiplication, students must understand the *consistent connection* of 3, 4, and 12, grounded in real-world meaning. (The accompanying CALP language in the previous list could be adjusted; for example, *equals* could be changed to *makes* as needed. But the real-world language that goes with the math concept must be practiced as well; also see Math Problem Vocabulary on page 182).

When CLD students are held accountable for those various *real-life* meanings of multiplicative relationships, then their concept understanding is being built simultaneously upon the concrete, in which they can become grounded and about which they know they are right. They should become able to quickly construct a meaningful word problem about any algorithm, which is worth its own structured practice.

When students practice multiplication facts for something like a two-minute drill, they should be practicing these various forms over time as opposed to just doing standard algorithms faster and faster:

$3 \times 4 = 12$	$12 \div 4 = ?$
$4 \times 3 = 12$	$12 \div \square = 3$
$4 \times 3 = ?$	$12 \div \square = 4$
$3 \times 4 = ?$	3, 4, 12 (i.e., the fact family)
$\square \times 3 = 12$	3, 4, _____
$\square \times 4 = 12$	_____, 4, 12
$3 \times \square = 12$	_____, 3, 12
$4 \times \square = 12$	$1/3 = 4/12$
$12 \div 3 = ?$	$1/3 = x/12$ (solve for x)

And so on.

This way, students are practicing fluency with all the ways the fact family 3, 4, and 12 are related in multiplication and division, *and* in the various forms they will come across it in the math curriculum. It is also a concrete way for students to base an understanding of the interrelationship between multiplication and division, because they use the same numbers. Plus, think about this: Students are unlikely to ever see just $3 \times 4 = \underline{\hspace{1cm}}$ as a problem to solve unless on a multiplication practice worksheet. So why have them practice it that way?

CLD students should *always* be developing number fluency skills to maximize space in working memory for developing concept understanding or solving a word problem so that they don't engage in an extended or random search for answers—especially given all the other possible intrinsic and extrinsic distractors that may still be present. Our intentionality and the student's reciprocity need to match exactly there.

The previous practice might look quite challenging for midgrade elementary school students, but it's quite possible to learn it well with time and effort, phasing in different forms over time. (And, as with Juan, some students need practice in *how* to study to commit things like math facts to memory.) Integrating all three types of math fluency is the best way to help CLD students in math. It's like a solid tripod in that all three legs should be the same length and strength.

Fluency with fact family relationships gives addition/subtraction and multiplication/division concepts meat on the bones. Students can then generate their own examples to check understanding and, more important, can understand *how and why* a concept works. Figure 6–1 illustrates the dynamic between math skills and schemata.

Meaning is being mediated when facts are practiced as a scaffold for developing conceptual fluency or are tied directly to solving problems. Inclusive practice with numbers deeply informs math concept learning.

We need to teach math in a way that balances number skills and conceptual understanding (and, of course, language, which is explored in more depth later in the chapter) because, in the end, that affords CLD students the best chance of acquiring the skills they need to further their education and get by the various gatekeeping mechanisms they will face in education and the society at large.

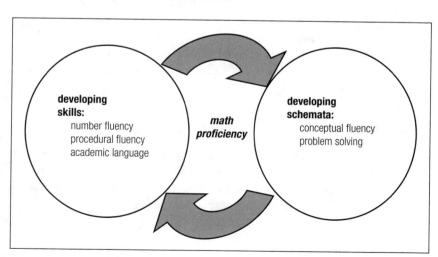

FIGURE 6–1. *Math Proficiency Chart*

Learning Must Be Grounded

I return to the reality that in most people's life experience, accurate calculation is the most important element of math. If we are adhering to the principle that *learning must be grounded*, then this is a key point. Students who primarily relate to math vis-à-vis calculation accuracy—because that's how they understand math in their real-life experience—may find themselves in a classroom where the teacher says that the answer doesn't matter as much as the thinking they do to get to the answer or where a right answer gets buried under a discussion of all the possible ways to *arrive* at that answer. Think of how painful this process must be for students who are reflective learners (see Chapter 1). In other words, how can I comfortably participate in a conversation with half-formed ideas or possibly mistaken ideas when I believe I will lose face that way? Such situations unintentionally privilege highly metacognitive, impulsive, dominant-culture students whose learning is firmly grounded in the classroom nearly all the time, who do not mind throwing out ideas even before they are fully formed or even wrong, and who have *already mastered at least one way to solve the problem*. Because they already know how the problem works, they have the luxury to compare the new way with the old.

> *Students who still need structured practice to get grounded in at least one way lose their practice time to a discussion of multiple ways that is beyond them.*

> *As Chapters 1–3 demonstrated, it's often the assumptions about learning, thinking, language, and culture that we make along the way that disempower CLD students. In math, it is no different.*

One of my students once blurted out to me in exasperation, "I wish she [the classroom teacher] would just teach me *one* way so I can learn to do it right!" CLD students know that in the end, they will be assessed by their right and wrong answers, if not by this teacher, then by the next, and certainly on standardized tests. CLD students' learning must be grounded in their own very valid reality and experience and build up from there. Then exploring how there could be more than one answer, or more than one way to arrive at an answer, is meaning-full.

Early Math

If a child comes to school unpracticed with numbers, she needs to be systematically helped to develop a foundational number sense as well as the language skills needed to support its use. The following are overlapping stages in developing number fluency and their connection to language:

- reciting the numbers one through ten[3]

- one-to-one correspondence for the numbers one through ten

- recognizing isolated numbers between one and ten quickly

- reciting numbers larger than ten

- reciting numbers backward from ten to one

- recognizing isolated numbers between ten and twenty quickly

- recognizing and producing patterns (visual, then numeric)[4]

- *quickly* saying the next number after a stated number from one to ten (e.g., "What is the next number *after* five?")

- counting on from a given number to ten

- quickly saying the next number before a stated number from one to ten (e.g., "What is the number *before* seven?")

- counting backward to one from a given number between two and ten

- basic addition facts with the numbers one through ten[5]

- quickly saying the next number after a stated number larger than ten

- counting on from a given number larger than ten

- counting backward from a given number larger than ten

- counting by twos

- counting by fives

- counting by tens

- unitizing (e.g., the grouping of five ones into a group of five, and being able to conceptualize and manipulate it as five instead of five separate ones; and obviously, ten becomes a very important, almost essential, unitizing concept)

Of course, many of these activities are standard practice in an early-elementary math curriculum. However, some students need practice with *all* of them, and the *amount* of practice needed and the *time line* for establishing fluency in each may well differ. In addition, language-based practice with *before* and *after* (or *next*, etc.) might not be a typical need of dominant-culture native English speakers. As concepts such as unitizing begin to take on multiple steps, narrative (see Chapters 2 and 4) comes into play, and students need to have the appropriate language skills and transition words in their independent repertoire to *apply* the concept. This is also true of organizational speech.

If a student seems very weak early on in the math curriculum, finding out his home community experiences with numbers and mathematical ideas can be very revealing and helpful, and can enable a teacher to build on that child's strengths. However, students also need to develop fluency with each of those various foundational elements of number sense to function independently in a school's formal math curriculum.

There are many fun ways to achieve the listed number and language skills, including games and songs. But intentionality and reciprocity must be focused appropriately for maximal learning to occur. In addition, if a child is pulled through these basic stages of number sense and number-related language skills faster than the pace of her own independent fluency development, or one or another of these number sense or language stages are skipped or remain spotty, the student will eventually struggle mathematically. A child without a practiced formal number sense upon entry into school needs to develop fluency with all of these skills and schemata, or it may end up looking like she has a special need down the road.

Math and Language

A *huge* problem for many CLD students is that language has taken on an increasingly greater role in contemporary math pedagogy. The language involved in explorations of concept learning is particularly CALP laden. A much greater emphasis is also put on communicating one's reasoning these days, and this privileges standard dialect, formal register, vocabulary-specific, academic English (along with well-developed logical thinking skills). We need to recognize and address the various ways language affects math learning and instruction for CLD students.

Creating math problems out of children's own stories helps them more easily develop conceptual fluency.

One excellent way to minimize the impact of language is to construct math problems and math contexts that are grounded in CLD students' real-life experiences. When math teaching and problem solving are approached in this way, CLD students' problem-solving skills increase (Lo Cicero, Fuson, and Allexsaht-Snider 1999). It both empowers students and allows us to see the extent of their math skills more clearly.

However, CLD students will still come face-to-face with preconstructed problems, especially on standardized tests, and we still use language to teach. So language may likely still be a big barrier to underachieving CLD student performance.

Talking About Math

I hope it goes without saying that when CLD students are talking about their learning, it is not the time to be correcting grammar or pronunciation. We also have to consider whether our classroom's discourse community norms will affect the degree to which CLD students want to, or are willing to, participate. Just having heterogeneous groups or allowing for all-class discussions about math thinking is not enough, as was discussed in Chapter 1. It is important to consciously create safe sociocultural spaces for dialogue and, at the same time, be careful to discriminate between a student's possible lack of full language control and her concept understanding.

It is very important for underachieving CLD students to have sufficient opportunity to talk about their math learning, both the result of their thinking as well as the process of their thinking.

Underachieving CLD students' performance may improve if they have an opportunity to talk out their thinking before they begin solving a problem or before they have to write how they solved it. This allows reciprocity and intentionality to be focused on the students' organizational speech. I have students who need practice with school-matched organizational speech coconstruct an appropriate script with me about some problem or concept learning, which I write up on the board. The students initially read verbatim what they need to think about and/or do to successfully engage with that task or concept the next time they face it. Then little by little, I erase a couple of words at a time, requiring the students to still provide the entire script before they do a new example, practice, or problem. They do not have to produce the script verbatim, but they must be linguistically accurate and include any important tier 3 vocabulary for that task or concept. Eventually, all the words are gone from the board, but the students are left with the script as independent internal speech, or at least it will not take much to activate it (Chapter 3).

Rubrics and models for problem solving and communicating one's thinking also provide clarity and support an elevated performance of all students. However, an *additional* talk-it-out time can enable things to fall into place better for CLD students, even with a model or rubric to refer to.

Vocabulary

Math concepts, instruction, and problems have their own vocabulary. Just as a limited tier 2 vocabulary base is a big obstacle to a CLD student's progress in reading, limited tier 2 and 3 vocabularies are big obstacles to progress in math.

Math Problem Vocabulary

I want to address the issue of the key words (i.e., CALP words) in math problems first. Key words, such as *altogether*, signal particular math operations. For example, *John has 2 cookies. Mary gives him 2 more. How many does he have altogether?* If you know the connection between *altogether* and addition, you know how to solve the problem. However, some recent thinking in math devalues a focus on key words (e.g., as in Investigations, a math series based on constructivist principles that emphasizes concept development and exploration). The argument against key words is twofold. First, they are misleading because they can be used in many ways. For example, *John has 4 cookies altogether. He gives 2 to Mary. Now how many does he have?* Using a mechanical application of the key word rule, a student might add instead of subtract. Second, not all problems have key words in them, so students really do need to ground their understanding in how the numbers interact in a problem first; a fixation with key words may even block a student from seeing the mathematical structure of a problem.

Although there is a grain of truth in these two arguments against key words, for the most part they are misleading. The reality is that a skillful understanding of key words is a *boon* to underachieving CLD math learners! Without getting anchored in language, understanding how numbers interact in a problem is very hard.

First of all, many key words have just *two* basic functions, not many:

> *By integrating language into structurally understanding math problems in this way, we increase comprehension.*

- They signal one type of reasoning when they are in the body of the *problem* (i.e., the part of the problem where the numbers and context are introduced).

- They signal the *opposite* kind of reasoning when they are in the *question* (i.e., the question students need to answer about the problem).

Again, take the word *altogether*: When it appears in the body of the problem, it sets up the following thinking in the reader's mind: "We are starting with the greatest amount." The logical conclusion is that we will be taking away from it (of course, some young children may find *counting on* an easier operation than subtraction when they actually solve the problem, but that does not change the fact that their answer will be a smaller number than that introduced in the problem). Conversely, when it is in the question, the word signals additive reasoning, "We are moving toward the greatest amount."

An extremely important key word in multiplication (or repeated addition) and division is *each*. *Each* in the body of a problem signals multiplicative reasoning,[6] while in the question, it signals divisive reasoning with the numbers it

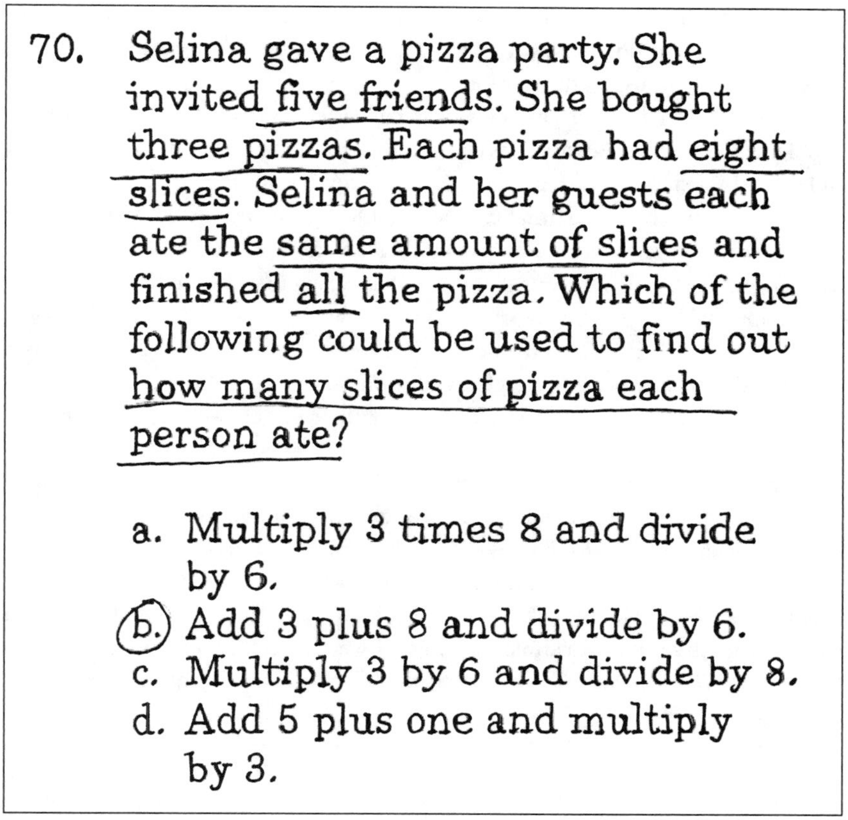

> 70. Selina gave a pizza party. She invited <u>five friends</u>. She bought <u>three pizzas</u>. Each pizza had <u>eight slices</u>. Selina and her guests <u>each</u> ate the <u>same amount of slices</u> and finished <u>all</u> the pizza. Which of the following could be used to find out <u>how many slices of pizza each person ate?</u>
>
> a. Multiply 3 times 8 and divide by 6.
> ⓑ. Add 3 plus 8 and divide by 6.
> c. Multiply 3 by 6 and divide by 8.
> d. Add 5 plus one and multiply by 3.

FIGURE 6–2. *Student Edits of Math Problem*

is linked to. The item in Figure 6–2 is from a page of four problems in a fifth-grade standardized test practice book. A classroom teacher had asked me to work with a student because his classroom math performance was shaky. I first wanted to get a sense of his language awareness, so I asked him to underline the important words in the problems and then solve them. I asked him to go through the problems at the speed he would do it on the real test. Figure 6–2 shows what he did.

As you can see, the student ignored the word *each* in the phrase *each pizza*. Note that it connects the three with the eight in the body of the problem, which means we should multiply 3×8. Then *each* reappears in the question, which signals division. Only the first answer satisfies the condition of multiplying 3×8 first, then dividing

> Key words are like linguistic beacons that help illuminate the appropriate cognitive paths students should take in problem solving. It is a very important amplifier.

later. In fact, *each* was present in every problem on that page, and he did not underline it in any problem—and he got *all* the problems wrong! He did not see how language connected the numbers.

In my experience, certain key words have very consistent meanings for the problems elementary-age students come across. We actually can map out an array of key CALP words in math problems and the operations they signal. Figure 6–3 is the beginnings of a chart that can be organically coconstructed with students as key words arise in problems, depending on the grade and the math being learned (where blank, it means that it is not as clear-cut as it is in the other cases, or not applicable).

And what if students come across an exception to something on the chart or a word that has been highlighted in some other way? Wonderful! What a great opportunity to explore why, deepening their understanding of the role of math vocabulary in the process. That's the essence of good learning!

The problem in Figure 6–4 was initially a stumbling block for a second-grade CLD student, "Samoeuth." She brought the problem from her classroom to the excellent math resource teacher with whom she worked.

On her first try, Samoeuth had drawn just ten trees in answer to the first question, so her answer to the second was "5." The math teacher determined that Samoeuth's initial vocabulary problems were threefold. First, she had to be told what *orchard* meant. Then *kind* needed some clarification. Samoeuth's in-

Word	In Body of Problem	In Problem Question
altogether	subtractive (e.g., the answer will be a smaller number)	additive
difference		subtractive
more/less, -er than	often additive, but not always	subtractive
each	additive (repeated) or multiplicative	subtractive (repeated) or divisive
every	additive (repeated) or multiplicative	subtractive (repeated) or divisive
left		subtractive

FIGURE 6–3. *Key Words Chart*

stinct was to grab onto the most obvious BICS meaning of *kind*, in the sense of a personal attribute (e.g., a kind person). Until that was straightened out, the problem was gobbledygook to her. Finally, because the math instructor was very sensitized to CLD student-related language issues, she sensed that *each* was the main problem. So she turned the instructional focus onto that word.

Indeed, it turned out that Samoeuth did not understand that *each* really meant "one by one" or, in this problem, "kind by kind." *Each* signals a need for using multiplicative reasoning (or in this case with a second grader, repeated addition), before the main operation that answers the question—subtraction.

FIGURE 6–4. *Samoeuth's Work with Fruit Problem*

Once that was clarified, the student used manipulatives to count out ten of each type of tree, did the math correctly, and transferred that to her solution paper, as shown in Figure 6–4.[7] In fact, Samoeuth knew what to do conceptually for the main problem-solving operation! She had the number fluency and the procedural fluency to subtract accurately. The stumbling block was the CALP language in the problem.

Other math words that can be confusing, especially to younger CLD students, are the sometimes subtle semantic differences between *some*, *several*, *a few*, *few*, *a little*, *many*, *much*, and *a lot*. In addition, the comparative form of adjectives (*-er* [*than*], *more* [*than*]) is an important grammatical signal that often shows up in math problems, and ESL students may not realize, or have a clear idea about, what it means.

Instructional Vocabulary

The language we use to convey and explain math concepts might itself be an obstacle to CLD students' comprehension. We have to learn to simplify our instructional language, highlighting our lesson goal while at the same time consciously highlighting and integrating valuable CALP vocabulary (usually verbs). In Chapter 3, an example from a math text showed how the word *find* in the context of an open-ended math activity might be misleading for CLD students. *Find* in a BICS meaning implies that a person *already knows* what he's looking for; for example, "I *found* my glasses on the table." In contrast, *find* in a

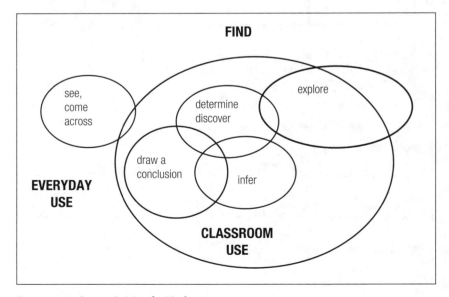

FIGURE 6–5. *Semantic Map for* Find

CALP sense means "discover," which implies that the student has to first draw conclusions about what he's looking for and then look for it. The CALP *find* requires high metacognitive ability and appropriate organizational speech. Figure 6–5 is an example of a semantic map using the word *find*.

Not *explicitly highlighting language hinders CLD students' progress in math.*

Focusing student attention on CALP instructional words as they arise, and having some way to graphically differentiate between their meanings, is an important element of successful math instruction for CLD students.

Language Goals and Math

We need to clarify important math content vocabulary and instructional vocabulary as needed in every math lesson. Setting a clear content goal to book-end a lesson (see Chapter 3) puts the lesson in sharper focus for students. Also, setting language goals *forces* us and the students to deal explicitly with language. Math content and language goals become the schemata and skills students will need to become experts, and on which they must have their intentionality and reciprocity brought to bear during the lesson. In math it is particularly important to have both content and language goals for CLD students.

The following is a list of general categories to mine in setting language goals in math. They exist in the math language of every grade (though the specific language of early math programs will obviously be much simpler than many of my examples here).

- academic vocabulary specific to subject (geometry terms, *factor*, *multiple*, etc.)

- academic vocabulary needed to do subject (often CALPS synonyms for common words, e.g., *show* = *illustrate*, *demonstrate*, *indicate*, *exhibit*, *explain*, *describe*, *diagram*, etc.)

- general tier 3 academic (CALP) vocabulary needed to learn math (*equivalent*, *operation*, *balance*, etc.)

- instructional vocabulary (usually CALP verbs)

- procedural vocabulary (*first*, *then*, *next*, etc.)

- hypothetical or logical thinking vocabulary (*if*, *therefore*, *further*, etc.)

- key word vocabulary

As noted previously with unitizing, facility with cohesive ties (e.g., *first*, *next*, *therefore*) is a function of narrative skill (see Chapters 2 and 4). Students with an undeveloped personal narrative may struggle in math problems that require logical reasoning and hypothetical thinking, which go along with a higher level of narrative development, or even in simpler problems that are organized sequentially if the students' narrative development is not even to that level.

Math Grammar

A deep understanding of math language must combine with a deep understanding of math concept schemata for a student to become expert at solving problems. This leads to the story grammar element of math problems. Aside from the many issues of vocabulary that naturally surface, the structure of math problems does not always parallel the logic of BICS communication. It can be very abstract, which is especially challenging for CLD students, or a problem may start very abruptly. By making the typical structure of word problems explicit, and making that a teaching goal, we can help clarify this important element of math.

In my experience, elementary school word problems typically set up the simple structure shown in Figure 6–6.

If the first decision is made correctly, then the rest of the problem falls into place, especially if supported by key words. I have used a photo or illustration of elevator buttons to remind students to make this determination early on in solving a problem (see Figure 6–7). The kids have to say, "Going up!" (meaning addition or multiplication) or "Going down!" (meaning subtraction or division) as if they were elevator operators.

However one wishes to focus student intentionality and reciprocity on this element of word problems, some students need separate practice with it. It can be a race through a number of problems to see how quickly students can decide what operation to use *and then justify their decisions,* or some visual reminder—but not *solving* the problem. However it is done, we need to

---

Near the start of the problem is one or more sentence(s) that introduce the context and the first number(s). The combination of context, language, and numbers very often signals one of two things:

- *the total*, so the problem is to find a part (subtraction or division); or
- *a part*, so the problem is to find the total (addition or multiplication)

Figure 6–6. *Structure of Elementary School Word Problems*

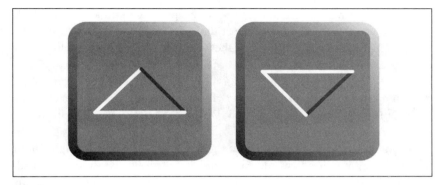

Figure 6–7. *Elevator Buttons*

take aim at just one number and the way it enters a problem allows us to have intentionality and reciprocity at the right point, frees up space in working memory to focus on the instructional goal (e.g., not having to worry about getting the answer), and enables students to develop this schema to apply in future problems.

One problematic issue of structure is that many math problems start with *if*. In real-world BICS communication, some shared circumstance, knowledge, or experience is most often already established between speaker and listener or writer and reader before a condition with *if* can be introduced; e.g., *If it rains, we can't go outside for recess* (in this case, recess is a given unless it rains). Most intermediate ESL students, not to mention English-dominant CLD students, know *if* in this usage. However, math word problems starting off with an *ungrounded condition* can be distracting. The following is pretty typical of a simple early-elementary math problem: *If Mary has 7 apples and she buys 5 more, how many apples does she have?* Many ESL students have a lot of difficulty with problems like this. There is no shared context—we don't know who Mary is or whether she has any apples to start with. Actually, in the BICS sense, "If Mary has 7 apples" implies she *doesn't* have seven to start with if you are familiar only with the most basic usage of *if*!

I might recast this problem for my students this way, by stating the circumstance or context: *Mary has 7 cupcakes. But she needs more to share for a class snack. So she buys 5 more. Now how many cupcakes does she have?* This version will be easier to understand and therefore solve.

Another important issue related to problem structure is realizing what the most significant words and numbers are in a problem. If a student gives all words equal import, it is very hard to get a handle on a problem. Highlighting important numbers and words (by underlining) to foreground them from the rest of the text should be standard procedure for CLD students when problem solving. However, as I noted in the previous chapter, some students find it hard to limit themselves to highlighting just the most important words. I often see students highlighting many if not *all* the words of a problem! If you look back at the problem illustrating the word *each* (Figure 6–2), the student had under-lined the distractive number *five* as an important number. Luckily for him, it did not appear in a reasonable answer choice, or he might well have chosen a wrong answer for that reason as well. Distractive numbers often trip weaker math learners up.

Consistently insisting throughout the year that CLD students highlight or underline any important words and numbers in problems—both the words that go with numbers in the problem and key words—is essential to helping them gain facility with these different structural elements of math problems. This holds true not only for their everyday work but especially for standardized tests when no teacher can remind them to do it.[8] It's like developing a certain procedural fluency for attacking word problems. It's not enough just to expose students to an issue and practice a bit; we must insist that the new skill be mas-tered and used independently every time. Only then can we be sure that our students will be likely to use that skill on their own.

Math Activities

Math activities centered in exploring math concepts are considered highly val-ued ways of helping children construct their own math understanding, but they can be particularly problematic for many CLD students. Such activities are an example of how particular cultural values are enacted through pedagogy. The linguistic and cognitive amplifiers required for open-ended problems are not similarly developed in children in all communities.

First, there is the organizational speech students need to orient themselves to the task. If students are not practiced in tasks in which they help set or even independently set the parameters and boundaries of learning, then they will not have developed the subvocalized speech needed for deciding what steps to take or even how to start. Then there is the cluster of independent thinking skills students need to perform this type of task. In an open-ended or ex-ploratory activity, students need to actively monitor their thinking (metacogni-tion); spontaneously compare the new experience with what they know; hypothesize; be able to go from whole to part as well as part to whole as thinkers, depending on the situation; be flexible; be organized; and be able to think logically. They need to have strong executive functioning ability. They cannot be satisfied with a quick, first answer. They also need to know the lan-guage of the problem. Finally, during the activity, a student must have the num-ber fluency and procedural fluency necessary to confirm and then enact what she envisions conceptually, without these acting as distractions or taking up working memory space. Wow—that's a lot of skills and schemata that have little, if anything, to do with *math* per se! Isn't it obvious how success in many contemporary math curricula is predicated on facility with literacy-oriented language and thinking skills and schemata? And how that disadvantages non-literacy-oriented students from the get-go, especially if no time is spent helping students explicitly develop those *quality* learning skills?

Think back to those Brazilian village mothers in Chapter 2 who explicitly directed their children's every move in the puzzle-making activity. How would a child from that learning environment do when plunked down in front of an exploratory math task? For an underachieving CLD student to participate successfully in an exploratory activity or work out an open-ended problem, any or many of those cultural, linguistic, and conceptual schemata and skills may need to be scaffolded as the student does the task. Further, the student's intentionality and reciprocity need to be brought to bear on whatever aspect of the process we want them to learn more about, and then we have to have practice opportunities for that particular schema or skill if the student is to further the process of internalizing it.

HOW BASIC ASSUMPTIONS WE HOLD DISADVANTAGE STUDENTS

In contemporary math pedagogy, understanding math concepts and processes has been conceived of by many as working in a certain way, designing the learning environment in a certain way, which resonates strongly with other contemporary pedagogies: whole language, process writing, inquiry-based learning, constructivism, and others. However, as Lisa Delpit noted so eloquently in *Other People's Children* (1995), contemporary pedagogy has most benefited the already most privileged because it echoes dominant-culture beliefs and values (see also Bailey and Pransky 2005). Remember that when the dominant culture is privileged in a classroom, others are disempowered by definition unless they have been explicitly initiated into the dominant discourse community norms of learning, thinking, and language.

Think of it this way: There may not be a more rigidly controlled, old-fashioned system of education in the world today than the British system in its onetime colonial possessions, yet India produces some of the greatest mathematical thinkers in the world! How could that be if only certain types of learning practices allowed for deep conceptual understanding? Children are not expected to think in sophisticated ways like miniature adults in all cultures. They are given time to grow and develop their metacognitive skills and expand their repertoire of thinking skills, and the expectation is that they will end up being just fine as adult thinkers. And it never fails—they do! Many CLD students in our schools are brought up in home communities that still are predicated on more traditional children's roles. The assumptions we hold are like blinders that prevent us from seeing how to be successful when working with them.

Our students bring different ways of learning, using language, and problem solving to our classrooms, along with different experience with numbers. We need to honor this reality in our classrooms, even as we try to help all students develop school-matched ways of thinking, using language, and problem solving.

Cognitive Load Addendum

Cognitive load theory was not developed with CLD students and cultural or linguistic issues in mind. It was conceived as a way to maximize students' working memory through the way problems and instructional materials are designed. From this perspective also, cognitive load theory can help us with underachieving math learners.

Cognitive load can become heavy in two ways. First, it may overload memory *extrinsically* (outside the context of the concept or information being learned). Poorly designed materials may increase the load by adding distractors or creating confusion where it might not otherwise occur. For example, a complex diagram with a key that is not very close to it increases the load by forcing attention to jump back and forth between two places, or else the load may increase if the key is itself not clear, or if information in the key replicates information already stated in the diagram. The load will be increased if, for example, the directions are just as complex as the math itself, or if a supporting visual is far away from the text it supports. There can be many ways in which our attention becomes distracted, overloaded, diffused, or confused by the way materials have been constructed.

The heavier the intrinsic load in a concept, the more the extrinsic load needs to diminish, or working memory will quickly become overwhelmed.

There also can be an *intrinsically* heavy cognitive load. That means a heavy cognitive load within the concepts themselves. Very abstract or complex concepts carry a heavy load for many students. Trigonometry and physics were subjects that had a very heavy intrinsic load for me! When grappling with intrinsically heavy concepts, our working memories should not be further burdened by poor materials design.

Cognitive load theory has some very thought-provoking ways of minimizing extrinsic load within materials design. One that resonates with me concerning conceptual schema building in math is *closing off a problem*. If we are focusing on schema *building*, we can eliminate a lot of the load that goes into a search for answers (which if random, can occupy the entire working memory) *by simply giving students the answer*. Think of the different way attention is channeled by these two problems:

- 7 times 3 is 21. Show how this works.

• What is 7 times 3? Show how you got your answer.

In the first problem, the student's attention is focused only on *how* 7 × 3 is 21. The student is *immediately and directly* working with the idea of *equal-sized groups* as a key to understanding multiplication. His intentionality and reciprocity are at the right place. In the second problem, the student's attention may get diffused between an answer search and schema building. It's a subtle yet important difference: if that has been the case, even a right answer would not be proof of schema building. If a student does not know that 7 × 3 = 21 *before* doing the activity or does not already have a conceptual understanding of multiplication, all the student's attention—or at least most of it—might be diverted from the real goal, which is developing a schema of equal groups as a key concept in multiplication, to an answer search.

The second problem would be a good assessment of how students have developed a schema of equal groups in multiplication but a less skillful way of enabling students to build that schema. Closing off problems also enables the content goal for a lesson to be quite explicit and easily communicable—for example, "Today you will learn how multiplication means counting equal-sized groups (of things or people)."

Another way to use the concept of cognitive load to think about teaching math is exemplified in using grid multiplication.[9] For example, let's assume I need to multiply 23 × 46. In case you are unfamiliar with this way of multiplying, Figure 6–8 shows how it would look with a grid.

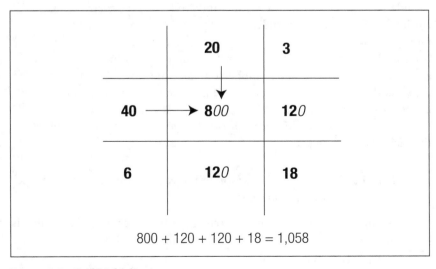

Figure 6–8. *Grid Multiplication*

As you can see, the numbers in the original algorithm need to be broken into their respective *place values* and placed on the grid. Arrows have been added to the grid to illustrate the following:

1. Do the simple math fact; for example, $4 \times 2 = 8$.

2. Add zeros on; for example, 8 becomes 800 (one zero from the 40 and one from the 20).

3. Repeat that process in each grid box.

4. Add the results of all the boxes up.

Once students know their simple multiplication facts and are taught that multiplying with zeros means just adding the zeros together and tacking them onto the product, they can quickly multiply larger numbers with a grid. In my experience, many students are more accurate and efficient multiplying this way. Also, the procedural fluency needed for it is less complex than in the standard two-digit multiplication algorithm. Finally, it has the benefit of reinforcing the concept of place value, which becomes an increasingly important concept as children do more advanced math.

Even if students do not initially understand what is happening with the zeros *conceptually*, the procedural and mechanical fluencies needed to do this multiplication are pretty easy. When students are well grounded with accurate mechanical and procedural fluency such as in a grid, they learn to appreciate how place value interacts with numbers in multiplication through cumulative practice, with their intentionality and reciprocity focused accordingly. I insist that my students use the grid form as soon as we begin to multiply two or more digits. I teach the standard algorithm *after* they are comfortable using this method. Then they can choose which to use. (Open-array multiplication becomes cumbersome beyond three digits, but by then students should already be comfortable and accurate using the standard algorithm anyway.)

Put in terms of cognitive load theory, the open-array form of multiplication does the following:

• It avoids the common distraction of lining up numbers incorrectly in a two-digit multiplication algorithm.

• It simultaneously develops and reinforces the schema of place value in long-term memory (though intentionality and reciprocity must be brought to bear at some point).

- The distraction of an answer search is minimized because each step is relatively easy:
  1. using simple math facts
  2. adding on zeros
  3. adding for the answer

Thinking about math learning and instruction via cognitive load theory has been very helpful to both me and my students.

Summary

As the NAEP and TIMSS results indicate, in spite of all the thinking about improving math instruction, we have not been as successful teaching the students who have always struggled the most in our classrooms, many of whom are CLD students, as we have been teaching school-matched students. It's not a particular pedagogy or methodology that will change this dynamic, nor how math teaching is enacted anywhere else in the world, but rather a better understanding of our students and ourselves, our students' and our own languages, how memory systems work in learning, the learning dynamics of our classrooms, and our own particular math curriculum. Keeping learning models firmly in mind, successful math instruction for CLD students should include the following:

- knowing there are three kinds of fluency and that students need to develop automaticity with the mechanical fluencies of facts and procedures, with conceptual fluency as the ultimate goal

- sufficient structured problem-solving practice (with a focus on thinking skills)

- teaching our instructional language and using it carefully

- scaffolding exploratory activities or open-ended problems as needed

- not assigning more value to certain types of math activity over others

- helping students learn how to profit from culturally unfamiliar math activities

- helping students develop school-matched quality-learning skills and schemata

- helping students develop appropriate organizational speech for all three fluencies

- setting clear content *and* language goals (and the latter across the spectrum of language use within the math curriculum)—language, language, language!

- grounding math concepts in real-world applications

- grounding math in the students' lives and experiences

- teaching key words and their value to understanding math problems

- teaching the story grammar of math problems

- grounding students' learning *in what they do best* whenever possible

- understanding cognitive load theory to minimize distractions

- understanding cognitive load theory to reduce the extrinsic load of materials and instruction

- ensuring that intentionality and reciprocity are always at the right place

- having an awareness that all students do not learn equally within *any* particular pedagogy

- knowing math better ourselves

- providing safe spaces for talking out students' math thinking

- *always* infusing instruction with meaning

- giving sufficient practice time

- combating disempowerment

This chapter is not meant to be the be-all and end-all about math instruction and learning. There are many elements of sound, creative math instruction that I did not touch on. My goal was to focus on how we conceptualize math and assume math instruction should be enacted through the lens of the sociocultural framework established in Chapters 1–3. It's not *what* we do, but *how* and *why* we do it, that we need to consider *first* when working with CLD students.

If we are trying to know more about ourselves and our CLD students from cultural and linguistic perspectives, and our students are working on becoming experts in math schemata and skills, language schemata and skills, and thinking schemata and skills, how can they go wrong, regardless of *how* they learn them?

Notes

1. The United States scored behind Singapore, Korea, Japan, Hong Kong, Netherlands, the Czech Republic, and Austria. See nces.ed.gov/pubs99/1999081.pdf. The TIMSS study does not break published results down by ethnicity, social class, or language groupings. Thus, it is quite possible that there are disparities in achievement between subgroups in these other countries, but because the percentages are small, we do not see an impact on overall scores.

2. Mel Levine (2002) specifically refers to math facts as an example of an essential automaticity that students *must* develop.

3. Connecting this practice to physical movement and ball games is very helpful for some students.

4. Of course, the roots of recognizing and using patterns stretches much further back in a child's life. Here I mean in a more explicit, extended way.

5. The Touch Math program combines visual and tactile learning channels with developing fact fluency and is extremely helpful for students who come to school unpracticed with numbers.

6. The one exception is the type of division problem where you need to find the number of groups (or packages, etc.) after being given the total, and the amount of things (or people) in each group. For example: Ms. Perez has 72 stickers and wants to give her kindergarten students 6 stickers each. If she has 13 students in her class, does she have enough stickers? Note this problem also introduces the largest number in the problem, implying that it will be a "take away" or division problem, and this fact trumps specific vocabulary words (also see the section "Math Grammar" in this chapter).

7. Note that her instinct was to grab onto the most obvious word in the problem (*cherry*, which was used twice) and create her answer around it. It appears that she also needed language goals concerning picking out important words in the question, how to use the question to help write an answer or explanation (understanding that the question asked about trees, so that word should be in her answer), and perhaps a sharp focus (with intentionality and reciprocity) on taking in and processing information clearly and carefully.

8. Periodically, I even give students a scoring rubric that awards six or seven points out of ten for highlighting important words and numbers in a problem, with just three or four points given for actually solving the problem. That both focuses attention on this issue as well as helps convey the message that it is important to use the strategy consistently.

9. This practice did not come out of cognitive load theory, but its value is easily seen when viewed through that lens.

Conclusion

ONE DELIGHTFUL aspect of my job is that the parents of my ESL students typically express traditional feelings of deep gratitude and respect for their children's teachers, feelings about teachers and the work we do that seem to be slowly seeping out of our culture. But as much as I enjoy being gushed over, when the parents of my literacy-oriented students thank me for helping their son or daughter, I deflect it.

After all, what can I take credit for? The parents, themselves, armed their children with just about all they would need to be successful in school. Sure, if they were non–English speakers, I helped early on when they were starting to acquire BICS skills. But even though I continued to work with them until they became English proficient, my taking credit for their academic success would be like taking credit for the delicious food at a banquet just because I brought some food to the table. I say to the parents, "If all my students were like your child, I'd be the most successful schoolteacher in the world."

The only credit I can take is for whatever contribution I make toward the academic success of my non-literacy-oriented CLD students. I'm sure many teachers would agree that most of their successful students would succeed without them, while other students succeed only because of them. This book has been an attempt to enable us be more successful with the students we take the most pride in teaching, to show us how we can become more empathetic and knowledgeable. It's hard to find a framework that helps us be consistent and keep our eyes on the prize, amid all the voices clamoring for our attention.

In brief, the following list summarizes some of the most important characteristics of empathetic and knowledgeable teachers of CLD students that were described within this framework.

- *We* actively *counteract the disempowerment dynamic.* Without doing this, we have no chance to be successful with underachieving CLD learners; it takes vigilance, understanding, and continual effort, but everything else hinges on it.

- *We build strong, positive relationships with students and their families.* Combating disempowerment is possible only if we build genuine, caring relationships with our students and their families.

- *We cultivate a reflective practice.* This need never ends as long as we are teachers because we never know everything, and linguistic and cultural assumptions constantly elbow their way into our consciousness as truth, unintentionally coloring what we do to the detriment of our CLD students.

- *We infuse content and teaching with a social justice perspective.* The reality is that for many reasons, many CLD students see this culture, society, and history through a very different lens than many of us from the dominant culture; we need to learn to teach multiple perspectives, and to think empathetically about what we do and what we teach through the lens of our students' eyes and experience.

- *We know ourselves, the school culture, and students from a sociocultural perspective, and we ground our teaching in that knowledge.* By definition, this becomes an imperative when we teach *culturally* and linguistically diverse students.

- *We make the tacit explicit in all areas of curriculum, language, and classroom culture.* As a part of our reflective practice, we have to deconstruct our assumptions about teaching and learning, so our classroom becomes a safe, comfortable, and productive sociocultural learning space for all students.

- *We look* first *for the cause of student difficulty in ourselves, our language, and the classroom culture or curriculum, not in students or their families.* We must always be on guard against falling into the trap of deficit thinking; yet as much as we may try to change the learning dynamics of our classrooms to help CLD students comfortably ground themselves in their preferred ways of learning, we also realize that successful, independent learning will not happen consistently until a student has mastered the learning dynamics and academic language of the formal learning, dominant-culture classroom (whether we think that's fair or not).

- *We ground learning in the students' background and experience when possible.* By doing this, we combat disempowerment and help students develop more academic skill.

- *We understand the impact of language on all areas of study and instruction.* By definition, this becomes an imperative when we teach culturally and *linguistically* diverse students.

- *We have a tier 2 vocabulary growth perspective.* Vocabulary instruction is a must for underachieving CLD students, in particular fostering the development of a larger tier 2 vocabulary; this should be thought of as an integral element of reading instruction.

- *We help CLD students understand the characteristics of formal register, standard dialect English.* The language of power is the language of school and has characteristics that not all speakers of English share; it must be a focus of study as well as the medium of study for CLD students who speak a different dialect and/or use a different register.

- *We help students develop school-matched organizational (planning) speech as needed.* School-matched organizational speech is essential to being able to independently and profitably interact with highly metacognitive, exploratory, and other school learning tasks.

- *We help students develop a school-matched personal narrative.* Some CLD students may have a different cultural narrative form, which needs to be understood and accommodated. Others may need to develop an age-appropriate personal narrative, which otherwise has a detrimental effect on text comprehension, writing, and thinking skills.

- *We have clear content and language objectives for lessons.* We need to articulate a clear (simply stated) learning goal as well as highlight those elements of language that will enable a student to comprehend or participate more successfully in our lesson.

- *We have opportunities for problem-solving practice every day as well as time for contextual language practice.* In combination with an understanding of how vocabulary, narrative, organizational speech, and the cultural nature of learning tasks impact CLD student learning, we should be having students apply new learning to solving problems.

- *We learn to sharply focus attention.* This means both our own *and* our students'; for underachieving CLD students, putting attention at the right spot is a key to better learning.

- *We infuse all learning interactions with meaning (for the learner).* Every learning interaction, and every element of the learning interaction, must be meaning-full to the learner.

- *We explicitly bridge new learning to old experience and future learning.* Many non-literacy-oriented CLD students do not spontaneously compare new learning with old or compose the appropriate organizational speech script to apply it to future learning.

- *We have students reflect on their* learning process *before, during, and after lessons.* Students must get a chance to systematically practice metacognitive reflection and develop metacognitively oriented organizational speech at least once a day.

- *We scaffold across as many domains as necessary.* Learning must be deep to stick, and for it to be deep enough, we may need to fill in some missing pieces of, or buttress, the learning environment or task or language.

- *We differentiate between* quantity *and* quality *learning.* We need to give *at least* equal time for *how*-we-learn instruction as well as what-we-learn instruction; all the areas we need to scaffold become part of the student's quality-learning curriculum; the quality curriculum targets crucial literacy-oriented amplifiers that students need, but do not all possess (*high vocabulary level, strong personal narrative, semantic memory, high metacognition, thinking skills that buttress independence in learning*).

- *We help students develop expertise in schemata and skills.* Only this enables us to become experts; through a quality-learning curriculum, students need to develop skill and schema expertise (building amplifiers) in the following:
  - the academic curriculum
  - classroom language
  - the classroom culture
  - classroom ways of thinking and problem solving

- *We give sufficient practice time.* On the way to learning, students need sufficient practice time with both the quantity curriculum and the quality curriculum.

- *We minimize intrinsic and extrinsic distractors (in as many domains as possible) in learning tasks.* Working memories are relatively small, and their capacity may get filled up quickly either with complex subject matter, or by distractions, confusions, or other space users in the language, task, or learning dynamics; one way to think about scaffolding is as a way to minimize distractors.

- *We realize that some students may come to school poorly mediated.* It is not a blame game, but it is crucial to understand that if students are poorly mediated for whatever reason, we have to systematically help them develop the underlying cognitive and linguistic skills on which successful independent learning is based.

Overall, the system is stacked against many CLD students. As empathetic and knowledgeable teachers, we need to be strong allies and advocates, both for our students for their families, and for ourselves as professionals. The system does not often value the home experiences, languages, or families of CLD students. As students of color, they are bound to bump into racist attitudes and institutional structures somewhere along the way, not to mention often being locked out of dominant-culture discourse communities. And most germane to the perspective in this book, many students are caught within the *quantity-quality* paradox in education: the more there is to learn, the more your preferred ways of learning and cognitive structures have to match school, but the more you need to develop those ways and structures because they don't match your own, the less time there is because of the amount that has to be learned. But if we give up this fight, we cease to be empathetic and knowledgeable teachers. We have to grab onto the quality-learning thread, start pulling, and not stop until we have no more time or the tangle comes undone.

Of course, the dynamics that perpetuate CLD student underachievement are all interconnected. Pull on one thread, and you tug on the others. Out of the various possible threads to pull, I have grabbed one I believe helps to directly unravel the underachievement tangle with patience and perseverance. To be successful teachers of underachieving CLD students, we must keep pulling, regardless of the time crunch, testing, and all the roadblocks our society, our government, and even our schools throw in our way. The goal of this book is to offer a road map for navigating through and around these roadblocks and to figure out the right roads for our students to travel on even as all the signs are pointing in just one direction.

Most of us believe that it is in a CLD student's long-term best interests to learn to negotiate the dominant-culture classroom at school, and develop independent levels of solid academic achievement, even as we also understand that objectively speaking, they and their home families are not missing or lacking anything. However, as empathetic and knowledgeable teachers, we also understand that this will not happen naturally, or just because we set up our classrooms in a particular way—according to some notion of best practices—or use the "best" techniques or program. All that guarantees *nothing* for our young CLD students! As empathetic and knowledgeable teachers, we know that the primary responsibility is on *us* to make our classrooms comfortable, empowering, and familiar places. We need to build on CLD students' experiences and cultural strengths as well as making the learning norms of the school comprehensible and the language and learning dynamics of the classroom accessible to CLD students. No program or methodology can do this for us.

We realize that it is not primarily on the students to adapt (at least initially), even if that means teaching in ways counter to what our professional training and cultural assumptions says is optimal or best. Our thinking and assumptions can disempower CLD students, no matter how sympathetic we may feel toward them or how fervently we believe in our pedagogy. It's so easy to get caught up in our field's best this and newest that and think it will *finally* solve our problems.

A story I once heard encapsulates the field of education as it swings from one best thing to the next, yet never fundamentally alters the overall achievement of CLD students:

> In Europe long ago, a Hasidic rabbi traveled around to small villages to teach. In one tiny village, there were three eager young students. The rabbi stayed to teach them for several days. Just before he left, he leaned forward and extended a finger heavenwards. "Life," he said, nodding sagely, "is like a barrel." And he left.
>
> The disciples were perplexed. Yet it seemed so deep! Life is like a barrel! What did that mean? That life was empty and had meaning only by how one filled it? Or was the emptiness itself the meaning? Or was it something else entirely? For many years, the three disciples devoted themselves to the struggle to understand the deep meaning of the barrel. They waited for the day that the rabbi would return and reveal the secret to his mysterious teaching.
>
> But one day, word came to the tiny village that the famous rabbi was ill and probably dying. The three disciples grew anxious. They needed to find the answer to their question! What if the rabbi died before they had a chance to speak to him again? So they quickly packed their meager belongings and went as fast as they could to Vilna. By the time they arrived at the rabbi's house, he was near death.
>
> The three disciples were admitted in, and they stood respectfully at the doorway. The old rabbi lifted his head and beckoned to them to come closer. They hurried to the bedside and kneeled down. "Oh Great Rabbi," they pleaded. "Help us! Years ago you came to our village. You gave us a mysterious and wonderful teaching that was too deep for us to fully understand. No matter how much we tried, we could not fathom your words. You said, 'Life is like a barrel.'"
>
> The rabbi thought for a second, then shrugged. "So maybe it's *not* like a barrel . . ."

We all fervently want *the answer*. In that pursuit, our field has run after many rabbis, year after year. And yet we always get the same answer: So maybe best practice for all students is *not* whole language, though it was initially touted that way. So maybe best practice for all students is *not* constructivism . . . or process writing . . . or exploratory learning . . . or whole language . . . or phonics . . . or a certain math program . . . or methodology . . . or philosophy, though they all were—and new ones continue to be—touted that way. Running after rabbis will never be the answer for underachieving CLD learners. Instead, like many things in life, the answers can be right in front of— and inside—us, if we are honest and take the time to look more carefully and in a different way.

As I have asserted several times, the road map laid out in this book is mostly not one of giving good answers about our CLD students. Things like culturegrams, technique menus, and other shortcuts are not the answer! Those rabbis are dead-end detours. Within cultures there are many discourse communities, and our students all bring unique life experiences with them to class. Without knowing your students, how can anyone answer your questions about them?

There is no shortcut to learning more deeply who our students not like us are.

Moreover, those shortcut rabbis blind us to *ourselves*, to *our own* use of language, to the characteristics of *our own* classroom learning environments, to how cultural beliefs and values shape *our* assumptions. As soon as we rely on abstract or stereotypical generalizations to tell us who our students are and how teach them, we have stopped the process of inquiry and reflection not only about our students but about ourselves as well. The process of disempowerment automatically begins *right there*. It's like a battery that is either charging or discharging—we either are aware of disempowerment and actively addressing it, or we are not aware, at which point disempowerment insinuates itself back into the learning environment, social interactions, and the curriculum.

The process of genuinely wishing to know more about our students—which means also needing to know more about ourselves, making the effort, and responding accordingly as educators and mentors—encapsulates what it means to be a successful teacher of CLD students.

The process of inquiry and reflection should not stop until all our students are successful. One teacher in one year cannot do it all. But while we each can do only what we can do, the positive impact we make as empathetic and knowledgeable educators cannot be undone. Ideally, the process is a collaborative, systematic, and shared endeavor among teachers that stretches over grades. The more teachers across grades who collaborate and cultivate a reflective practice around a shared understanding of how to look at students, language, and the learning process, and how to develop a quality-learning curriculum, the more likelihood there is that their school's underachieving CLD students will become successful, independent learners.

Only collaborative efforts can really begin to tackle institutional barriers (be they cultural, linguistic, class oriented, or racist) that exist in schools and communities. For institutional change, there has to be a genuine desire among teachers to dive into this endeavor and an administrator who supports teachers and makes sure there is enough water in the pool they're diving into. CLD students in schools where staff members both individually and collectively engage in a reflective process around these issues are fortunate, indeed!

But even lacking supportive, knowledgeable administrators or even other similarly engaged colleagues to tackle problems at the institutional level, you can still be an extremely effective teacher of the students who need you the most by developing a reflective practice based on the road map laid out in this book. As I said in the introduction, you just need to be sure you keep smelling the burning wood as you go.

Finally, I am reminded of a famous Zen saying: "First there is a mountain, then there isn't a mountain, then there is a mountain again." In the Zen sense, it means that there is the everyday reality of the moment—our attachment to the identities of things and ourselves, our likes and dislikes and fears—that we are all constantly caught up in. Then if one become enlightened, the distinctions between things and their separate identities vanish; one transcends apparent reality. And when one returns to regular consciousness to live in the world, one again sees the distinctions and identities of the world, but now sees them as transitory phenomena, and relates to them in a much healthier way. One's actions become much more proactive and positive.

Similarly, there are a great many wonderful techniques, ways of working, and insights that we all know and can learn about in the field of elementary education. We model our teaching after them, or have to use them whether we want to or not, or we look to them for answers. However, in order to rethink language, cognition, and the process of learning and teaching, we need to temporarily put *all* of those aside. Then when we return to thinking of *what* to do in our classrooms, armed with empathy, knowledge, and a reflective practice, we again have all those things to choose from, and lots more besides, but we will no longer relate to them in the same way. Rather than leading us, they become subservient to our new understanding of our students, ourselves, language, and the teaching-learning process. They become more powerful, positive tools in our hands.

You perform such a wonderful service to society and have such a powerful, transformative effect on children. May you become even more empathetic and knowledgeable teachers than you already are, for the sake of your neediest students!

Glossary

Affective filter—one's openness to language learning, based on one's motivation to belong to the new language community, or not belong

Amplifiers—the underlying language and cognitive skills developed by a literacy orientation, upon which academic success is predicated

BICS—basic interpersonal communication skills (communicative, everyday language)

Bottom-up—a cultural learning style where the student is more comfortable learning small pieces that synthesize into larger understandings as he matures over time.

CALP—cognitive academic language proficiency (academic language skills)

CLD—culturally and linguistically diverse

Cognitive load—a view of learning which states that learning is what happens in working memory toward the creation of skills and patterns of thinking that can be stored in long-term memory for future use

Comprehensible input—language input based in what a student knows, which is provided by regulating vocabulary level, pausing, and speed, and using rephrasing, visuals, etc.

Dialect—a variety of a language distinguishable by pronunciation and/or vocabulary and/or language structures

Discourse community—a group that shares ways of thinking, feeling, believing, and acting and is identified by language use

Disempowerment—not being a valued member of the classroom discourse community

Distractor—an unfamiliar or misunderstood element of a learning task that, instead of helping maximize working memory space and scaffolding deeper learning, takes up working memory space and makes learning more problematic; may also be worry, feelings of disempowerment, or misunderstanding

Dominant culture—in this country, typically thought of as predominantly white, Judeo-Christian, middle class/affluent and English-speaking, generally privileging the individual; I have added "literacy-oriented" to this description

EFL—English as a foreign language

ELL—English language learner

ESL—English as a second language

Field dependent (or, field sensitive)—a cultural learning style that favors learning tied more to a particular context, so in that sense is more concrete and less generalized; more comfort learning more cooperatively and less competitively

Field independent— a cultural learning style that is comfortable with more generalized, abstract learning that transcends a particular context; learning can be more individualistic, more competitive, and less cooperative

Impulsive—a cultural learning style where making errors or partially formed thoughts in public or vis-à-vis the teacher does not inhibit active learning

Intentionality and reciprocity—when the focus of the student's and teacher's attention matches and is very clear, and the learner has the opportunity to respond at that point

Interpretive literacy—literacy that requires the reader to make sense of text and apply his own personal thinking to it; a foundational aspect of western schooling

L_1—second language

Literacy oriented—being acculturated for success in a society based on literacy skills

Long-term memory—in cognitive load theory, the storehouse of a person's skills and schemata that can be applied to new learning contexts

Mediation—culturally grounded learning that helps the learner transcend the moment

Mediation of meaning—every aspect of a learning interaction is made meaningful

Metacognition—a person's awareness of her own thinking, both content and process

MLE—mediated learning experience; a specific learning interaction employing mediation

Organizational speech—the subvocalized speech that we use to orient to a task or problem and that we use to perform the task or solve the problem

Quality learning—a focus on how learning is processed internally in a school-matched way; also the preferred learning dynamics, thinking skills cluster, and language skills of classroom learning

Quantity learning—the school curriculum (e.g., reading, writing, math, science, etc.)

Reflective—a cultural learning style where mistakes and partially formed ideas are avoided

Register—language regulated relative to social context

Schema(-ata)—thinking that creates patterns out of data

School matched—ways of thinking, feeling, believing, acting, and using language that the dominant culture (i.e., school) prefers and expects

School success paradigm—academic success as an extension of dominant-culture expectations and norms

Semantic memory—the organization of the world based in language by attribute categories

Short-term memory—where sensory information first goes before being sent to working memory; tied to a student's attention and focus

Tier 2 vocabulary—sophisticated synonyms of basic vocabulary, typically not taught in academic curricula, but essential for academic success

Top-down—a cultural learning style where learners are comfortable grappling with big concepts and ideas, and in the process, learn many of the relevant details

Transcendence—a characteristic of mediation; learning is bridged to the past and the future

Working memory—where learning happens as the creation of skills and schemata that can be stored in long-term memory to be applied later to future learning

ZPD—zone of proximal development (learning slightly beyond the ability of someone to achieve without assistance or support)

Bibliography

ALUIN, H. S. 2005. "Critical Language Awareness in the United States: Revisiting Issues and Revising Progress in a Resegregated Society." *Educational Researcher* 34 (7): 24–31.

ASHER, J. 1979. *Learning Another Language Through Actions: The Complete Teacher's Guidebook.* Los Gatos, CA: Sky Oaks Productions.

AU, K. 1980. "Participation Structures in a Reading Lesson with Hawaiian Children: An Analysis of a Culturally Appropriate Instructional Event." *Anthropology and Education Quarterly* 11: 91–115.

BACKHURST, D., and S. SHANKER, eds. 2001. *Jerome Bruner: Language, Culture, Self.* Thousand Oaks, CA: Sage Publications.

BAILEY, F., and K. PRANSKY. 2003. "To Meet Your Students Where They Are, First You Have to Find Them: Working with Culturally and Linguistically Diverse At-Risk Students." *Reading Teacher.* 26 (4): 370–83.

———. 2005. "Are 'Other People's Children' Constructivist Learners, Too?" *Theory into Practice* 44 (1): 19–26.

BAZRON, B., D. OSHER, and S. FLEISCHMAN. 2005. "Creating Culturally Responsive Schools." *Educational Leadership* 63 (1): 83–84.

BECK, I., and M. MCKEOWN. 2005. Enhancing Young Children's Vocabulary Development. Presentation at the American Educational Research Association, Montreal, Canada.

BECK, I., M. MCKEOWN, and L. KUCAN. 2002. *Bringing Words to Life.* New York: Guilford.

BEN-HUR, M. 1994. *On Feuerstein's Instrumental Enrichment: A Collection.* Arlington Heights, IL: IRI/Skylight Training and Publishing Co.

———. 2001. *FIE as a Model for School Reform.* Paper presented at the "Unlocking Human Potential to Learn" Conference. Canada.

BEYKONT, Z. F., ed. 2002. *The Power of Culture: Teaching Across Language Difference*. Cambridge, MA: Harvard Education Publishing Group.

BIEMILLER, A., and C. BOOTE. 2005. Selecting Useful Word Meanings for Instruction in the Primary Grades. Presentation at the American Educational Research Association, Montreal, Canada.

BLOCK, C. C., L. L. ROGERS, and R. B. JOHNSON. 2004. *Comprehension Process Instruction*. New York: Guilford.

BOYKIN, A., and R. CUNNINGHAM. 2001. "The Effects of Movement Expressiveness in Story Context and Learning Context on the Analogical Reasoning of African-American Children." *Journal of Negro Education* 70 (1–2): 72–83.

BOYKIN, A., K. TYLER, K. WATKINS-LEWIS, and K. KIZZIE. 2006. "Culture in the Sanctioned Classroom Practices of Elementary School Teachers Serving Low-Income African-American Students." *Journal of Education for Students Placed at Risk* 11 (2): 161–73.

BROOKS J., and M. BROOKS. 1999. *In Search of Understanding: Making the Case for Constructivist Classrooms*. Alexandria, VA: ASCD.

BROWN, D. H. 2000. *Principles of Language Learning and Teaching*. White Plains, NY: Addison Wesley Longman.

BRUNER, J. 1985. "Narrative and Paradigmatic Modes of Thought." In *Learning and Teaching: The Ways of Knowing*, edited by E. Eisner, 97–115. Chicago: Univ. of Chicago Press.

———. 1990. *Acts of Meaning*. Cambridge, MA: Harvard Univ. Press.

———. 1996. *The Culture of Education*. Cambridge, MA: Harvard Univ. Press.

BURNS, M. 1992. *About Teaching Mathematics: A K–8 Resource*. Sausalito, CA: Math Solutions.

CANAGARAJAH, A. 1999. *Resisting Linguistic Imperialism in English Teaching*. Oxford, UK: Oxford Univ. Press.

CARREON, G. P., C. DRAKE, and A. C. BARTOB. 2005. "The Importance of Presence: Immigrant Parents' School Engagement Experiences." *American Education Research Journal* 42 (3): 465–98.

CAZDEN, C. 1988. *Classroom Discourse*. Portsmouth, NH: Heinemann.

CHANDLER, J., et al. 1986. "Parents as Teachers: Observation of Low-Income Parents and Children in a Homework-like Task." In *The Acquisition of Literacy: Ethnographic Perspectives*, edited by P. Gilin and B. Schiefflin, 171–87. Norwood, NJ: Ablex Publishing Corporation.

CHENOWETH, K. 2007. *It's Being Done: Academic Success in Unexpected Schools*. Cambridge, MA: Harvard Univ. Press.

CLAY, M. 1991. *Becoming Literate: The Construction of Inner Control*. Portsmouth, NH: Heinemann.

COLE, M. 1996. *Cultural Psychology: A Once and Future Discipline.* Cambridge, England: Cambridge Univ. Press.

COLE, M., and S. COLE. 2001. *The Development of Children.* New York: Scientific American Books.

COLE, M., and M. GAUVAIN, eds. 1993. *Readings on the Development of Children.* Oxford, England: Scientific American Books.

COLE, M., P. GRIFFIN, and D. NEWMAN, eds. 1989. *Working for Cognitive Change in School.* New York: Cambridge Univ. Press.

COLE, M., D. NEWMAN, and P. GRIFFIN. 1989. *The Construction Zone.* Cambridge, England: Cambridge University Press.

COLLIER, V. P. 1995. "Acquiring a Second Language for School." Excerpted from *Directions in Language and Education* 1 (4): National Clearinghouse for Bilingual Education. Accessed at www.readingrockets.org/articles/100.

COLLINS, J. 2001. *Selecting and Teaching Focus Correction Areas: A Planning Guide.* Rowley, MA: Collins.

CUMMINS, J. 1986. *Bilingualism in Education: Aspects of Theory, Research, and Practice.* New York: Longman.

———. 2000. *Language, Power and Pedagogy: Bilingual Children in the Crossfire.* Buffalo, NY: Multilingual Matters.

DeLOACHE, J. S. 1995. "Early Understanding and Use of Symbols: The Model." *American Psychological Society* 4: 109–13.

DELPIT, L. 1995. *Other People's Children.* New York: New Press.

DELPIT, L., and T. PERRY, eds. 1998. *The Real Ebonics Debate.* Boston: Beacon.

ECHEVARRIA, J., D. SHORT, and M. VOGT. 2008. *Making Content Comprehensible for English Learners: The SIOP Model.* 3d ed. New York: Pearson Education.

ECONOMOPOULOS, K., C. TIERNEY, and S. J. RUSSELL. 1998. *Arrays and Shares.* White Plains, NY: Dale Seymour.

EKEY, R. 1999. *Fire! in Yellowstone.* Boston, MA: Houghton Mifflin.

ENGEL, S. 1995. *The Stories Children Tell: Making Sense of the Narratives of Childhood.* New York: W. H. Freeman.

EVANOVICH, J. 1999. *High Five.* New York: St. Martin's Press.

FALTIS, C. J. 2006. *Teaching English Language Learners in Elementary School Communities: A Joinfostering Approach.* 4th ed. Upper Saddle River, NJ: Pearson Education.

FERGUSON, R. 2008. *Toward Excellence with Equity.* Cambridge, MA: Harvard Education Press.

FEUERSTEIN, R., Y. RAND, M. B. HOFFMAN, and R. MILLER. 1980. *Instrumental Enrichment: An Intervention Program for Cognitive Modifiability.* Baltimore, MD: Univ. Park Press.

Fireman, G., T. E. McVay Jr., and O. J. Flanagan, eds. 2003. *Narrative and Consciousness.* New York: Oxford Univ. Press.

Fischer, K. W., and C. C. Knight. 1990. "Cognitive Development in Real Children: Levels and Variations." In *Learning and Thinking Styles: Classroom Interaction,* edited by B. Presseisen, et al., 55–65. Washington, DC: NEA Professional Library, National Education Association.

Fountas, I. C., and G. S. Pinnell. 1996. *Guided Reading.* Portsmouth, NH: Heinemann.

Freeman, Y., and D. Freeman. 1998. *ESL/EFL Teaching: Principles for Success.* Portsmouth, NH: Heinemann.

———. 2004. "Connecting Students to Culturally Relevant Texts." *Talking Points* (April–May): 2–7.

Fry, P. 1992. *Fostering Children's Cognitive Competence Through Mediated Learning Experiences: Frontiers and Futures.* Springfield, IL: Charles C. Thomas.

Garner, B. 2007. *Getting to Got It!* Alexandria, VA: Association for Supervision and Curriculum Development.

Gauvain, M. 2001. *The Social Context of Cognitive Development.* New York: Guilford.

Gee, J. 1990. *Social Linguistics and Literacies: Ideology in Discourses.* London: Falmer.

Genesee, F. 1994. *Educating Second Language Children.* Cambridge, UK: Cambridge Univ. Press.

Gleason, J. B. 1989. *The Development of Language.* Columbus, OH: Merrill.

Goodman, Y., K. Goodman, and W. Hood. 1991. *Organizing for Whole Language.* Portsmouth, NH: Heinemann.

Gorski, P. C. 2005. *Savage Unrealities: Uncovering Classism in Ruby Payne's Framework.* Highlands, TX: EdChange.org.

Graves, A. W., R. Gersten, and D. Haager. 2004. "Literacy Instruction in Multiple-Language First Grade Classrooms: Linking Student Outcomes to Observed Instructional Practice." *Learning Disabilities Research & Practice* 19 (4): 262–72.

Green, L. C. 2007. "Bilingual Word Power: Research-Based Vocabulary Strategies for English Language Learners." *Intercultural Development Research Association.* Accessed at: www.idra.org/IDRA_Newsletters/April_2004_Self_Renewing_Schools_Reading_and_Literacy/Bilingual_Word_Power.

Halliday, M. A. K. 1987. *Language as Social Semiotic.* Baltimore, MD: University Park Press.

Healy, A. F., ed. 2005. *Experimental Cognitive Psychology and Its Applications.* Washington, DC: American Psychological Association.

HEALY, J. M. 1999. *Endangered Minds.* New York: Simon and Schuster.

HEATH, S. 1983. *Ways with Words.* Cambridge, UK: Cambridge Univ. Press.

HEDEGARD, M. 1998. "Situated Learning and Cognition: Theoretical Learning and Cognition." *Mind, Culture and Activity* 5 (2): 114–26.

HEDGE, T., and N. WHITNEY. 1996. *Power and Pedagogy.* Hong Kong: Oxford Univ. Press.

HERMAN, D., ed. 2003. *Narrative Theory and the Cognitive Sciences.* Stanford, CA: CSLI.

HOLDAWAY, D. 1980. *Independence in Reading.* Portsmouth, NH: Heinemann.

HOLLINS, E. 1996. *Culture in School Learning: Revealing the Deep Meaning.* Mahwah, NJ: Lawrence Erlbaum.

HOWARD, G. R. 1999. *We Can't Teach What We Don't Know: White Teachers, Multiracial Schools.* New York: Teachers College Press.

HUBBARD, R. S., and B. M. POWER. 1996. *Language Development: A Reader for Teachers.* Englewood Cliffs, NJ: Merrill.

HUGHES, D. L. 1997. *Guide to Narrative Language: Procedures for Assessment.* Eau Claire, WI: Thinking Publications.

HUGHES, J., and O. KWOK. 2007. "Influence of Student-Teacher and Parent-Teacher Relationships on Lower Achieving Readers' Engagement in the Primary Grades." *Journal of Educational Psychology* 99 (1): 39–51.

IRVINE, J. J., and D. E. YORK. 1995. "Learning Styles and Culturally Diverse Students: A Literature Review." In *Handbook of Research on Multicultural Education*, edited by J. A. Banks and C. A. M. Banks, 484–97. New York: Macmillan Publishing USA.

ISRAEL, S. E., C. C. BLOCK, K. L. BAUSEMAN, and K. KNUCCAN-WELSCH. 2005. *Metacognition in Literacy Learning.* Mahwah, NJ: Lawrence Erlbaum.

JACOBSON CHERNOFF, J., K. D. FLANAGAN, C. MCPHEE, and J. PARK. 2007. *Preschool: First Findings from the Preschool Follow-Up of the Early Childhood Longitudinal Study, Birth Cohort (ECLS-B)* (NCES 2008-025). Washington, DC: National Center for Education Statistics, Institute of Education Sciences, U.S. Department of Education.

JOHNSON, D. 1999. "Critical Issue: Addressing the Literacy Needs of Emergent and Early Readers." Accessed at www.ncrel.org/sdrs/areas/issues/content/cntareas/reading/li100.htm.

KAGAN, S. 1995. *Cooperative Learning.* San Juan Capestrano, CA: Resources for Teachers.

KERMANI, H., and H. A. JANES. 1999. "Adjustment Across Task in Maternal Scaffolding in Low-Income Latino Immigrant Families." *Hispanic Journal of Behavioral Sciences* 21 (2): 134–53.

KEY, A. 1965. *The Forgotten Door.* New York: Scholastic, Inc.

KHISTY, L. L. 1995. "Making Inequality: Issues of Language and Meanings in Mathematics Teaching with Hispanic Students." In *New Directions for Equity in Mathematics Teaching*, edited by Walter Secada, 279–97. New York: Cambridge University Press.

KIRSHNER, D., and J. WHITSON, eds. 1997. *Situated Cognition*. Mahwah, NJ: Lawrence Erlbaum.

KLEIN, P. 1987. "Promoting Flexibility in Young Children's Mind Within the Family—A Cross Cultural View." *International Journal of Early Childhood* 19 (2): 51–60.

———. 1997. "A Mediational Approach to Early Intervention." *The Journal of Development and Learning* 1: 61–85.

KOZULIN, A. 1998. *Psychological Tools*. Cambridge, MA: Harvard Univ. Press.

———. 1999. "Cognitive Learning in Younger and Older Immigrant Students." *School Psychology International* 20 (2): 177–90.

———. 2001a. "Mediated Learning Experiences and Cultural Diversity." Accessed at www.umanitoba.ca/unevoc/conference/papers/kozulin.pdf.

———. 2001b. *Psychological Tools: A Sociocultural Approach to Education*. Cambridge, MA: Harvard University Press.

———. 2002. "Sociocultural Theory and the Mediated Learning Experience." *School Psychology International* 23 (1): 7–35.

KOZULIN, A. et al., eds. 2003. *Vygotsky's Educational Theory in Cultural Context*. Accessed at: http://books.google.com/books?hl=en&id=mfCHutwHT-cC&dq=Kozulin&printsec=frontcover&source=web&ots=uenVmgs-qC&sig=wDmEcMIXG5M7Qo6u5XWQkp16bz4#PPP1,M1.

KRASHEN, S., H. DULAY, and M. BURT. 1982. *Language 2*. New York: Oxford Univ. Press.

KRASHEN, S., and T. TERRELL. 1983. *The Natural Approach: Language Acquisition in the Classroom*. San Francisco: Alemany Press.

LADSEN-BILLINGS, G. 1994. *The Dreamkeepers: Successful Teachers of African-American Children*. San Francisco: Jossey-Bass.

———. 1995. "But That's Just Good Teaching! The Case for Culturally Relevant Pedagogy." *Theory into Practice* 34: 159–65.

LANTOLF, J. P., ed. 2000. *Sociocultural Theory and Second Language Learning*. Oxford, UK: Oxford Univ. Press.

LAVE, J., and E. WEGNER. 1991. *Situated Learning: Legitimate Peripheral Participation*. Cambridge, UK: Cambridge Univ. Press.

LEE, S. J. 2006. "Additional Complexities: Social Class, Ethnicity, Generation, and Gender in Asian-American Student Experiences." *Race, Ethnicity, and Education* 9 (1): 17–28.

LEVINE, M. 2002. *A Mind at a Time*. New York: Simon and Schuster.

LEVITT, S., and S. DUBNER. 2005. *Freakanomics*. New York: William Morrow.

LIEBERMAN, D. A. 1997. "Culture, Problem Solving and Pedagogical Style." In *Intercultural Communication*, ed. Samovar and Porter, 191–207. Boston: Wadsworth.

LO CICERO, A. M., K. C. FUSON, and M. ALLEXSAHT-SNIDER. 1999. "Mathematizing Children's Stories, Helping Children Solve Word Problems, and Supporting Parental Involvement." In *Changing the Faces of Mathematics: Perspectives on Latinos*, edited by L. Ortiz-Franco, N. G. Hernandez, and Y. De La Cruz, 59–70. Reston, VA: National Council of Teachers of Mathematics.

LYONS, C. 2003. *Teaching Struggling Readers*. Portsmouth, NH: Heinemann.

MA, L. 1999. *Knowing and Teaching Elementary Mathematics*. Mahwah, NJ: Lawrence Erlbaum.

MARZANO, R. J., and D. J. PICKERING. 2005. *Building Academic Vocabulary Teacher's Manual*. Alexandria, VA: Association for Supervision and Curriculum Development.

MEADOWS, S. 2006. *The Child as Thinker: The Development and Acquisition of Cognition in Childhood (2nd edition)*. New York: Routledge.

MELTZER, L., ed. 2008. *Executive Function Education*. New York: Guilford.

MIURA, I. T., and Y. OKAMOTO. 1999. "Counting in Chinese, Japanese and Korean." In *Changing the Faces of Mathematics: Perspectives on Asian Americans and Pacific Islanders*, edited by C. Edwards. Reston, VA: National Council of Teachers of Mathematics.

MONTANO-HARMON, M. R. 1991. "Discourse Features of Written Mexican Spanish: Current Research in Contrastive Rhetoric and Its Implications." *Hispania* 74 (2): 417–25.

MONTGOMERY, W. 2001. "Creating Culturally Responsive, Inclusive Classrooms." *Teaching Exceptional Children* March/April: 4–9.

MOORE, J. A. 1998. *Black English Speakers: An Examination of Language Register of High and Low Achieving Black Elementary School Students*. Report.

MORAN, P. 1984. *Lexicarry*. Brattleboro, VT: Pro Lingua Associates.

MOREAU, M. R., and B. S. WECH. 2007. *Talk to Write, Write to Learn*. Springfield, MA: MindWing Concepts, Inc.

MOREAU, M. R., and S. ZAGULA. 2005. *Braidy, the Story Braid*. Springfield, MA: MindWing Concepts, Inc,.

MORGAN, W. R., D. F. ALWIN, and L. J. GRIFFIN. 1979. "Social Origins, Parental Values and the Transmission of Inequality." *American Journal of Sociology* 85 (1): 156–66.

MOSCHKOVICH, J. "Learning Mathematics in Two Languages: Moving from Obstacles to Resources." In *Changing the Faces of Mathematics: Perspectives on Multicultural and Gender Equity*, edited by W. Secada, 85–92. Reston, VA: National Council of Teachers of Mathematics.

NAEYC. 1995. "Responding to Linguistic and Cultural Diversity: Recommendations for Effective Early Childhood Education." Position Statement adopted November. Washington, DC: National Association for the Education of Young Children.

National Center for Education Statistics website. nces.ed.gov.

NELSON, K. 1998. *Language in Cognitive Development: Emergence of the Mediated Mind.* New York: Cambridge Univ. Press.

NIETO, S. 2000. *Affirming Diversity.* New York: Addison Wesley Longman.

———. 2002. *Language, Culture and Teaching: Critical Perspectives for a New Century.* Mahwah, NJ: Lawrence Erlbaum.

NORTHEAST AND ISLANDS REGIONAL EDUCATIONAL LABORATORY. 2002. *The Diversity Kit: An Introductory Resource for Social Change in Education.* Providence, RI: Brown Univ.

OGBU, J. U. 1982. "Socialization: A Cultural Ecological Approach." In *The School Life of Children in a Changing Society*, ed. K. M. Borman, 253–67. Hillsdale, NJ: Lawrence Erlbaum.

OLSON, D. R., and N. TORRANCE, eds. 1996. *Modes of Thought: Explorations of Culture and Cognition.* New York: Cambridge Univ. Press.

OVANDO, C., V. COLLIER, and M. COMBS. 2003. *Bilingual and ESL Classrooms: Teaching in Multicultural Contexts.* 3d ed. New York: McGraw Hill.

PAYNE, R. K. 1998. *A Framework for Understanding Poverty.* Highlands, TX: RFT Publishing.

PEASE-ALVAREZ, C., and O. VASQUEZ. 1994. "Language Socialization in Ethnic Minority Communities." In *Educating Second Language Children*, ed. F. Genesee, 82–102. Cambridge, UK: Cambridge Univ. Press.

PEREGOY, S. F., and O. F. BOYLE. 2005. *Reading, Writing and Learning in ESL.* Boston: Pearson Education.

PERRY, T., and J. W. FRASER, eds. 1993. *Freedom's Plow.* London: Routledge.

PORTES, P. R., T. E. CUENTAS, and M. ZADY. 2000. "Cognitive Socialization Across Ethnocultural Contexts: Literacy and Cultural Differences in Intellectual Performance and Parent-Child Interaction." *Journal of Genetic Psychology* 16 (1): 79–98.

PORTES, P. R., et al. 1994. Assistance in Science-Related Parent-Child Interactions: Problem-Solving in the Zone of Proximal Development (ZPD). Paper presented at the annual meeting of American Educational Research Association, New Orleans.

POWER, B. M., and R. S. HUBBARD. 1996. *Language Development: A Reader for Teachers.* Englewood Cliffs, NJ: Merrill / Prentice Hall.

RAGEN, A. 2005. "Teaching the Academic Language of Textbooks: A Preliminary Framework for Performing a Textual Analysis." *The ELL Outlook* (November–December): Accessed at www.coursecrafters.com/ELL-Outlook/2005/nov_dec/ELLOutlookITIArticle1.htm.

RAMIREZ, J, D. 1991. *Final Report: Longitudinal Study of Structured English Immersion Strategy, Early-Exit and Late Exit Transitional Bilingual Education Programs for Language Minority Children.* Washington, DC: US Department of Education.

RASINSKI, T. 2003. *The Fluent Reader.* New York: Scholastic Professional Books.

REIBER, R., and D. ROBINSON, eds. 2004. *The Essential Vygotsky.* New York: Plenum.

RESEARCH FOR BETTER TEACHING. 2007. Acton, MA.

ROBERTS, T. 2005. Vocabulary Instruction for Preschool English Language Learners: What Was Learned and Questions Raised. Presentation at the American Educational Research Association, Montreal, Canada.

ROGOFF, B. 2003. *The Cultural Nature of Human Development.* New York: Oxford Univ. Press.

ROGOFF, B., and K. GUTIERREZ. 2003. "Cultural Ways of Learning: Individual Traits or Repertoires of Practice." *Educational Researcher* 32 (5): 19–25.

ROGOFF, B., and J. LAVE. 1999. *Everyday Cognition: Development in Social Context.* Cambridge, MA: Harvard Univ. Press.

SACO-POLLITT, C., E. POLLITT, and D. GREENFIELD. 1985. "The Cumulative Deficit Hypothesis in the Light of Cross-Cultural Evidence." *International Journal of Behavioral Development* 8: 75–97.

SCHLEIN, M. 1999. *The Year of the Panda.* Boston, MA: Houghton Mifflin.

SCRIBNER, S., and M. COLE. 1981. *The Psychology of Literacy.* Cambridge, MA: Harvard Univ. Press.

SHADE, B. J. R., ed. 1997. *Culture, Style and the Educative Process: Making Schools Work for Racially Diverse Students.* 2d ed. Springfield, IL: Charles C. Thomas.

SHADE, B. J. R., C. KELLY, and M. OBERG. 1997. *Creating Culturally Responsive Classrooms.* Washington, DC: American Psychological Association.

SHAH, I. 1972. *The Exploits of the Incredible Mullah Nasruddin.* New York: E. P. Dutton.

SNOW, C., S. BURNS, and P. GRIFFIN. 1998. "English Language Learners and Reading Difficulties." Excerpted from C. E. Snow, S. M. Burns, and P. Griffin, eds. 1998. "Predictors of Success and Failure in Reading." In *Preventing Reading Difficulties in Young Children.* National Research Council, National Academy of Sciences. Accessed at www.readingrockets.org/articles/291.

SOLOMON, J., and N. RHODES. 1995. "Conceptualizing Academic Language." Abstract. Center for Applied Linguistics, National Center for Research on Cultural Diversity and Second Language Learning.

STERNBERG, R., and R. WAGNER. 1994. *Mind in Context.* Cambridge, UK: Cambridge University Press.

STEWART, E. 1972. *American Cultural Patterns.* Chicago: Intercultural.

STIGLER, J. W., and J. HIEBERT. 1999. *The Teaching Gap.* New York: Free Press.

SUMMERS, J. 2006. "The Effects of Collaborative Learning in Math in Sixth Graders' Individual Goal Orientation from a Socioconstructivist Perspective." *The Elementary School Journal* 106 (3): 273–91.

SWANSON, H. L., and M. BEEBE-FRANKENBERGER. 2004. "The Relationship Between Working Memory and Mathematical Problem Solving in Children at Risk and Not at Risk for Serious Math Difficulties." *Journal of Educational Psychology* 96 (3): 471–91.

SWELLER, J., and J. J. G. VAN MERRIENBOER. 2005. "Cognitive Load Theory and Complex Learning: Recent Developments and Future Directions." *Educational Psychology Review* 17 (2): 147–77.

SWELLER, J., J. J. G. VAN MERRIENBOER, and F. G. PAAS. 1998. "Cognitive Architecture and Instructional Design." *Educational Psychology Review* 10 (12): 251–96.

THARP, R., and R. GALLIMORE. 1988. *Rousing Minds to Life.* Cambridge, UK: Cambridge Univ. Press.

TILESTON, D. W. 2004. *What Every Teacher Should Know About Diverse Learners.* Thousand Oaks, CA: Corwin.

TIMM, J. T. 1999. "The Relationship Between Culture and Cognitive Style: A Review of the Evidence and Some Reflections from the Classroom." *Mid-Western Educational Researcher* 12 (2): 36–44.

TOMASELLO, M. 1999. *The Cultural Origins of Human Cognition.* Cambridge, MA: Harvard Univ. Press.

TOOMELA, A., ed. 2003. *Cultural Guidance in the Development of the Human Mind.* Westport, CT: Ablex.

TSE, L. 2001. *"Why Don't They Learn English?": Separating Fact from Fallacy in the U. S. Language Debate.* New York: Teachers College Press.

TZURIEL, D. 1996. "Mediated Learning Experience in Free-Play Versus Structured Situations Among Preschool Children of Low-, Medium- and High-SES." *Early Childhood Development and Care* 125: 57–82.

VALSINER, J., ed. 1988. *Child Development Within Culturally Structured Environments: Comparative Cultural and Constructivist Perspectives.* Vol. 3. Westport, CT: Ablex.

———, ed. 1989. *Child Development in Cultural Context.* Lewiston, New York: Higrefe and Huber.

———. 1997. *Culture and the Development of Children's Action: A Theory of Human Development.* New York: John Wiley and Sons.

———. 2007. *Culture in Minds and Societies: Foundations of Cultural Psychology.* New Delhi: Sage.

VYGOTSKY, L. S. 1978. *Mind in Society.* Cambridge, MA: Harvard University Press.

———. 1986. *Thought and Language.* Cambridge, MA: MIT Press.

WANG, A. 1993. "Cultural-Familial Predictors of Children's Metacognitive and Academic Performance." *Journal of Research in Childhood Education* 7 (2): 83–90.

WANG, L., and E. LIN. 2005. "Comparative Studies on US and Chinese Mathematical Learning and the Implications for Standards-Based Mathematics Teaching Reform." *Educational Researcher* 34 (5): 3–13.

WAXMAN, S. 2002. "Early Word Learning and Conceptual Development: Everything Had a Name and Each Name Gave Birth to a New Thought." In *Blackwell Handbook of Childhood Development*, ed. U. Goswain, 102–26. Malden, MA: Blackwell.

WERDENSCHLAG, L. B. 1993. Characteristics of Parent-Child Interactions: How Do They Affect Children's Acquisition of Metacognitive Skills? Paper presented at the biennial meeting of the Society for Research in Child Development, New Orleans.

WHORF, B. L. 1956. *Language, Thought and Reality.* Cambridge, MA: MIT Press.

WIGGINS, G., and J. McTIGHE. 2006. *Understanding by Design.* 2d ed. Upper Saddle River, NJ: Pearson Education.

WILLIAMS, N., and M. BROGAN. 1991. *Developing Literacy in At-Risk Readers.* Springfield, IL: Charles Tuttle.

WOZNIAK, R. H., and K. W. FISCHER. 1993. *Development in Context: Acting and Thinking in Specific Environments.* Hillsdale, NJ: Lawrence Erlbaum.

YOUNG, T. A., and N. L. HADAWAY, eds. 2006. *Supporting the Literacy Development of English Learners.* Newark, DE: International Reading Association.

Index